Samuel Johnson
his Friends and Enemies

Frontispiece: Samuel Johnson in old age;
portrait by James Barry.

Samuel Johnson
his Friends and Enemies

Peter Quennell

Weidenfeld and Nicolson
5 Winsley Street London W 1

Designed by Alan Bartram.

Filmset by Keyspools Ltd, Golborne, Lancashire
Printed in England by C. Tinling & Co. Ltd, Prescot and London.

ISBN 0 297 99536 8

Contents

Acknowledgments

Photographs and illustrations were supplied by or are reproduced by kind permission of the following. The photographs on pages 148 and 172 are reproduced by gracious permission of H.M. The Queen; on page 40 (*right*) by permission of His Grace the Duke of St Albans; on page 92 by permission of His Grace the Duke of Marlborough; on page 15 by permission of the Marquis of Lansdowne; on pages 61 and 146 by permission of Earl Spencer; on page 111 by permission of Lady Galway; the two pictures on page 105 by permission of Lord Lambton; on page 93 by permission of Lord Sackville from his collection at Knole; on page 59 (*right*) by permission of Sir Richard Sykes; on page 249 (*right*) by permission of Captain H. M. Denham; on page 201 by permission of H. I. T. Gunn; on page 106 (*right*) by permission of Mrs Peggy Hickman; on pages 13 and 30 by permission of Mrs Donald Hyde; on page 53 by permission of Revesly Sitwell, Esq.; on pages 113 and 115 by permission of the Master and Fellows of University College, Oxford; on page 255 (*left*) by permission of the Faculty of Music, University of Oxford; on pages 8, 34, 37, 78, and 79 by permission of the Trustees of Dr Johnson's House, Gough Square. Chris Barker: 37, 124; Beaverbrook Art Gallery, Frederickon, New Brunswick, Canada: 243; British Broadcasting Corporation: 56/2, 89; British Museum: 17, 19, 23, 38, 40/1, 42, 47/1, 56/1, 66, 81, 95, 102/2, 102/3, 107, 123, 129, 139, 145, 170, 171, 177, 189, 249/1, 256, 259; Musée Condé, Chatilly: 207; A. C. Cooper: 123, 139; Courage Ltd: 181; Courtald Institute of Art: 71, 215, 222, 225; R. B. Fleming: 19, 23, 66, 81, 107, 129, 145, 256,; John R. Freeman: 21, 38, 40/1, 42, 47/1, 95, 102/2, 102/3, 170, 171; Giraudon: 207; Greater London Council, Department of Architecture and Civic Design: 35; Hawkley Studios Assoc. Ltd.: 93; Leeds City Art Galleries: 58, 59/1; Leggatt Bros. on behalf of a private collection: 32; London Borough of Lambeth, Director of Library and Amenity Services: 21, 69; London Museum: 60, 117; Louvre: 208; Metropolitan Museum of Art: 91; National Gallery of Scotland: 211; National Portrait Gallery: 28, 39, 46, 87, 106/1, 108, 109, 121, 128/2, 131, 134, 137, 157, 161, 185, 187, 214, 218, 239, 255/2, 260, 261; National Trust: 56/2, 89; Herbert K. Nolan: 181; Gerald M. Norman Gallery: 151; Peter Quennell: 50, 118, 143/1, 162, 175; Radio Times Hulton Picture Library: 143/2; Shakespeare Birthplace Trust: 102/1; Scottish National Portrait Gallery: 45, 128/1, 213; Tate Gallery: 141/2; Victoria and Albert Museum: 25, 26, 55, 64, 73, 132, 235, 257; Trustees of the Walker Estate, on loan to the London Museum: 168–9; Reece Winstone: 101; Derick Witty: 25, 26, 64, 73, 246.
Picture research by Jasmine Spencer.

Foreword

'Dr Samuel Johnson's character, religious, moral, political, and literary, nay his figure and manner, are, I believe, more generally known than those of almost any man', wrote James Boswell in his *Journal of a Tour to the Hebrides*; and to add yet another volume to the immense Johnsonian bibliography may seem a somewhat presumptuous undertaking. Many admirable books on Johnson and his associates have been published during the last fifty years. My object, however, has been not so much to attempt a portrait of Johnson himself as to produce a literary conversation-piece, in which my hero stands at the centre of the picture, surrounded by his friends and enemies, against the background of his social period.

Meanwhile, I should like to express my gratitude to Professor James L. Clifford, not only for his excellent books on *Hester Lynch Piozzi* and *Young Samuel Johnson*, but for the advice and help that he has given me; to Mrs Donald Hyde, for permitting me to quote from Mrs Thrale's *Children's Book*, now in her collection; to Dr Katherine C. Balderston, for her invaluable edition of *Thraliana* (1942: 2nd edition 1951), from which I have quoted extensively by kind permision of the Clarendon Press; to the John Rylands Library at Manchester and its Librarian, Dr F. Taylor, for leave to quote from letters exchanged by Johnson and Mrs Thrale, among the Rylands English MS; and for Lord and Lady Lansdowne for so kindly entertaining me at Bowood, and showing me their precious collection of Johnsoniana.

P.Q.

Streatham Place, as enlarged by Henry Thrale; drawing by W. H. Brooke.

Streatham Place I

By the splendid standards that prevailed in its own age, Streatham Place, sometimes called Streatham Park, was neither a very large nor a particularly impressive building; but, with its gardens, paddock, lawns and avenues, it had a prosperous, dignified and consequential air. The whole estate, which filled up the acute angle between Tooting Upper and Tooting Lower Commons,* covered approximately a hundred acres; and the house itself, built for a rich businessman named Ralph Thrale about the middle of the eighteenth century, possessed an unassuming classic frontage, a neatly pedimented central block and modest single-storeyed wings. It was originally, wrote Ralph's daughter-in-law, 'but a little, tidy Brick House', 'a little squeezed miserable Place'. Henry Thrale, however, who had inherited the property from his father in the year 1758, though he left the façade almost untouched, had greatly altered and improved his residence, enclosing some noble elms opposite his main gate, absorbing various 'fields and closes', and adding a library, a drawing-room and an 'Eating Parlour'.

Mr Thrale had a deep regard for books; but he was also an accomplished gourmet, and took an especially keen interest in the cultivation of his kitchen gardens. Protected by lofty red-brick walls, they stretched alongside a broad avenue nearly as far as Tooting Lower Common; and under the lee of the house, where he could inspect them at his ease, he had established not only an excellent orchard, but 'graperies' and a 'melon ground'. The park, too, was carefully redesigned, to include a shrubbery, coppices and wandering lines of trees, a picturesque summer-house and an oval 'spring pond'.

Hither, before he began to enlarge his property, Henry Thrale had brought a young wife. In some respects, Hester and Henry Thrale

---

* Since re-named Tooting Bec and Tooting Graveney Commons. The house was demolished in 1863; and the estate has now been overrun by a labyrinth of dull Victorian buildings, known collectively as Streatham Park.

appeared a somewhat ill-assorted couple. Mr Thrale's origins were undistinguished; but, thanks to his energetic father and grand-uncle, he had been educated amid an atmosphere of riches; while Hester Thrale, though she came of an ancient Welsh family, who traced their lineage back to an eleventh-century adventurer named Adam of Salzburg, as a child had experienced many of the hardships of a struggling poor relation. Her parents had never agreed; when Hester Maria Cotton, a spirited and beautiful girl, married John Salusbury, her 'flashy cousin', a perverse and irritable young man, they had plunged, their daughter tells us, into ten long years of 'mutual Misery'; and during those years Mrs Thrale was so poor that only once could she afford to buy herself a new dress, which she purchased for a guinea from a wandering pedlar when he visited their lonely farm.

At home, Mrs Salusbury was obliged to make her own candles, salt her own meat, and iron her own and her child's and husband's linen. Yet she declared that she would still have been happy enough, had Salusbury 'been but good-humour'd'. Alas, he was by no means good-humoured; among his numerous defects, he had a dreadfully explosive temper; and his ill-treatment had caused her several miscarriages before at last, on 16 January 1741, she managed to provide him with a living child.

Mrs Salusbury would never bear again; and the child, whom they christened Hester Lynch, soon discovered that she must form a 'Centre of Unity' between her aggrieved, unhappy parents. Her mother employed her to amuse and distract the despot, and taught her, she said, 'to play a thousand pretty tricks, and tell a thousand pretty stories', as often as Mr Salusbury, aggrieved, disappointed and 'gloriously out of humour', happened to return home. Her efforts succeeded. 'Rakish Men seldom make tender Fathers, but a Man must fondle something'; and 'I therefore grew a great favourite ... in spite of his long continued Efforts to dislike me ...'.

Meanwhile, the family's position had not improved; but John Salusbury eventually secured an appointment that took him off to Nova Scotia, and set sail, when his daughter was eight, 'leaving my Mother and myself to scrattle on' as best they could. During his two years' absence, they usually spent their time with rich relations in the country – in Wales, at Offley Court in Hertfordshire, or in Bedfordshire at East Hyde, the seat of Hester's paternal grandmother. Hester was a lively, courageous child; and at East Hyde, it pleased her to recollect, she had captivated the entire household:

When my Mother hoped I was gaining Health by the Fresh Air, I was kicking my Heels on a Corn Binn, and learning to drive of the old Coachman

... Grandmama kept four great ramping War-horses; *chevaux entiers* for her Carriage, with immense long Manes and Tails which we buckled and Combed – and when after long Practice I showed her and my Mother how two of them (poor Colonel and Peacock) would lick my hand for a lump of Sugar or fine white Bread, much were they amazed! much more when my skill in guiding them round the Courtyard on the Break, could no longer be doubted or denied ...

Thus, Hester had quickly developed into an expert charmer and diplomatist. She had also adopted the habits of fashionable life. Should they leave the country, she and mother would retire to small and inexpensive London lodgings, where Mrs Salusbury 'made our Bed, and swept our Room' herself. But still, they were surrounded by 'quality people'; and 'Duchesses, Countesses, and Baronets' Ladies ... visited us in our little Parlour ...'. At the same time, Hester, who always read eagerly, had begun to scribble verse and prose; and, before she was fifteen, she had contributed a number of amusing pieces to the *St James's Chronicle*.

As an adolescent, she was shrewd beyond her years. From the sad example of her careless scapegrace father she had learned that men were apt to be selfish, passionate and headstrong, but could be managed with the help of charm; and from her parents' unending talk of money, inheritances, mortgages, settlements and the tragedies and comedies of the marriage-market, that money was a decisive factor in life, and a 'good marriage' the passport, if not to happiness, at least to some degree of reasonable well-being.

She, too, had worldly expectations. Offley Court had come into her uncle's possession through his marriage to an heiress; and Lady Salusbury, though plump, amiable and handsome, was a stammering epileptic who seemed unlikely to produce a child. On Sir Thomas' death, it was thought, he would bequeath his house and estate to Hester; for she and Mrs Salusbury were constant guests at Offley, and she had become her aunt's darling and her uncle's 'favourite plaything'. The Salusburys' Hertfordshire house was now her true home; and there, in 1761, she had first encountered Henry Thrale, a rich young Londoner, then about thirty-three, personable, accomplished, self-assured and, according to Sir Thomas, '*a real sportsman*'.

He was not, however, a product of the English upper classes. His father, indeed, had been the ambitious son of a cottager at Offley, who had left the village to join an uncle, Edmund Halsey, at his successful brewery in Southwark. Himself the son of a Hertfordshire miller, Halsey had originally inherited the concern by marrying his employer's daughter, and had risen to such heights that he had married his eldest girl to the future Lord Cobham. When he died, the industrious apprentice had been able to acquire the brewery; and, with its revenues, he had 'educated his Son and three Daughters quite in a high Style'. Ralph Thrale, honoured and affluent, had expired in 1758; and by that time there was nothing to differentiate Henry from any other fashionable man of pleasure, except that, despite his devotion to pleasure and the rakish company he kept, he had not ceased to be a man of business.

Although he had passed some lazy years at Oxford and, accompanying his friend, William Henry Lyttleton, afterwards Lord Westcote, had subsequently enjoyed a Grand Tour, he himself managed the brewery, which he attended every morning; and, besides the country house his father had built at Streatham in Surrey and a hunting-box at Croydon, whence he rode out with his own hounds, he had a London house near the brewery's walls amid the sweltering alleys of the Borough. Nor did he seek to disguise his humble origins. Sir Thomas had first met Thrale at a party given by Henry Levinz, Receiver-General of the Customs; and, the conversation happening to turn to Hertfordshire, Mr Thrale, 'it seems with some Emotion', remarked 'that Offley was the place of his Father's Birth'.

When he returned home and undertook further enquiries, Sir Thomas 'found out that the House he was born in, was our Dog Kennel.... Growing more and more intimate, Sir Thos. press'd his new Friend to come and see the Place of his Father's Nativity.' Her husband, Mrs Thrale adds, 'was the more willing to comply ... as he too was an eminent sportsman', and did not at all object to hounds being bred and reared beneath his father's old roof. He therefore duly arrived at Offley, escorting an elderly aunt named Mrs Smith, whom the authoress of *Thraliana* dismisses as 'a very ordinary old Woman indeed', but to whom Mr Thrale, she noted, 'paid a mighty polite attention'.

Mrs Salusbury was particularly pleased by their visitor and his civil, unpretentious ways. 'She had no Notion ...', she told her daughter that evening, 'of a Man so handsome, so well educated, and so well bred, being thus totally insensible to the apparent Shame of acknowledging an old Cottager in our Village for his Grandfather....' Thrale was delighted to describe 'how his Family had prospered by the Ingenuity of his Father, whom he talked on with Rapture'; and, next

Right Henry Thrale (1742?–81) painted by Reynolds for the library at Streatham; 'a man', wrote his wife, 'exceedingly comfortable to live with', yet cold, lethargic, inconsiderate and self-centred.

day, she was charmed to see him put his hand into his pocket and present 'five Shillings to a white headed Lad who was lying on a Bank', because, he said, he imagined that his father might once have been just such a boy.

Hester's attitude was a good deal more reserved. Though 'a very handsome and well accomplished Gentleman', Thrale was evidently not a courtier, and took 'less Notice of Me', she recalled, 'than any other Man I had ever seen come to the House almost'. Yet it soon became clear that he meant to seek her hand in marriage – an idea that enchanted Mrs Salusbury, though it angered both her jealous and selfish father and the eccentric Dr Collier, her devoted tutor. Sir Thomas, of course, was on Thrale's side. But, as luck would have it, by now he had lost his wife, and had recently fallen in love with 'a young and blooming Widow'.

If the widow married him, as she presently did, Hester would cease to be her uncle's heiress. There followed a dramatic family quarrel; and, while it was still raging, John Salusbury, having set out to walk across Offley park, suddenly collapsed 'and was brought us home a Corpse ...'. During this crisis in the Salusbury's affairs, Thrale remained a firm friend. Though he seldom paid Hester much attention, he continued to visit her mother and obstinately pressed his suit; and, when Sir Thomas announced that he would provide his niece with a dowry of £10,000, she finally submitted to Mrs Salusbury's pleas. The couple were married at St Anne's, Soho, on 11 October 1763.

Thrale immediately carried her off to Streatham. It had been a surprising courtship. 'Except for one five minutes', Mrs Thrale recorded, she had never seen her suitor alone 'till quite the Evening of the Wedding Day'. Yet she did not repine. Mrs Salusbury, who, after the marriage ceremony, had driven with the Thrales to Streatham Place, was still her daughter's close companion; and Mrs Thrale regarded her mother as 'the most accomplished Female that ever my Eyes beheld. Her Shape so accurate, her Carriage so graceful, her Eyes so brilliant, her Knowledge so extensive, and her Manners so pleasing that it was no wonder She had such a choice of Lovers in her Youth, and Admirers in her advanced Age.'

Zoffany's picture of the widowed Mrs Salusbury shows a tall and slender personage, wearing a widow's cap and sable weeds, as she

Right Mrs Salusbury (1707–73), Hester Thrale's widowed mother; 'the most accomplished Female that ever my Eyes beheld'. Portrait by Zoffany.

stands beneath her husband's portrait, and an expression that combines pensive dignity with a pleasant gleam of humour. Thrale had been her choice – it was to the mother rather than to the daughter that he had originally paid his court; and Mrs Salusbury's influence, calming and steadying, now kept the marriage on an even keel.

Her own experience of marriage had not been happy; and Mrs Thrale seems to have accepted her mother's view that men were strange, incalculable creatures. Yet, whatever she had expected of Henry Thrale, during the early years of their marriage she must often have been disappointed. He neither loved, nor pretended to love his wife. His was essentially a frigid nature. Methodical, punctilious, self-absorbed, he maintained a steady, unhurrying pace through life, which he obstinately refused to quicken. Mrs Thrale was fond of relating, for instance, how one night they had been roused by the news that his favourite sister's house had caught fire; whereat Mr Thrale had ordered the servant who woke them to hasten to his sister's rescue, but had then turned over in bed and quietly gone to sleep again.

When she had already been married for thirteen years, Mrs Thrale decided that the time had come to draw a literary portrait of her husband. 'Mr Thrale's Person', she wrote, 'is manly, his Countenance agreable, his Eyes steady and of the deepest Blue.' His look is 'neither sprightly nor gloomy, but thoughtful and Intelligent'; his behaviour, devoid of 'every kind of Trick or Particularity', but 'unaffectedly civil and decorous'. Though he loves money and seeks it diligently, 'he loves Liberality too, and is willing enough both to give generously and spend fashionably'. Either his passions are 'not strong, or else he keeps them under such Command that they seldom disturb his Tranquillity or his Friends'; and she thinks that 'it must . . . be something more than common which can affect him strongly either with Hope, Fear, Anger, Love or Joy'. As for his conversation, it is remarkably decent and sober, 'wholly free from all Oaths, Ribaldry and Profaneness'. This makes Mr Thrale 'a Man exceedingly comfortable to live with, while the easiness of his Temper and slowness to take Offence add greatly to his value as a domestic Man'.

Yet, for all his estimable qualities – and here a more caustic note begins gradually to creep through – 'I think his Servants do not much love him, and I am not sure that his Children feel much Affection for him'. By 'low People' he is generally shunned and disliked, as he lacks any kind of *bonhomie*, and has 'none of that officious and Cordial Manner' which the lower classes find appealing. Even among his equals, he often appears ungracious, 'and *confers* a Favour less pleasingly than many a Man refuses one'. Nothing could break down his stolid reserve.

Yet, however unaffectionate he might seem, he is not entirely un-appreciative; 'with Regard to his Wife, tho' little tender of her Person, he is very partial to her Understanding . . .'.

Five years earlier, a caricature, entitled 'The Southwark Macaroni', had been exhibited in the windows of the London print-shops. It represents Thrale as a contemporary man of fashion, wearing one of the diminutive saucer-shaped hats then affected by the younger dandies. He has keen eyes, an aquiline nose, a stubborn chin and an expansive stomach; and he carries a walking stick that may be the gold-headed cane once given him by Mrs Thrale. She had inherited

Henry Thrale as dandy and man of pleasure;
a caricature of 1772.

it, we know, from John Salusbury; and he had himself inherited it from a certain 'French Marquise', who was said to have died in his arms after he had helped her to run through her fortune. Perhaps, when Hester handed it on to Thrale, she was making a symbolic gift. Although Henry Thrale was cold and aloof, whereas John Salusbury had been rash and violent, he had quickly taken over the parental rôle; and, having learned to tolerate an awkward father, she found no difficulty in coming to terms with an almost equally mysterious husband.

'My Mother lived with me and I was content', she wrote. 'I re'd to her in the Morning, played at Back Gammon with her at Noon, and worked Carpets with her in the Evening.... We visited nobody.' Meanwhile, Mr Thrale 'went every day to London and returned either to dinner or Tea'. When he came home, he remarked, 'he always found two agreable Women ready to receive him, and thus we lived on Terms of great Civility and Politeness, if not of strong Alliance and Connection'.

Occasionally, he brought back a London friend; and in London, his wife was well aware, he had not given up his old amusements. Before his marriage he had been a fashionable rake; and, at home, he soon began to display a keenly affectionate interest in her charming kinswoman, Miss Hetty Cotton. This, too, she accepted without a qualm; 'for as I never was a fond Wife, so I certainly never was a Jealous one'.

Thrale had married her, she was not ashamed to admit, largely 'from prudential Motives'; Hester was well-educated and well-bred; and, as she afterwards learned, none of the other girls he had considered would have agreed to spend a part of the year at Southwark, in an inconvenient, old-fashioned house next door to his obnoxious brewery. Until he had refurnished it, Hester was never allowed to see the house in Dead-Man's Place; but, once the old building was fit for habitation, she found that she was expected to divide her time between Streatham and the crowded, nasty Borough. Again she submitted. Wherever they lived, it was Thrale who supervised their household; and, being passionately addicted to the pleasures of eating, he ordered every meal himself.

The nursery alone was under his wife's charge. Though Mr Thrale might often be selfish and negligent, he never failed in the regular performance of his matrimonial duties. Besides requiring an agreeable hostess, he also needed worthy children; and, during the course of his married life, he succeeded in begetting twelve. The Thrales, however, were no more fortunate than the majority of eighteenth-century parents. 'The death of a new-born child ...' wrote Edward Gibbon, himself the sole survivor of a brood of seven, 'may seem an unnatural but it is strictly a probable event; since of any given number the greater part are extinguished before their ninth year.' Both the Thrales' sons were doomed to die in childhood; and of the ten daughters who completed the family, only four reached adult life.

Mrs Thrale's first child, christened Hester Maria but presently nicknamed 'Queeney', a girl who grew up to be her mother's pride

Arthur Murphy (1727–1806), Johnson's 'dear Mur', who first introduced him to Henry and Hester Thrale; after a contemporary portrait by Dance.

and scourge, was born on 17 September 1764. Next year, 'on the second Thursday of the Month of January', a new visitor appeared at Dead-Man's Place. Among Thrale's oldest friends was the versatile Irishman, Arthur Murphy, actor, dramatist, journalist, author and professional diner-out. Though Mrs Thrale had learned to resent and distrust many of the boon-companions her husband brought from London, particularly the profligate and sharp-tongued Topham Beauclerk, she seems always to have been fond of Murphy – a middle-aged man with 'full light eyes' and a heavily pock-marked face, 'so unassuming, so unaffected, so friendly in his *manner* and *Address*: so willing to amuse *you*, to direct your *Company*, to *inform*, to *sooth* ...'.

One of his many engaging traits was his conversational adaptability. If your guests were 'People of high Rank and Accomplishments', nobody outshone Murphy, yet nobody was eclipsed by him. 'Have you a set of low Fellows, Burgesses of a Boro' or Freeholders of a County? Murphy sets them on a continual Roar....' Yet, should you happen to be alone, 'Murphy appears not to be disappointed ... he'll lay out all his Talents for *your* Amusement, or if you are not in a humour to be amused, will talk to you of your children ...'. Like other good-humoured men, he did his best to bring his friends together; and it was Murphy who, early in 1765 while he was dining with the Thrales at Southwark, originally talked to them of Samuel Johnson.

He was anxious that they should meet the great man, 'of whose Moral and Literary Character', Mrs Thrale relates, 'he spoke in the most exalted Terms; and so whetted our desire of seeing him soon, that we were only disputing *how* he should be invited, *when* he should be invited, and what should be the pretence'. Finally, they decided to employ 'one Woodhouse, a Shoemaker who had written some Verses, and been asked to some Tables', as the necessary social bait. Dr Johnson would surely not refuse to meet this unknown but deserving rhymer. Nor did he refuse; it was never his way to decline an invitation that promised him both a delicious dinner and a flow of good talk. And, accordingly, at four o'clock, on that momentous Thursday, accompanied by his 'dear Mur', a friend to whom he had long been devoted, he arrived in Dead-Man's Place.

During the highly enjoyable party that followed, poor Woodhouse played a secondary rôle. He had been 'informed at the time', he would afterwards write, not perhaps without a certain bitterness, 'that Dr Johnson's curiosity was excited, by what was said of me in the literary world, as a kind of wild beast from the country'. But, although Johnson recommended him to read the *Spectator* – 'Give days and nights, Sir', said he, 'to the study of Addison, if you mean either to be a good writer, or ... an honest man' – he was evidently much more interested in his dinner and the Thrales. Both his host and hostess, even at their first meeting, he found immediately sympathetic. 'We liked each so well that the next Thursday was appointed for the same Company to meet – exclusive of the Shoemaker, and since then' Mrs Thrale adds, 'Johnson has remained ... our constant Acquaintance, Visitor, Companion and Friend.'

Such were the chance beginnings of a friendship that would last for more than twenty years. Johnson appreciated Henry Thrale, whose gravity, dignity and impassive courtesy gratified his natural sense of order. But the emotions that Mrs Thrale aroused had a very different

Streatham Place; early-nineteenth-century engraving from a picture by C. Stanfield, which shows the additions that Henry Thrale had made to the house, and Dr Johnson in the foreground.

and far deeper source. Though his present life was resolutely chaste, Johnson always loved women; and Mrs Thrale was a woman who, despite the scrupulous propriety of her conduct and the apparent coolness of her nature, instinctively attracted men. But she was not beautiful. In 1778, having already drawn a portrait of her husband, she was to compose a no less elaborate description of her own physical and moral qualities.

She is somewhat diminutive, the portraitist begins by announcing – only four feet eleven inches tall – and has a proportionately slender waist, a neck 'remarkably white' and 'rather longish', chestnut hair and strongly defined eyebrows above 'a pair of large – but light Grey Eyes'. Her skin is radiant, 'perfectly clear – the Red very bright, and the White eminently good and clean'. Hers is not an expressive appearance; '*Expression* there is *none* I think . . .'. And, though she does not deny that she can claim some bodily grace, it is 'more acquired than natural; for Strength and not Delicacy was the original Characteristick of the Figure'.

That grace has been largely acquired through art – 'by Keeping genteel Company . . . and looking much at Paintings, learning to Dance almost incessantly, and chusing Foreign Models . . . as patterns of Imitation'. She is proud of her foreign air, and knows that some of her English acquaintances probably suspect that she must paint her face. As to her temper, though it may derive something from her Welsh origins, she believes that it has an Italian warmth and brio. She is irritable, she says, but tender and affectionate; and she expects a return for any affection she shows that 'busy People have no Time to pay, and coarse people have no Pleasure in paying'. A diligent friend, she is also 'by Nature a rancorous and revengeful Enemy'; but she has 'conquered that Quality thro' God's Grace,' and does not harbour long grudges. In money matters, she declares, she is both acquisitive and extravagant. As to her education, 'her Knowledge of Ancient Languages is superficial enough'; but her command of modern tongues is 'rather skilful'. 'Universal Grammar', of which she possesses an uncommon grasp, Geometry, Astronomy and Poetry are among the other subjects she has studied.

Mrs Thrale, in short, was a small, plumpish, rosy-cheeked young woman, energetic, quick and neatly built, whose greatest charm, no doubt, was the air of alert intelligence that irradiated everything she said or did. Melancholy, introspective and painfully morbid himself, Johnson at once responded to her warmth and gaiety. Not only did he recognize the strength of will that underlay her blithe, impetuous manner; but, as a lonely, unhappy spirit, he valued her gift of dispensing happiness and her large capacity (hitherto seldom employed) for feeling and communicating real affection.

When they met, she was nearly twenty-four; Samuel Johnson, fifty-five. Life had scarred him deeply. In 1765 his appearance was so alarming that those who encountered him for the first time were invariably somewhat astonished, and often shaken and appalled. His face was hideously marked. Born on 7 September 1709, he had come into the world a sickly, weak-eyed child, who, during his early infancy, developed scrofula, the tuberculous infection of the skin and the lymphatic glands, then popularly named the King's Evil, that English sovereigns, by administering their royal 'touch', were reputed to have the privilege of curing.

In childhood, Johnson had been taken from Lichfield, his Stafford-shire birthplace, to be touched by Queen Anne, of whom, in later years, he said that he retained 'a sort of solemn recollection' as a lady wearing 'diamonds, and a long black hood'. But the Queen's magical touch did not effect a cure; and the disease, besides pitting and seaming his face, soon did irremediable harm both to his hearing and to his eyesight. He was strong, however; and, once he had struggled through the perils of early childhood, he became a stout and powerful boy.

Sarah had passed the age of forty when her elder son was born, her husband being some twelve years older. Michael Johnson was naturally proud of his son; but Johnson, writes Mrs Thrale, seemed always

Michael Johnson (1657–1731); he was 'a pious and a worthy Man', his son told Mrs Thrale, but 'wrong-headed, positive, and afflicted with Melancholy'. Engraving by E. Finden after a contemporary drawing.

somewhat exasperated 'at the recollection of the bustle his parents made with his wit ... "That (said he to me one day) is the great misery of late marriages; the unhappy produce of them becomes the plaything of dotage: an old man's child ... leads much such a life, I think, as a little boy's dog, teized with awkward fondness, and forced, perhaps, to sit up and beg ... to divert a company".'

'Poor people's children, dear Lady', he said on another occasion, 'never respect them: I did not respect my own mother, though I loved her....' Even so, his attachment, he felt, had not been entirely unselfish; and he admitted, for example, that he 'should never have so loved his mother as a man, had she not given him coffee she could ill afford, to gratify his appetite when a boy'. Mrs Johnson, it is clear, had adored her elder son. Besides spoiling him, she taught him to read, assisted by 'her old Maid Catharine', and, on their famous visit to London, bought him a little silver cup and spoon, bearing the engraved inscription SAM. I.

The elderly Lichfield bookseller was a very different personage. Though 'a pious and a worthy Man', his son informed Mrs Thrale, he was 'wrong-headed, positive, and afflicted with Melancholy' – the 'vile melancholy' that Samuel Johnson afterwards accepted as a part of his inheritance. It was a gloomy household. 'My father and mother', he declared, 'had not much happiness from each other. They seldom conversed; for my father could not bear to talk of his affairs; and my mother, being unacquainted with books, cared not to talk of anything else.' Michael Johnson's affairs were usually ill-starred; and 'the perpetual Pressure' they involved kept him travelling round the country.

Samuel Johnson rarely talked of his childhood, and then customarily with some hesitation; 'one has', he remarked, '*so* little pleasure in reciting the anecdotes of beggary'. Nevertheless, he could not forget his parents; and, near the end of his life, when he was revisiting Lichfield and remembered how, on that very day, fifty years ago, his father, who was lying ill at home, had asked him to open his bookstall in a neighbouring market town, and he had proudly and obstinately refused his help, he drove to the place, humbly uncovered his head, 'and stood with it bare an hour before the stall which my father had formerly used, exposed to the sneers of the standers-by and the inclemency of the weather; a penance' he explained, 'by which I trust I have propitiated heaven for this only instance, I believe, of contumacy towards my father'.

Although his contumacious behaviour had caused him bitter regrets, Johnson's pride, and deep-rooted sense of his own value, continued to distinguish him throughout his whole existence. 'That superiority over his fellows', observes Boswell, 'which he maintained with so much dignity in his march through life, was not assumed from vanity and ostentation, but was the natural and constant effect of those extraordinary powers of mind.... From his earliest years his superiority was perceived and acknowledged. He was from the beginning *Anax andrōn*', a king of men.

Many stories were afterwards told of the benevolent tyranny he exercised. The band of favourites he had collected would await his appearance every morning and, offering their shoulders as an improvised chair, carry him bodily to school. He did not join in the usual

The Grammar School at Lichfield, to which the young Johnson's three devoted friends used to carry him upon their backs; after an early-nineteenth-century drawing by John Buckler.

schoolboy sports – he was already far too short-sighted; but, during the winter months, he sometimes took pleasure 'in being drawn upon the ice by a boy barefooted, who pulled him along by a garter fixed round him; no very easy operation, as his size was remarkably large'.

Similarly, at Pembroke College, Oxford, where he entered as a

Commoner in October, 1728, he very soon made himself the centre of a circle of appreciative friends, among whom he 'was generally seen lounging' on the threshold of the College gate, entertaining them with his conversation and keeping them from their academic studies, 'if not spiriting them up to rebellion against the College discipline ...'. In those days, he was accounted 'gay and frolicsome' – a boldly impertinent undergraduate, who avoided and despised the dons. His gaiety, however, was superficial; and, later, reviewing his Oxford life, he declared that what his contemporaries had mistaken for 'frolick' had been merely bitterness and frustration, and that, at Oxford, he

Pembroke College, Oxford, in 1744. Johnson was usually to be found lounging on the threshold of College, keeping his friends from their studies, or 'spiriting them up to rebellion against College discipline'. Engraving by George Vertue.

had been 'mad and violent', miserably poor, determined to fight his way; with the result that he had 'disregarded all power and authority'.

Then the ancestral malady struck him down. When he returned home, during the college vacation of the year 1729, he suddenly experienced the full force of the disease he had inherited, and 'felt himself overwhelmed', according to Boswell's narrative, 'with an horrible hypochondria, with perpetual irritation, fretfulness, and impatience; and with a dejection, gloom, and despair, which made existence misery. From this dismal malady he never afterwards was perfectly relieved.' Johnson himself, who took a keen, indeed an almost morbid interest in the history of his own sufferings, dated them back to that hideous early crisis. Since those dreadful days, he observed at sixty-nine, 'my health has been ... such as has seldom afforded me a single day of ease'.

Thenceforward he was never a free man; his melancholia, and the necessity of combatting and, if possible, concealing it, was to govern all his actions. Not only did it transfix him with a terrible sense of dread – he was a sinner, he believed, who, having sinned beyond redemption, was destined to eternal punishment; but it dulled his perceptions, crippled his faculties, and gradually reduced him to a state of overpowering sloth and languor. In 1729, he told a friendly acquaintance, 'he was sometimes so languid and inefficient, that he could not distinguish the hour upon the town-clock'.

Thus Johnson had grown up under the influence of two conflicting but equally dominant sensations – the pride he felt in himself as king among men, and a conviction of weakness and wickedness that would remain with him until his death. How he had acquired his sense of sin is one of those problems we cannot hope to solve; but there are moments when he reminds us of a character described by George Borrow – another life-long melancholic – in his picaresque novel, *The Romany Rye*, who imagined that many years earlier, while he was still almost a child, he had committed the mysterious 'sin against the Holy Ghost'. Soon after the crisis of 1729 – probably during the December of that year* – Johnson seems to have abandoned Oxford; and we next hear of him in 1731 endeavouring, though unsuccessfully, to obtain a position at a country school. Such a position he obtained a year later, but found the drudgery it demanded highly tedious and uncongenial; and thereafter he drifted away to Birmingham, where he tutored a friend's son and did some hackwork for a local printer.

It was not that the young man wanted a patron. He had already secured a valuable supporter in Gilbert Walmesley, Chancellor of the diocese of Lichfield, a rich, amiable and cultured gentleman, at whose house he was frequently entertained, and with whom he met the youthful David Garrick. Walmesley had the reputation of being 'the finest gentleman in Lichfield'; but he had taken an immediate fancy to 'the huge, overgrown, mis-shapen' stripling, and welcomed him 'as man to man, as friend to friend'; though Mr Walmesley was 'a zealous Whig', and Johnson, even in his boyhood an impassioned Tory, 'maintained his opinions on every subject' (wrote the poetess Anna Seward, who herself had been brought up at Lichfield) 'with the same sturdy, dogmatic and arrogant fierceness with which he now overbears all opposition ...'.

*Boswell believed that Johnson stayed on at Pembroke until 1731. But recent researches appear to prove him wrong. See Joseph Wood Krutch: *Samuel Johnson*.

The earliest known portrait of Samuel Johnson; executed by Joshua Reynolds in 1756, a year after his triumphant completion of the *Dictionary*.

None of his Lichfield or Oxford friends, however, could do much to help him on his way through life. He was still wretchedly poor. When Michael Johnson died in December 1731, he had left his nearly bankrupt business to the care of his widow and his younger son, Nathaniel, and to Samuel, a legacy of twenty pounds. Thus he continued to drift, translating a travel-book from the French*, and making abortive efforts to interest a London editor. But then, a sudden shaft of light transfigured the whole murky prospect. At Birmingham he encountered a middle-aged widow, Mrs Elizabeth Jervis Porter – she had three children, the eldest, her daughter, Lucy, being nearly grown up – and immediately fell deep in love.

During his earlier life, Boswell assures us, his 'attachments to the fair sex' were always brief and unimportant; 'and it is certain that he formed no criminal connections whatsoever.... In a man whom religious education has secured from licentious indulgences, the passion of love, once it has seized him, is exceedingly strong.... This was experienced by Johnson, when he became a fervent admirer of Mrs Porter, after her first husband's death.' To her daughter Lucy, Boswell was indebted for a vivid account of Mrs Porter's earliest impressions of the strange young Lichfield genius:

... His appearance was very formidable: he was then lean and lank, so that his immense structure of bones was hideously striking to the eye, and the scars of the scrophula were deeply visible. He also wore his hair, which was stiff and straight, and separated behind: and he often had, seemingly, convulsive starts and odd gesticulations, which tended to excite at once surprize and ridicule. Mrs Porter was so engaged by his conversation that she overlooked all these external disadvantages, and said to her daughter, 'this is the most sensible man that I ever saw in my life'.

Samuel Johnson, aged twenty-six, married the forty-six-year-old Elizabeth Porter on 9 July 1735. 'It was a love-marriage', he told Topham Beauclerk; but, apart from the married pair themselves, no one could explain their union. Though Mrs Johnson, Boswell conjectured, 'must have had a superiority of understanding and talents', her 'person and manner were by no means pleasing ...'. Garrick described her to Mrs Thrale as 'a little painted Poppet; full of Affectation and rural Airs of Elegance'; while Dr Levett, latterly Johnson's perpetual guest and cantankerous private pensioner, alleged that 'She was always drunk and reading Romances in her Bed ...'. But the only

*Father Jerome Lobo's *Voyage to Abyssinia*, which may afterwards have inspired him to write his Abyssinian novel, *Rasselas*. Johnson used a French version of the Portuguese Jesuit's text.

The only surviving portrait of Elizabeth, or 'Tetty', Johnson (1689–1752), whom Garrick remembered as 'a little painted Poppet; full of Affectation and rural Airs of Elegance'.

serious early quarrel that Johnson cared to recollect was said to have taken place as they rode to church upon their wedding day. The bride complained that her bridegroom rode too fast, and, when he slackened his pace and she passed him, that he was riding far too slowly. But he had soon perceived, he remarked to Mrs Thrale, 'that it was Coquettry only', and without more ado jogged straight ahead. At which she had submissively followed behind; 'but I believe', he said 'there was a Tear or two – Pretty dear Creature!'

Johnson's next step was to set up his own school, presumably with assistance from his wife's capital, which amounted to about £700; and in 1736 the *Gentleman's Magazine* carried a succint advertisement: 'At Edial, near Lichfield, in Staffordshire, young gentleman are boarded and taught the Latin and Greek languages, by SAMUEL JOHNSON.' The school failed; only three boys, David and George Garrick and 'a Mr Offely*, a young gentleman of good fortune who died early', ever presented themselves at Johnson's door. David Garrick was a lively, but inquisitive and somewhat malicious pupil; and Boswell admits that, according to Garrick's evidence, Johnson does not appear to have been deeply respected by his charges:

His oddities of manner, and uncouth gesticulations, could not but be the subject of merriment to them; and, in particular, the young rogues used to listen at the door of his bed-chamber, and peep through the key-hole, that they might turn into ridicule his tumultuous and awkward fondness for Mrs Johnson, whom he used to name by the familiar appellation of *Tetty* or *Tetsey*. . . . Mr Garrick described her to me as very fat, with a bosom of more than ordinary protuberance, with swelled cheeks of a florid red, produced by thick painting, and the liberal use of cordials; flaring and fantastick in her dress, and affected both in her speech and general behaviour.

Long after her death, Boswell saw Garrick imitating Mrs Johnson, with his 'exquisite talent for mimickry, so as to excite the heartiest burst of laughter'; and among those who loved and admired Johnson his married life was usually treated as a grotesque and unbecoming episode. But Johnson himself, though he allowed that Tetty was occasionally capricious and difficult, always regarded his seventeen years of marriage as a period of real happiness. For a while, however, once his school had failed, he found it necessary to desert his wife; and in February 1737, he and David Garrick – Johnson claimed that

---

*Laurence Offley; according to Johnson's first biographer, Sir John Hawkins, Johnson's pupils may have been slightly more numerous, but, 'at no time, exceeded eight', of whom 'not all were boarders'.

On the left, David Garrick (1717–79) and his friend William Windham of Felbrigg; portrait by Francis Hayman.

they had had less than sixpence between them – left Staffordshire and rode to London.

Late in the summer, Johnson returned home, having accomplished apparently very little; but, that autumn, he decided to make a second journey south. This time his travelling-companion was Tetty; and, during the next few years, the Johnsons inhabited a series of cheap London lodgings, which Tetty, still the provincial housewife, did her best to keep clean. Her domesticated habits caused many disputes. She had 'a particular reverence for cleanliness', he told Mrs Thrale – a reverence he himself never shared – and Tetty was one of those women who are slaves to their brooms and look forward to 'the hour of sweeping their husband out of the house' along with other dirt and rubbish. 'A clean floor is *so* comfortable' she would remark by way of teasing Johnson.

Presumably, Tetty's small capital had been long ago exhausted; and he was now an industrious journalist, wringing a weekly income out of London booksellers and editors. They were poor, of course, though perhaps not quite so hopelessly poor as would appear from Johnson's later stories – yet, at one moment, certainly poor enough to be obliged to sell his mother's silver cup and spoon. Poor they remained; and his years of bohemian obscurity left an indelible mark upon his character. It was then that he had first become acquainted with another struggling bohemian, Richard Savage.

Despite the fact that he judged the world as a moralist and, if he distrusted or disliked a man, customarily emphasized his moral failings, for those whom he happened to like or love he was always ready to make large exceptions. Savage's warmest admirers could not have pretended that he had led a virtuous life – his conduct, Boswell announces, was a mixture of 'profligacy, insolence, and ingratitude'. But he possessed 'a warm and vigorous, though unregulated mind'; and, since he 'had seen life in all its varieties, and been much in the company of the statesmen and wits of his time, he could communicate to Johnson an abundant supply of such materials as his philosophical curiosity most eagerly desired...'.

Edward Cave (1691–1754), proprietor of the *Gentleman's Magazine*, whose hireling journalists included Johnson and Savage.

They met at the offices of the *Gentleman's Magazine*, then edited by Edward Cave from St John's Gate, Clerkenwell, the former gate-house of an ancient monastic foundation, which both journalists regularly visited to dash off occasional essays and reviews. Their labours were ill-rewarded; and sometimes 'all the money they could both raise was less than sufficient to purchase for them the shelter and sordid comforts of a night cellar', and they found it necessary to walk the streets. Johnson afterwards spoke to Sir Joshua Reynolds of 'one night in particular, when Savage and he walked round St James's square.... They were not at all depressed by their situation; but in

St James Square, 1752. Johnson remembered that Savage and he had once spent all night walking round and round it.

high spirits and brimful of patriotism, traversed the square for several hours, inveighed against the minister, and "resolved they would *stand by their country*".'

No doubt they also talked of the reverses they had known themselves. At least in his own eyes, Savage's history was a classic case of oppression and injustice; for he asserted that, although born out of wedlock, he was a man of noble lineage, the bastard son of Lady Macclesfield by

her lover, Lord Rivers; and that his 'inhuman' mother, now divorced
and remarried, had callously ignored his pleas, assuring Lord Rivers
that their child had died, and that she believed Savage to be the
legitimate son of a shoemaker whose wife she had employed as nurse.
Savage was proud of his illegitimate origins; and in 1728 he had
published a poem, *The Bastard*, dedicated, 'with all due reverence',
to his mother, Mrs Brett, proclaiming that a love-child was naturally
superior to the commonplace offspring of the marriage-bed:

> Blest be the Bastard's birth! thro' wond'rous ways,
> He shines excentric, like a comet's blaze!
> No sickly fruit of faint compliance He!
> He stampt in nature's mint of exstacy!
> He lives to build, not boast a generous race:
> No tenth transmitter of a foolish face.
> His daring hope, no sire's example bounds:
> His first-born lights, no prejudice confounds.
> He, kindling from within, requires no flame;
> He glories in a Bastard's glowing name . . .

Savage had little or no corroborative evidence to support his far-
fetched story; but Johnson, who, if it suited his thesis, seldom paid
much heed to evidence, readily accepted the whole tragic tale; and,
when Savage died in 1743, he hastened to do literary justice to his
'unfortunate and ingenious' friend. 'I wrote', he said, 'forty-eight of
the printed octavo pages of the *Life of Savage* at a sitting.' But then,
he had 'sat up all night'. The work created a considerable stir. 'Upon
his return from Italy', Reynolds assured Boswell, 'he met with it in
Devonshire, knowing nothing of its author, and began to read it while
he was standing with his arm leaning against a chimney-piece. It
seized his attention so strongly, that, not being able to lay the book
down till he had finished it, when he attempted to move, he found his
arm totally benumbed.'

What had interested Johnson in Savage was perhaps not so much
the injustices he claimed to have suffered as the essential strangeness
of his personality; and Sir John Hawkins, whose *Life of Johnson* came
out in 1787 – Boswell's long-delayed masterpiece would not appear
until 1791 – suggests that he was also captivated by Savage's 'dress
and demeanour ... for it must be noted of him, that, though he was ...
an admirer of genteel manners, he at this time had not been accustomed to the conversation of Gentlemen; and Savage ... was, to a
remarkable degree, accomplished: he was a handsome, well-made man,
and very courteous in the modes of salutation. I have been told, that

in taking off his hat and disposing it under his arm, and in his bow, he displayed as much grace as those actions were capable of; and that he understood the exercise of a gentleman's weapon, may be inferred from the use he made of it in that encounter which is related in his life, and to which his greatest misfortunes were owing.'*

Savage's loneliness, despite his brilliant gifts, and the deep mystery that surrounded his parentage, may have added to his fascination. He was 'a man dropped into the world as from a cloud'; and his story moved Johnson's imagination, just as the somewhat similar legend of '*le pauvre Gaspard*'** was presently to charm the French Romantics. Moreover, he had a fund of curious knowledge. It was he who, like Virgil conducting Dante, introduced Johnson to the modern inferno of poverty and vice and crime. Neither Hawkins nor Boswell felt that his influence on the younger man had been altogether salutary. 'How far his conversations with Savage', writes Hawkins, 'might induce him ... to delight in tavern society, which is often a temptation to greater enormities than excessive drinking cannot now be known, nor would it serve any good purpose to enquire.'

'I am afraid ...', Boswell admits, 'that by associating with Savage, who was habituated to the dissipation and licentiousness of the town, Johnson ... was imperceptibly led into some indulgencies which occasioned much distress to his virtuous mind.' Throughout the whole period of his marriage, he is said to have drunk only water; but, at taverns and other places of resort, he was not averse from meeting prostitutes. These brief contacts, however, would appear to have been largely innocent. He enjoyed hearing the young women talk and persuading them to tell the stories of their lives.

Later, the recollections of his past sins, committed, no doubt, under his friend's amoral influence, often troubled and alarmed him. He possessed none of Savage's coarse effrontery; and, notwithstanding his odd bohemian habits, he was always a devoted husband. Though he and Tetty were frequently separated – he visiting his friends near Lichfield, she retiring to take the waters at Hampstead – their marriage never broke up; and in 1748, when he began his work on the *Dictionary*, which had been commissioned a year earlier by a group of enterprising London publishers, they moved into 17 Gough Square, a fairly

---

* Savage had killed a man in a drunken squabble and stood trial at the Old Bailey. When Hawkins asserts that Johnson was not accustomed to the society of gentlemen, he seems to have forgotten his association with the cultivated Gilbert Walmesley.

** Kaspar Hauser, who inspired one of Paul Verlaine's most beautiful lyrics, was a mysterious changeling, believed by some to be the child of the Empress Josephine's niece, Stéphanie de Beauharnais; by others, to be the bastard offspring of Napoleon himself.

Top The dining-room of Johnson's house in Gough Square, built about 1700 by
a successful London tradesman. Here Johnson lived from 1749 to 1759.
Above Johnson's house; the staircase.

spacious house off Fleet Street, where Johnson's six assistants occupied an upper room, and 'he gave to the copyists their several tasks'.

He himself steadily 'tugged at his oar', skimming through innumerable volumes and marking the passages he had chosen for reference with a heavy black-lead pencil. The *Dictionary* was published in 1755, an achievement that brought him 'great fame', if not the wealth he had expected. But meanwhile, three years earlier, Tetty had died, leaving him (wrote Sir John Hawkins, who did not respect her memory) 'a childless widower, abandoned to sorrow, and incapable of consolation'. So long as he lived, he preserved her wedding-ring

St Dunstan's, Fleet Street, with a distant view of Temple Bar; drawing by Thomas Malton.

'in a little round wooden box'*; and his dead wife was thenceforward seldom absent either from his thoughts or from his secret prayers.

Against the sense of solitude that now enveloped him Johnson battled with despairing courage. He became the man who felt most at home in a tavern, and announced that a tavern chair was 'the throne of human felicity', and that, as for a tavern itself, there was no other

---

* Inside the lid he pasted an inscription:

> *Eheu!*
> *Eliz: Johnson*
> *Nupta Jul. 9 1736,*
> *Mortua, eheu!*
> *Mart. 17 1752*

written out 'in fair characters'.

institution 'contrived by man, by which so much happiness is produced'. At the same time, he filled his empty rooms with a 'family'
of starveling pensioners; for, among these often ungrateful waifs and
strays, his life, otherwise so erratic and desultory, appeared to have a
Christian purpose. But he was still alone; and loneliness remained
the keynote of Johnson's existence from the death of his wife in 1752
until, through Murphy's good offices, he met the Thrales in 1765.

During that period, however, thanks to his two long poems, *London*
and *The Vanity of Human Wishes*, his tragic drama, *Irene* (which
David Garrick had produced, though unsuccessfully, at Drury Lane)

George III (1738–1820); from the studio of Allan Ramsay. Johnson was an avowed
Jacobite, though he became a royal pensioner.

his novel, *Rasselas*, and, above all else, his *Rambler* essays, he had been
slowly building up a reputation. In the year that saw the appearance of
the *Dictionary*, he was awarded an honorary degree by the University
of Oxford – an honour that delighted him – and, finally, in 1762,
granted a royal pension of £300 per annum.

The grant was unexpected, even a trifle embarrassing; for it reached
Johnson through Lord Bute, now the young King's Prime Minister –
George III had succeeded to his grandfather's throne in October 1760 –
who, both as a Scotsman and as a servant of the Hanoverian line,
should have ranked among his chief aversions. It was nonetheless
extremely welcome; and Johnson accepted it with good grace. In 1756
he had been actually arrested for debt – the amount involved was five

pounds eighteen shillings*; and when his mother died at Lichfield, in January 1759, he was obliged to write his Abyssinian novel – it was produced, he said, 'on the evenings of one week', sections of the narrative, which he never read again, being sent off by the printer's devil as soon as he had finished them – to pay her modest funeral expenses.

Having at last secured a decent yearly income, Johnson was secure from want; but neither financial security nor public fame and honours could alleviate his moods of black depression. They recurred with hideous regularity; and, during the year 1764, the thoughts that

Left Bennet Langton (1737–1801). A portrait by George Dance of Langton in his latter years.
Right Topham Beauclerk (1739–80); chief among Johnson's younger friends: 'Everything comes from Beauclerk so easily', he remarked, 'that it appears to me I labour if I say a good thing'. A pastel portrait by Francis Cotes of Beauclerk at the age of seventeen.

oppressed him seem to have been particularly dark and doleful. Thus, on Good Friday, 20 April, he added some poignant sentences to the notebook that enshrined his *Meditations*: 'I have made no reformation; I have lived totally useless, more sensual in thought, and more addicted to wine and meat.' And, a day later:

My indolence, since my last reception of the sacrament, has sunk into

* In a letter, dated 16 March, Johnson applied for help to Samuel Richardson, the veteran novelist, referring to his 'former obligations'.

grosser sluggishness, and my dissipation spread into wilder negligence. My thoughts have been clouded with sensuality; and, except that from the beginning of this year I have, in some measure, forborne excess of strong drink, my appetites have predominated over my reason. A kind of strange oblivion has overspread me, so that I know not what has become of the last year. . . .

These were the reflections, we must remember, not of a self-tormenting solitary, but of an active, exceptionally gregarious man, who, if he had a free choice between society and solitude, very seldom passed an hour alone. Many new friends had recently come his way, including Joshua Reynolds and two rich and fashionable young gentlemen, the serious, cultured Bennet Langton and the 'gay, dissipated' Topham Beauclerk. He loved the young, and always enjoyed their company; but the last was a friendship that astonished Garrick. Did Johnson propose to wander the streets with Beauclerk, get drunk and perhaps assault the watch? 'What a coalition!' he remarked. 'I shall have my old friend to bail out of the Round house.'

More important was the friendship that, on Monday, 16 May 1763, had begun in the back-room of Tom Davies' bookshop, when a young Scotsman, as he peeped through the glass door, beheld the great moralist and lexicographer advancing majestically towards him. Boswell's own vivid account of their meeting, and of the succession of tremendous snubs with which Johnson, enraged by a tactlessness he mistook for vulgar impertinence, almost immediately felled him to the ground, need not be repeated here. Though, at the time, he says, he felt a good deal stunned, Boswell very soon recovered; and Davies bade him pluck up his spirits, observing somewhat unexpectedly, 'I can see he likes you well'.

It was on the 24th that, encouraged by Davies' words, Boswell dared to cross the great man's threshold. His reception was reassuring:

. . . But it must be confessed, that his apartment and furniture, and morning dress, were sufficiently uncouth. His brown suit of cloaths looked very rusty; he had on a little old shrivelled unpowdered wig, which was too small for his head; his shirt-neck and knees of his breeches were loose; his black worsted stockings ill drawn up; and he had a pair of unbuckled shoes by way of slippers. But all these slovenly particularities were forgotten the moment that he began to talk. Some gentlemen . . . were sitting with him; and when they went away, I also rose; but he said to me, 'Nay, don't go.' 'Sir, (said I,) I am afraid that I intrude upon you. It is benevolent to allow me to sit and hear you'. He seemed pleased with this compliment . . . and answered, 'Sir, I am obliged to any man who visits me.'

On a subsequent occasion, when Boswell reminded Johnson of

No. 1, Inner Temple Lane, where, on 24 May 1763, Boswell visited Johnson at home for the first time. 'He received me very courteously; but it must be confessed, that his apartment, and furniture, and morning dress, were sufficiently uncouth'.

the rough treatment he had received at Tom Davies' bookshop, 'Poh, poh! (said he, with a complacent smile,) never mind these things. Come to me as often as you can, I shall be glad to see you.' Thereafter the friendship grew and prospered; and Boswell was often privileged to dine in Johnson's company, told him the story of his own life, and heard him deliver his opinions on a large variety of absorbing topics, which included ghosts, the evidences of Christianity, Methodism, governments good and bad, insanity, the virtues of the young (whom he had always preferred to the old) and the inferiority of the French writers. But Boswell was just then bound for Europe; and early in August he left London to undertake an extended Grand Tour. Johnson – a singular proof of his affection – bore him company as far as Harwich. From the deck of the packet-boat, Boswell writes, 'I kept my eyes upon him for a considerable time, while he remained rolling his majestick frame in his usual manner: and at last I perceived him walk back into the town, and he disappeared.'

When they parted, both Johnson and Boswell seem to have experienced a genuine pang of loss. Boswell moped and desponded in Holland; and, next year, a fearful resurgence of his old malady, 'the hypochondriack disorder, which was ever lurking about him', temporarily laid Johnson low. It was a severe attack. 'He was so ill', reports Boswell, 'as, notwithstanding his remarkable love of company, to be entirely averse to society, the most fearful symptom of that malady. Dr Adams told me, that ... he was admitted to visit him, and that he found him in a deplorable state, sighing, groaning, talking to himself, and restlessly walking from room to room. He then used this emphatical expression of the misery which he felt: "I would consent to have a limb amputated to recover my spirits".'

Although Murphy had been careful to warn them that his appearance was surprising, the Thrales had little previous knowledge of the guest they entertained at Southwark. Johnson, in his mid-fifties, was a huge, ungainly man, nearly six feet tall without his shoes, large-boned, broad-shouldered and thick-necked. His legs and feet, Mrs Thrale noted, were both 'eminently handsome, his hand handsome too, in spite of Dirt, and of such Deformity as perpetual picking his Fingers necessarily produced'. His face was rugged, pitted and scored. He was, moreover, extremely myopic, and had lost the sight of one eye. The colour of his eyes was light blue; and they were 'so wild, so piercing, and at Time so fierce; that Fear was I believe the first Emotion in the hearts of all his Beholders'.

No less alarming were Johnson's fashion of speech and the series of convulsive tics that regularly shook his frame:

While talking or even musing as he sat in his chair, [runs Boswell's vivid description] he commonly held his head to one side towards his right shoulder, and shook it in a tremulous manner, moving his body backwards and forwards, and rubbing his left knee in the same direction, with the palm of his hand. In the intervals of articulating he made various sounds with his mouth, sometimes as if ruminating, or what is called chewing the cud, sometimes giving a half whistle, sometimes making his tongue play backwards from the roof of his mouth, as if clucking like a hen, and sometimes protruding it against his upper gums in front, as if pronouncing quickly under his breath, *too, too, too*. . . . Generally when he had concluded a period in the course of a dispute, by which time he was a good deal exhausted by violence and vociferation, he used to blow out his breath like a Whale.

A profoundly superstitious man, obsessed by the idea of numbers, which for him possessed an arcane meaning, Johnson had also contracted the habit of counting the steps that it took him to reach a door, and was careful to leave a room either with his left or with his right foot – Boswell had forgotten which; '. . . I have upon innumerable occasions, observed him suddenly stop, and then seem to count his steps with a deep earnestness; and when he had neglected or gone wrong in this sort of magical movement, I have seen him go back again, put himself in a proper posture to begin the ceremony, and, having gone through it, break from his abstraction, walk briskly on, and join his companion'.

These psychological quirks, like his melancholia, he apparently attributed to his ancestral heritage. His father's sanity, he believed, had hung by a thread. Mrs Thrale learned that, although the bookseller's workshop, 'a detached building, had fallen half down for want of money to repair it', Michael Johnson had not been 'less diligent to lock the door every night', despite the fact 'that any body might walk in at the back part. . . . "This (says his son) was madness, you may see, and would have been discoverable in other instances of the prevalence of imagination, but that poverty prevented it from playing such tricks as riches and leisure encourage".'

In middle age, Johnson himself frequently gave the impression of being either mad or partially deranged; and William Hogarth, not only a great painter but an accomplished physiognomist, used to relate how he had encountered him with Samuel Richardson. He had 'perceived a person', said Hogarth, 'standing at a window in the room, shaking his head, and rolling himself about in a strange ridiculous manner. He concluded that he was an ideot, whom his relations had put under the care of Mr Richardson, as a very good man. To his great surprize, however, this figure stalked forwards to where he and Mr Richardson were sitting' – they were discussing a belated victim of the Jacobite revolt of 1745 – 'and all at once took up the argument, and burst out into an invective against George the Second. . . . He

Right James Boswell as young man; portrait by George Willison.

displayed such a power of eloquence, that Hogarth looked at him with astonishment, and actually imagined that this ideot had been at the moment inspired.'

During the last few years, Johnson's aspect had not grown any less wild, nor his manners more accommodating; and it says much for Henry and Hester Thrale that they should have given him so warm a welcome. They must have presented a remarkably incongruous picture – the host, large, polite, impassive, presiding with firm, yet good-natured authority over the splendid meal he had himself ordered; the hostess, small, alert and talkative, quietly deferring to her husband, yet full of verve and conversational spirit; and their guest, whose clothes were old-fashioned and whose hands perhaps not very clean, grimacing and twitching as he dominated their table and keenly

Left Samuel Richardson (1689–1761); portrait by Joseph Highmore, 1750.
Right William Hogarth (1767–1864); bust by L. F. Roubiliac. At their first meeting, he mistook Johnson for a harmless lunatic, who had been entrusted by his family to Samuel Richardson's care.

Top Leicester Square, 1753. William Hogarth occupied a house on the right.
Above Brighthelmstone in 1778. Here Johnson had his first glimpse of the open sea.

scrutinized the various dishes, or rolling back in his chair to deliver some majestic peroration, from which he emerged at length with whale-like grunts and sighs.

By the time they separated that evening, Johnson had made the Thrales' conquest; and he was soon dining at Southwark every Thursday. In the autumn of 1765, learning that his friends had departed for Brighthelmstone (the newly fashionable seaside resort that has since become Brighton), he decided he would join them there; and, when he arrived and found them already gone, 'he wrote us a letter expressive of anger, which', remarks Mrs Thrale, 'we were very desirous to pacify ... Mr Murphy brought him back to us again'; and from that day his visits became more frequent. In 1766, however, 'his health ... grew so exceedingly bad' that he could not leave his sickroom. It was Henry Thrale who then suggested that he must be induced to quit his unhealthy urban surroundings, and that they should carry him off to enjoy the solid domestic comforts and the wholesome breezy airs of Streatham.

2 'Thralia Dulcis'

Some while before Johnson reached his new home and joined the
Thrales at Streatham Place, he had often lamented to them 'the
horrible condition of his mind', which, he said, was near distraction.
'He charged *us*', writes Mrs Thrale, 'to make him solemn promises of
secrecy'; and, when she and her husband visited his London sick-
room, they were surprised to hear him, as he bade goodbye to a learned
clergyman named Dr Delap, beg that the doctor would remember to
pray for him, couching his request, they noted, 'in the most pathetic
terms'. Mrs Thrale 'felt excessively afflicted with grief'; and even the
stolid Henry Thrale showed signs of being deeply troubled. She well
remembered, Mrs Thrale records, that her husband had 'involuntarily
lifted up one hand', as though to shut the speaker's mouth, on 'hearing
a man so wildly proclaim what he could at last persuade no one to
believe; and what, if true, would have been so very unfit to reveal'.

Soon afterwards Thrale was called away, and left Johnson and his
wife alone. But, meanwhile, he had suggested that she should persuade
their friend to quit his 'close habitation' off a busy London street and
join them as their guest at Streatham. Johnson agreed; and, once she
had finally taken charge of his health, Mrs Thrale 'had the honour and
happiness of contributing to its restoration'. The task, however, was
sometimes 'distressing enough'; and it would have been a great deal
easier 'had not my mother and he disliked one another extremely, and
teized me often with perverse opposition, petty contentions, and
mutual complaints'.

Both were positive, strong-minded characters; and, as elderly
people are always apt to do, they frequently squabbled about 'the
daily prints'. Mrs Salusbury was fond of reading the newspapers
and discussing foreign politics. Not only did Johnson despise all
foreigners; but this 'superfluous attention' to a subject with which
no well-bred woman need concern herself clearly exasperated him
beyond endurance. If he were sufficiently annoyed, Johnson did not

spare his enemy; and now, alleges Mrs Thrale, he went so far as to concoct fictitious news-items regarding 'the division of Poland perhaps, or the disputes between the states of Russia and Turkey', and cause them to be printed in the London press. Poor Mrs Salusbury was at first deceived, until the writer's style betrayed him. She was then 'exceedingly angry'; and a bitter feud sprang up that disturbed the Streatham household – though Mr Thrale presumably remained aloof – for another six years.

Since she had become accustomed to managing her daughter's life, Mrs Salusbury was also deeply vexed by the signs she detected of Johnson's powerful influence. A born teacher, gifted with a penetrating insight into every sort of human problem – apart, of course, from the problems that bedevilled his own mind and senses – Johnson, once he had gained a friend, immediately set to work upon that friend's improvement. As his affection for Hester Thrale grew, she acquired the privileges of a favourite pupil; and she received a particularly important piece of advice during the earliest period of their friendship, when she 'first had the Pleasure of getting acquainted with Johnson', and he had begun patiently opening her eyes to the 'odd kind of Life' she led at home:

One Day that I mentioned Mr Thrale's cold Carriage to me, tho' with no Resentment, for it occassioned in me no Dislike; He said in Reply – Why now for Heaven's Sake Dearest Madam should any Man delight in a Wife that is to him neither Use nor Ornament? He cannot talk to you about his Business, which you do not understand; nor about his Pleasures which you do not partake; if you have Wit or Beauty you shew them nowhere, so he has none of the Reputation; if you have Economy or Understanding you employ neither in Attention to his Property. You divide your Time between your Mamma & your Babies, & wonder you do not by that means become agreable to your Husband.

This somewhat brutal review of her situation was 'so plain', Mrs Thrale remarks, 'that I could not fail to comprehend it'. Why not take an interest in the affairs of the Southwark brewery, where, as she rightly suspected, two meddlesome counsellors, Henry and Humphrey Jackson, who had published a learned treatise on the use of isinglass to clarify fermented liquors, were seriously injuring her husband's business? But first she consulted Mrs Salusbury, and 'gently hinted that I had some Curiosity about the Trade ...'. Her mother was astonished and indignant, pointing out that 'I had my Children to nurse, & to teach, & that She thought that was better Employment than turning into *My Lady Mashtub* ...'.

Such had been her mother's very words; and 'so I went on in the old Way, brought a Baby once a Year, lost some of them & grew so anxious about the rest, that I now fairly cared for nothing else, but them & her; and not a little for Johnson, who I felt to be my true Friend, though I could not break thro' my Chains to take his Advice as it would only have helped to kill my poor Mother, whose health now began to decline, & who was Jealous enough of Mr Johnson's Influence as it was'.

During the earlier years of her marriage, her social amusements had been few indeed; never once did she put her head into a theatre,

The Promenade at Carlisle House, 1781, where Henry Thrale, according to his wife, very often spent his evenings; from a drawing by John Raphael Smith.

'or any Place of publick Resort, till my Eldest Daughter in her sixth Year was carried by Lady Lade to see the King at an Oratorio; & I went too, that I might take proper Care of *her*'. Meanwhile, Mr Thrale continued his usual round, 'in his Counting house all Morning, at Carlisle House*, or the Opera, or some public Place all Evening. . . .'

*Seat of the famous 'assemblies', conducted by Casanova's former mistress, Mrs Cornelys, a haunt of the most expensive London demi-mondaines.

When Mrs Thrale had given birth to her eldest child, Queeney, Mr Thrale was evidently proud and pleased; he was 'very glad to see his little Girl, his beautiful daughter as he called her'. But it had not occurred to him to change his mode of life; 'as for poor me, I believe he might visit my Chamber two or Three Times a Week in a sort of formal Way, which my Mother said was *quite right*, – so therefore I appeared to think so too'.

It was a dull, frustrating round; and the seeds of ambition that Johnson had planted still lay hidden deep beneath the surface. True, in 1770, after nearly seven years of marriage, she decided to make an independant journey – to visit her ailing uncle, Sir Thomas Salusbury, at Offley Park – and set forth unaccompanied, despite her husband's derisive laughter and her mother's furious protests. But, when she returned home 'jocund ... and highly pleased', she soon dropped back again, cheerfully enough, into her 'usual Employments and Amusements'. Indeed, she was now so 'fond of my Poultry, my Dairy etc etc', that she felt 'no other Desire than that of sitting down safely & quietly at Streatham to which of late I had begun rather to attach myself'.

Johnson had frequently scoffed at her interest in her farmyard, and would tell her that, 'while she was feeding her chickens, she was starving her own understanding'. But he would not have presumed to advise a young wife to revolt against her husband; and she might never have succeeded in breaking her chains had it not been for the calamities that threatened to overwhelm Thrale during the summer of the year 1772. Prompted by the Jackson brothers, he had made a long series of imprudent speculations, among others the purchase of an enormous copper vessel, which cost him some £2,000, and of no less than thirty new vats, capable of holding gigantic quantities of beer. It was a costly scheme; his elaborate new equipment spoiled the produce of a whole twelve months. Simultaneously, a sudden financial panic shook the London money market. A number of important firms collapsed; Thrale himself was nearly bankrupt; and, at this crisis of his affairs, he revealed an unexpected lack of resolution.

So distraught was he, and so bewildered, that he temporarily resigned control and permitted his wife and her adjutant, Johnson, to deal with his difficulties as they thought best. Mrs Thrale now emerged in the guise of an efficient businesswoman, confronting rebellious employees, writing innumerable letters and, although she was once again pregnant, hurrying about the country to solicit loans. She triumphed; the Southwark brewery was saved. But the child she bore – a daughter named Penelope – died, 'poor little Maid!', in a few hours.

Thereafter, she never quite returned to her previous state of mild subjection. Johnson's excellent advice began at last to bear fruit; and even Thrale gradually developed a habit of respecting and consulting her. Before long, as the friend and hostess of Johnson, she herself became a social personage; and the visitors who drove from London to Streatham grew increasingly numerous and distinguished. Joshua Reynolds had already appeared, in September 1766; but many of the other friends she collected around her at Streatham did not arrive until the early 1770s, when Henry Thrale was slowly receding into the background, and Mrs Thrale, with Johnson beside her, was the principal ornament of Streatham Place.

A French historian might say that she had founded a *salon*; but this description of the part she played would be somewhat misleading. Hester Thrale bore no resemblance, either in her own personality or in the position she occupied, to such Parisian ladies as the marquise du Deffand, Horace Walpole's bitter, brilliant old admirer, the marquise's faithless protégée, Mademoiselle de Lespinasse, or the temperate and cautious Madame Geoffrin. Like them, she appreciated good talk; and her greatest friends were all tremendous talkers. But she and the French *salonnières* seem to have regarded the art of conversation from very different points of view.

In France, conversation was a substitute for political and social action; and the flood of talk that swept throughout Parisian drawing-rooms helped to undermine, and ultimately bring down the existing fabric of society. During the reign of Louis XV, writes Talleyrand in his memoirs, one or two literary men had found their way into the guarded world of power and privilege; but Fontenelle, Montesquieu, Buffon, brought up under the Sun King, had respected the conventions of the previous epoch, carefully preserving '*ces égards, cette liberté, cette aisance noble qui ont fait le charme et l'illustration des réunions de Paris*'.* Under Louis XVI, '*tout se dénatura*'; every social barrier crumbled: '*Alors l'esprit général de la société subit des modifications de tout genre. On voulait tout connaître, tout approfondir, tout juger. Les sentiments furent remplacés par des idées philosophiques; les passions, par l'analyse du cœur humain; l'envie de plaire, par les opinions; les amusements, par des plans, des projets. ...*'**

Although Madam Geoffrin, that sober and sensible lady, made a

* 'those marks of esteem, that of air of freedom and that patrician easiness, which had given social gatherings in Paris their peculiar charm and dignity'.

** 'Then the mood of society in general suffered every kind of change. People were determined to know everything, investigate everything, judge everything. Sentiments were replaced by philosophical notions; passions, by attempts to analyse the workings of the human heart; the desire to please, by the parade of opinions; amusements, by designs and projects . . . .'

practice of checking her guests' talk should it become too wild and dangerous – '*Voilà qui est bien*', she used to remark, before she directed the conversation towards another, less explosive subject – she was surrounded by the free-thinking *Philosophes*, all literary supporters of the social revolution. Meanwhile, the classes mingled; *esprits forts* consorted with the proudest members of the aristocracy:

Delille dînait chez madame de Polignac avec la reine; l'abbé de Balivière jouait avec M. le comte d'Artois . . . Chamfort prenait le bras de M. de Vaudreuil. . . . Le jeu et le bel esprit avait tout nivelé. . . . Tout les jeunes gens se croyaient propres à gouverner. On critiquait toutes les operations des ministres. Ce que faisaient personellement le roi et la reine était soumis a la discussion et presque toujours a l'improbation des salons de Paris!*

If the Roman Empire had gone laughing to its end, the *Ancien Régime*, as established by Louis XIV, gaily talked itself to death.

Georgian family life; the Warneford and Sitwell families. On the right, Francis Hunt Sitwell and his wife, with their children, Mary and Sitwell Sitwell.

There was nothing, however, in the least subversive about the conversations held at Streatham. Mrs Thrale's delightful drawing-room had a peculiarly English atmosphere; none of the friends she assembled was, in Gallic sense, an '*esprit fort*'. Hers was a middle-class world, one that reflected the profound, though gradual change

*'At Madame de Polignac's house, Delille dined with the Queen; the abbé de la Balivière played cards with M. le comte d'Artois; Chamfort took M. de Vaudreuil's arm. . . . Gambling and the love of wit had had a levelling effect on the whole social system. . . . Every young person felt capable of governing. All the actions of the royal ministers were criticized; and the private behaviour of the King and Queen was talked about, and usually disapproved of, in Parisian drawing-rooms!'

that was now overtaking eighteenth-century England. Aristocratic persons often attended her parties; but her most conspicuous guests were Johnson, Reynolds and Burke, Goldsmith, Burney, Baretti and Boswell, all – with the possible exception of Boswell – gifted descendants of the hard-working *bourgeoisie*; while Johnson, Mrs Thrale admitted, was unquestionably 'a Man of Mean Birth'.

As to Mr Thrale's fortune – now happily restored after the disasters of 1772 – had it not originated in a brewer's vat? And Boswell, who was proud of his own descent from a long line of romantic Scottish lairds, when he was describing Johnson's early relationship with 'the eminent brewer' and his wife, gave a slightly malicious account both of the brewer's humble ancestry and of his rapid progress up the social ladder:

Foreigners [he remarks] are not a little amazed when they hear of brewers, distillers, and men in similar departments of trade, held forth as persons of considerable consequence. In this great commercial country it is natural that a situation which produces much wealth should be considered as very respectable; and, no doubt, honest industry is entitled to esteem. But, perhaps, the too rapid advance of men of low extraction tends to lessen the value of that distinction by birth and gentility, which has ever been found beneficial to the grand scheme of subordination.

This was a state of affairs that Boswell could not approve:

There may be some who think that a new system of gentility might be established, upon principles totally different from what have hitherto prevailed.... Why, in civilised times, we may be asked, should there not be rank and honours, upon principles, which ... are certainly not less worthy.... Why should not the knowledge, the skill, the expertness, the assiduity, and the spirited hazards of trade and commerce, when crowned with success, be entitled to give those flattering distinctions by which mankind are so universally captivated?

Such are the specious, but false arguments for a proposition which always will find numerous advocates, in a nation where men are every day starting up from obscurity to wealth.

Boswell, of course, had a grudge against the Thrales, whom he had once suspected of trying to monopolize the great man's company; but his views were not entirely biased. He was shrewd enough to perceive that a momentous transformation, exemplified by the rise of men like Henry Thrale, was now occuring in the social structure. Though the English eighteenth century is often regarded as, above all else, an aristocratic age, when the nobility and gentry still maintained

'There is in London all that life can afford'; the city's size and mercantile greatness were a source of unending pride to its inhabitants. The Old Custom House Quay by Samuel Scott.

a firm hold on the conduct of the nation's business, and a nobleman, wearing the emblems of his rank,* was still received with general deference, since the end of the seventeenth century a prosperous middle class, cultivated, intelligent, self-assured, had been becoming more and more powerful.

Its emergence left a lasting mark on the arts. Among the vast and splendid houses raised by the Augustan aristocracy lie scattered the

---

* Johnson strongly insisted that a nobleman should wear such emblems. Having been reproached by Mrs Thrale for turning his back on Lord Bolingbroke, Lady Diana Beauclerk's first husband, he grumbled that Lord Bolingbroke did not condescend to advertise his rank. 'What are stars and other signs of superiority made for?'

elegant smaller houses, designed for merchants, lawyers, doctors and parsons, usually the work of an unknown builder, but each in its own way a minor monument of English architectural taste. Literature, too, was coloured by middle-class standards; and both the famous novelists who visited the Thrales at Streatham – Oliver Goldsmith and Fanny Burney – wrote books that described the existence of homely, unpretentious characters, and owed their resounding popular success to vivacious episodes of 'low life'.

The aristocracy themselves had begun to cast aside some of their previous resplendent trappings; and Lord Glenbervie tells us that, at a slightly later period, Charles James Fox used to declare 'that the neglect of dress in people of fashion had, he thought, contributed much to remove the barriers between them and the vulgar, and to propagate levelling and equalizing notions'. The attire of the rich, when they appeared *en grande tenue*, was still elaborate and expensive – and a man's wardrobe, it seems, was no less expensive than a woman's*; but there was a gradual move towards simplicity, as the idea of quiet, unstudied elegance replaced that of ceremonious splendour. Gold-laced suits, of the kind beloved by Boswell**, would at length be given up; and, while women's dresses tended to adopt a simpler, straighter and more fluid line, men's coats had lost the heavy skirts and cuffs that had encumbered them during the earlier half of the century.

Among the other characteristics of Johnson's contemporaries was their ebullient self-esteem, to which even the loss of the American Colonies did comparatively little damage. As they examined the daily newsprints, they might despair of Britain's future; but nothing could shake their belief that they were living in a period of continuous social progress, and that, at least since the days of the Antonine Emperors, no civilization had outshone their own. When Lord Chesterfield blandly announced that 'the present age has ... the honour and pleasure of being extremely well with me', he had expressed the general view; for not only, in private life, were morals and manners improving, but, in the public sphere, a series of brave reforms had eliminated many old abuses. London, since Hogarth depicted it, had

*Johnson and Mrs Thrale's friend, Mrs Strickland, once 'entered into a Dispute whose Dress was most expensive – a Gentleman's or a Lady's'. See *Thraliana*. Dec. 1777.

**Topham Beauclerk, an authentic man of fashion, often made fun of Boswell's gaudy coats, which already seemed provincial.

Left above Beaufort Buildings on the south side of the Strand, a typical eighteenth-century street, lined with commodious brick-built houses; drawing by Thomas Sandby.
Left below An aristocratic eighteenth-century interior, designed by Robert Adam; the Eating Room at Saltram. The graceful design of the carpet seems to be reflected in the ceiling.

ANNE HIS WIFE DAUGHTER
TO CHARLES 3:3 EARL OF CARLISLE.

RICH INGRAM THE FIFTH
VISCOUNT IRWIN

Three stages in the development of masculine fashion between 1720 and 1786.
1. The 5th Viscount Irwin and his wife, painted by Jonathan Richardson about
1720. He wears a heavily skirted coat and square-toed shoes, which give him an
air of ponderous equine dignity.

become a cleaner, quieter, less alarming city. It was better-lighted and,
thanks to a special act passed in 1762, considerably better-paved.
Gin-drinking, the scourge of the London populace from the 1720s to
the 1740s, had been drastically reduced by legislation; and Henry
Fielding's war against crime, launched after the dreadful crime-wave
of 1749 (when a gang of desperadoes had stormed the Gatehouse
Prison) had helped to rid the London streets of pickpockets and high-
way robbers.*

The Age of Anne had been a coarse, out-spoken period; and
women were as rough as men. But Mrs Thrale's feminine contem-

* Surrounding districts, however, were still dangerous; and, in 1763, driving through the
six miles of open country that separated Streatham Place from Southwark, Henry Thrale was
held up at pistol-point and robbed of his silver shoe-buckles and gold watch. The highwayman,
Samuel Beaton, was hanged in August 1763, near the scene of his crime on Kennington Common.
See James L. Clifford: *Hester Lynch Piozzi*.

2. *Left*. Colonel Charles Ingram with his children by P. Mercier, 1741. His coat
is long and gold-laced. 3. *Right*. Sir Christopher and Lady Sykes. His red cutaway
coat lacks any type of meretricious ornament, and has an elegantly simple line.
Portrait by George Romney.

poraries affected an extreme refinement. How great a Change [she
wrote on 4 November 1782] has been wrought in Female Manners
within these few Years in England! I was reading the Letter in the
3d Vol: of the Spectator 217. where the Man complains of his in-
delicate Mistress. I read it aloud to my little daughters of 11 & 12 Years
old, & even the Maid who was dressing my Hair, burst out o'laughing
at the Idea of *a Lady* saying her Stomach ach'd, or that something
stuck between her Teeth. Sure if our Morals are as much mended as
our Manners, we are grown a most virtuous Nation!

In any account of the social life of the later eighteenth century,
Samuel Johnson bulks large. Yet, although the figure he cut was
wonderfully bold and imposing, it was by no means representative;
a great many of Johnson's opinions and attitudes would appear to
have run directly counter to the spirit of his own age. It was a refined
age, one that had evolved a complicated code of good manners. When

Mrs Thrale set out to classify her male friends according to their moral and intellectual worth, she decided that she would conduct her examination under seven different heads. Having begun with 'Religion', 'Morality' and 'Scholarship' – here Johnson dropped a single mark: his Greek scholarship, Mrs Thrale suspected, was not so perfect as it might have been – she added 'General Knowledge', 'Person and Voice', 'Manner', 'Wit, Humor, and Good humor'. Thus, of the virtues she demanded in a man, only two were connected with the life of the spirit. The rest, except for scholarship, had a purely mundane value, and were calculated to assist the orderly working of

Rustic Mayfair; the corner of White Horse Street and Piccadilly, opposite the Green Park. Drawing by James Miller, 1775.

the modern social system.

In this intensely gregarious period, every educated person who went out into society was expected to play an honourable part and, if not to shine, at least to please. The adjective 'pleasing', used as a term of high praise, occurs again and again in eighteenth-century records; and pleasing manners appear to have been those which combined an air of formal dignity with a certain admixture of engaging informality. Boswell was generally liked; but he did not always please; once he was excited and had drunk a bottle of wine, he invariably went too far. Still less did Johnson please, though he commanded deep respect; his behaviour in society was much too rough and overbearing. Neither personal refinement nor social civility distinguished him among his fellows.

True, he believed, and often loudly asserted, that he was one of the politest men alive. 'He always wished', Mrs Thrale observes, 'for the Praise of good Breeding.... He would not sit forward nor on your right hand in a Coach.... He would not go into dinner till you arrived if he was ever so hungry, or the hour ever so late; would not displace an Infant if sitting in the Chair he chose, & always said he was more attentive to others than any body was to him – & yet says he *People call me rude.*'

The Green Park in 1760. To the left, Spencer House and the towers of Westminster Abbey; to the right, Buckingham House. Rosamond's Pond, scene of many romantic suicides, occupies the foreground.

Johnson's physical passions had always been strong; and – apart from concupiscence, which he very rarely mentioned save in the pages of his secret notebooks – he seldom troubled to disguise them. Certainly he did not disguise his greed; during later life, his powerful sexual appetites seem to have been largely diverted into a gigantic appetite for food. Since the nervous illness that had afflicted him in the year 1765, he customarily refused wine; but the deprivation he decided to impose on himself had served merely to increase his love of eating.

Mr Johnson's ... pleasures [noted Mrs Thrale] except those of conversation, were all coarse ones: he loves a good Dinner dearly – eats it voraciously, & his notions of a good Dinner are nothing less than delicate – a Leg of Pork boyl'd till it drops from the bone almost, a Veal Pye with Plumbs and Sugar, and the outside Cut of a Buttock of Beef are his favourite dainties, though he loves made Dishes, Soups etc: sowces his Plumb Pudden with melted Butter, & pours Sauce enough into every Plate to drown all Taste of the Victuals. With regard to Drink his liking is for the *strongest*, as it is not the Flavour but the Effect of Wine which he ever professes to desire, and he used often to pour Cappillaire* into his Glass of Port when it was his Custom to drink Wine which he has now left wholly off. To make himself amends for this Concession, he drinks Chocolate liberally. . . .

Boswell, too, was astonished, and a little perturbed, by his old friend's herculean appetite:

I never knew any man who relished good eating more than he did. When at table, he was totally absorbed in the business of the moment; his looks seemed rivetted to his plate; nor would he, unless in very high company, say one word, or even pay the least attention to what was said by others, till he had satisfied his appetite, which was so fierce, and indulged with such intenseness, that . . . the veins of his forehead swelled, and generally a strong perspiration was visible. To those whose sensations were delicate, this could not but be disgusting; and it was doubtless not very suitable to the character of a philosopher. . . . But it must be owned, that Johnson, though he could be rigidly *abstemious*, was not a *temperate* man either in eating or drinking. He could refrain, but he could not use moderately.

Gluttony was among the characteristic vices of the eighteenth-century Englishman; and none of Johnson's acquaintances was surprised to notice that he evidently enjoyed his meals. What offended them was his lack of gentlemanly restraint – the surly enthusiasm and expression of barely concealed ferocity with which he flung himself upon a good dinner, and the intemperate gusto with which he wolfed it down. His table-manners were by no means prepossessing. 'He is more beastly in dress and person', exclaimed a squeamish lady, who had watched him at table for the first time, 'than anything I ever beheld. He feeds nastily and ferociously, and eats quantities most unthankfully.' If his dinner proved to be disappointing, as very often dinners were, though he might excuse his negligent host or hostess, he would sternly inveigh against the knavish cook.

Nor was he prepared to tolerate high-flown sentiment. In an age that had coined the adjective 'sentimental', he was fiercely straightforward. Laurence Sterne, a writer he detested, had first introduced

---

* 'A syrup flavoured with orange-flower water': *Oxford English Dictionary*.

the word as early as 1741; and in 1748 Lady Bradshaigh, writing to her friend Samuel Richardson, begs him to enlighten her about the exact significance of the term now 'so much in vogue among the polite.... Everything clever and agreable is comprehended in that word.' The year 1768 had seen the publication of *A Sentimental Journey*; but, while Sterne had taught the world to mourn over a dead ass and sympathize with the loneliness of a caged starling, Johnson resolutely declined to shed tears unless he had the strongest reasons – which usually meant, of course, unless he were himself the sufferer.

The majority of men and women, he was inclined to believe, exaggerated the importance of their own emotions. He hated hyberbole, ridiculed displays of grief; and, when Mrs Thrale lamented the death of a near relation recently killed in the American War, '"Prithee, my dear (said he), have done with canting: how would the world be worse for it, I may ask, if all your relations were at once spitted like larks, and roasted for Presto's supper?" Presto was the dog that lay under the table while we talked.' One might grieve, perhaps, for a beloved wife, an only child or a greatly valued friend. Even then, one should set a limit to mourning. 'Grief', he considered, 'has its time.'

A realist in an age of sentiment, Johnson also pretended to dislike the arts in a period that had witnessed the rise of some of the most distinguished English artists. Sir Joshua Reynolds was an old friend; but Johnson was too honest to claim that he had the smallest taste for painting. 'Indeed', writes Mrs Thrale, 'Dr Johnson's utter scorn of painting was such, that I have heard him say, that he should sit very quietly in a room hung round with the works of the greatest masters, and never feel the slightest disposition to turn them if their backs were outermost, unless it might be for the sake of telling Sir Joshua that he *had* turned them.' His insensitiveness was evidently much increased by the fact that he was half-blind; and, since he had long been hard of hearing, he was equally oblivious to the charms of music.

His contemporaries delighted in sightseeing, and were charmed by any natural prospect that stirred the literary imagination. Thrale, for example, had always 'loved prospects'; and, when they journeyed together, he was 'mortified that his friend could not enjoy the sight of those different dispositions of wood and water, hill and valley, that travelling through England and France affords a man. But when he wished to point them out to his companion: "Never heed such nonsense", would be the reply: "a blade of grass is always a blade of grass, whether in one country or another: let us if we *do* talk, talk about something; men and women are my subjects of enquiry; let us see how these differ from those we have left behind".'

'View on the Pont Neuf'. Johnson shared the average middle-class Englishman's contempt for foreigners.

Sightseeing with Johnson was, therefore 'tiresome enough';* and, just as French landscapes failed to interest him, he was remarkably little concerned about the intellectual life of modern France. The French Enlightenment was now in full flower; but, although Boswell had visited Voltaire and Rousseau, and paid them almost fulsome homage, while David Hume, having absorbed the spirit of the Enlightenment abroad, had carried it home across the English Channel, Johnson bitterly condemned the *Philosophes*, and stigmatized Voltaire and Rousseau as a pair of arrant rogues.

This was one of the controversial topics on which Boswell loved to tease his mentor. When Johnson attacked him for having visited Rousseau, he 'answered with a smile "My dear Sir, you don't call Rousseau bad company. Do you really think *him* a bad man?" JOHNSON. "Sir, if you are talking jestingly of this, I don't talk with you. If you mean to be serious, I think him one of the worst of men; a rascal who ought to be hunted out of society.... Rousseau, Sir, is a very bad man. I would sooner sign a sentence for his transportation, than that of any felon who has gone from the Old Bailey these many

*The most adventurous sightseeing expedition that Johnson undertook with the Thrales was to Paris during the autumn of 1775. He found Paris 'not so fine a place as you would expect', though the palaces and churches were splendid, and decided that the French way of life was neither 'commodious' nor 'pleasant'. At Fontainebleau, where they saw the King and Queen dining in public, Queeney Thrale was noticed and admired by Marie-Antoinette.

years. Yes, I should like to have him work in the plantations."
BOSWELL. "Sir, do you think him as bad a man as Voltaire?"
JOHNSON. "Why, Sir, it is difficult to settle the proportions of iniquity
between them".'

Finally, despite the ministrations of John and Charles Wesley, and
the birth of the Evangelical movement – William Wilberforce became
a convert to Evangelicalism as early as 1784 – the second half of the
eighteenth century, at least in the 'polite world' inhabited by Johnson's
friends, was not a period of deep religious faith. Men like David Hume
and Edward Gibbon were determined unbelievers; elsewhere a
gentlemanly Deism had been grafted on to Christianity. Johnson,
however, was a Christian Fundamentalist, who admitted no com-
promise, but asserted the unshakable truth of every major point of
Christian doctrine. Indeed, he clung to his rugged beliefs with an
embittered pertinacity. Perhaps his pertinacity was bred of a secret
despair. 'A very old gentleman, who had known Johnson intimately',
writes Samuel Rogers in his *Table Talk*, 'assured me that the bent of
his mind was decidedly towards scepticism; that he was literally
afraid to examine his own thoughts on religious matters; and that hence
partly arose his hatred of Hume and other such writers.'

Johnson's strict adherence to the doctrines of Christianity seems to
have been closely connected with his fear of death; and the fact that
the dying Hume had remained so calm and courageous made his
record all the more offensive. During his own life, he declared, there
had never been 'a moment in which death was not terrible to him';
and, if he shuddered at the prospect of complete extinction, which
Hume was said to have accepted with good-humoured equanimity,
no less appalling was the idea that he might be destined to eternal
punishment. He was no Calvinist – salvation he did not regard as 'the
effect of an absolute decree'. It was 'conditional', he believed; and,
'as I cannot be *sure*', he announced, when he himself was nearing death,
'that I have fulfilled the conditions on which salvation is granted, I am
afraid I may be one of those who shall be damned'.

His interlocutor was 'the amiable Dr Adams', whom he had visited
at Pembroke College, and who had already suggested, when they
walked around the garden, that the God they both worshipped was
infinitely good. 'What do you mean by damned?' Adams now enquired.
'JOHNSON. (passionately and loudly) "Sent to Hell, Sir, and punished
everlastingly".' A far more typical product of his age, Adams was
surprised and shocked; but neither he nor Boswell, who was hovering
nearby, could do anything to reassure their friend; though Adams
quietly opined that 'being excluded from Heaven will be a punish-

St Clement Dane's in the Strand, where Johnson punctually performed his devotions. He always occupied the same bench, at the end of the gallery on the northern side of the church, immediately above the pulpit, a post from which he could follow the sermon with the keen attention it deserved.

ment', and that otherwise 'there may be no great positive suffering'; while Boswell asked whether a man might not 'attain to such a degree of hope' as to overcome his fear of death.

Johnson angrily brushed them aside:

'A man may have such a degree of hope as to keep him quiet. You see I am not quiet, from the vehemence with which I talk; but I do not despair.' MRS ADAMS. 'You seem, Sir, to forget the merits of our Redeemer.' JOHNSON. 'Madam, I do not forget the merits of my Redeemer; but my Redeemer has said that he will set some on his right hand and some on his left.' He was in gloomy agitation, and said, 'I'll have no more on't.'

Johnson's religious beliefs, however, formed a separate part of his existence. Elsewhere, as his modern biographer has pointed out, he was always 'a rationalist and a rationalizer'.[1] The same authority quotes from Mrs Thrale, who, having reported Hogarth's remark that Johnson, 'not contented with believing the Bible ... fairly resolves, I think, to believe nothing *but* the Bible', adds that 'Mr Johnson's incredulity amounted almost to disease'. The more irrational side of his temperament made him long for the support of faith; but his reason had a strongly sceptical tendency; and his innate scepticism extended to every sphere of human life and thought.

Johnson was recently described as 'the least optimistic of eighteenth-century literary men'[2]; and he might also be regarded, if we are to judge from the opinions he professed and the advice he gave, as among the most cynical. Every human activity, he maintained, could at length be traced back to some selfish motive. 'The vacuity of Life', says Mrs Thrale, 'had ... so struck upon the mind of Mr Johnson, that it became by repeated Impressions his favourite hypothesis ... the Things therefore which other Philosophers attribute to various & contradictory Causes, appeared to him uniform enough; all was done to fill up the Time.' If a man were profligate, and 'followed the Girls or the Gaming Table, – why, Life *must* be filled up ...'. If he were industrious, managed his estates and 'delighted in domestick economy: Why a *man must do something*, and what so easy to a narrow Mind as hoarding halfpence....'

Moral qualities, too, such as the tenderness that a devoted mother showed her brood, might have developed, he thought, simply through the lack of any more amusing occupation. 'Enquire', he demanded, 'and you will probably perceive that either her want of health or Fortune prevented her from tasting the Pleasures of the World.' Though he valued friendship, he would not allow that it was often based upon disinterested feelings. Mrs Thrale had 'once talked to him of a Gentleman who loved his Friend – he has nothing else to do, replies Johnson; Make him Prime Minister, and see how long his Friend will be remembered.' There was another unlucky occasion when the parson at Southwark spoke of friendship from the pulpit. Mrs Thrale enjoyed and praised his discourse; but Johnson very soon grew fretful. Why, he wished to know, did 'the blockhead preach about Friendship in a busy Place like this where no one can be thinking of it.... The men ... are thinking of their Money, & the Women are thinking of their Mops.'

For himself, loneliness and idleness were both conditions that he deeply dreaded – loneliness, because 'the solitary Mortal' was 'certainly luxurious, probably superstitious, and possibly mad'*; idleness, because it 'is apt to give opportunities for the Cultivation of that Sensibility' which regular employment helped to blunt, and which, if it were given free rein, became the nurse of 'all evil and prurient Passions'.

* 'It is observable that even Brutes cannot be happy in Solitude. When a cat is alone she never purrs': Johnson, quoted in *Thraliana*, June 1777.

Thus, for moral as well as for practical reasons, human life, in a bleak and empty world, where vices are more numerous than virtues, and the pains of living outnumber the pleasures, must be carefully, methodically 'filled up'. A wise man rejected 'no positive good.... There is in Life ... so very little Felicity to be possessed with Innocence, that we ought surely to catch diligently all that can be had without the hazard of Virtue....' This notion had made him a warm supporter of the conventional amusements of society. 'Cards, Dress, Dancing' Mrs Thrale observes, 'all found their Advocate in Johnson, who inculcated upon Principle the Cultivation of Arts which others reject as Luxuries, or consider as Superfluities.' If a lady refused to touch the cards, he would ask, 'how then does She get rid of her Time.... Does She drink Drams?'

Having himself an unbounded appetite for company, he explained that 'the most public Places are safest for those whose Passions are easily inflamed'; and were he ill, or reluctant to join the company, he usually distracted his thoughts with some ingenious private game. Frequently, these games were mathematical. According to Mrs Thrale, he had 'a consummate Knowledge of Figures', and liked working out fantastic problems. Once, for example, when, at the Thrales' house, 'he was greatly indisposed ... with Spasms in his Stomach', he consoled his enforced solitude by attempting 'an odd Calculation: no other than that the National Debt ... would, if converted into Silver, make a Meridian of that Metal for the real Globe of the Earth'. Alternatively, he might endeavour to decide how much money a man would save 'by laying up five Shillings a day'. Always his chief object was to repel the host of shadows that gathered threateningly about a vacant mind.

Johnson's domestication with the Thrales and their family not only occupied his days but had helped to fill his heart. It also greatly increased his domestic comforts; there were some who hinted that his affection for his host and hostess at Streatham Place included a considerable element of cupboard love. He enjoyed his easy journeys between Fleet Street and Streatham Place in their handsome, well-sprung coach. Even more keenly did he appreciate the sumptuous meals that Henry Thrale had carefully and punctually ordered. Only on two occasions, he said, had he ever had 'his Bellyful of Fruit ... once at Ombersly the Seat of my Lord Sandys – once at our House', writes Mrs Thrale, when he was devouring the exquisite peaches and nectarines produced by Henry Thrale's orchard.

Incidentally, both at Streatham Place and at Southwark he now occupied his own room*; and, as he was apt to damage his wigs by

The thatched summer-house, built by Henry Thrale at Streatham; an early-nineteenth-century engraving by E. Finden after a drawing by C. Stanfield.

his habit of reading in bed – so that 'the fore-top of all his wigs were burned by the candle down to the very network' – Mr Thrale's valet would meet him at the parlour door with a new wig 'when the bell had called him down to dinner, and as he went upstairs to sleep in the afternoon, the same man constantly followed him with another'. If he chose to take exercise, he had the run of a spacious garden; and the

*At Streatham Place, Johnson's bedroom was situated in the left wing. Before the end of the 1770s, the house included twelve bedrooms. The drawing-room and dining parlour were on the first floor. See James L. Clifford. *Op. Cit.*

thatched summer-house that Thrale had erected soon became a
favourite refuge.

Johnson accepted these benefits readily and unselfconsciously, but
not by any means ungratefully. While he loved his hostess, he liked
and respected her husband, whom he regarded as the almost perfect
type – if only he had been a little more talkative: Thrale's silences
were long, portentous and heavy – of the modern English gentleman.
He admired Thrale's air of quiet authority; though shaken by the
calamities that had threatened to overtake him in the year 1772,
Thrale remained the master of his household. There were moments,
Boswell was quick to notice, when Johnson spoke with deep respect
of Mr Thrale, but almost disparagingly about his hostess, at least about
her intellectual powers: 'I know no man, (said he), who is more
master of his wife and family than Thrale. If he but holds up a finger,
he is obeyed. It is a great mistake to suppose that she is above him in
literary attainments. She is more flippant; but he has ten times her
learning: he is a regular scholar; but her learning is that of a schoolboy
in one of the lower forms.'

Among his guests, though it may have been Mrs Thrale who
attracted them, he was equally authoritative. Johnson himself was
occasionally reduced to order by Mr Thrale's sudden displays of
firmness. Thus, when a vehement discourse on education was deafening the entire party, 'There, there,' he remarked, 'now we have had
enough for one lecture. . . . We will not be upon education any more till
after dinner, if you please.' At another gathering, he demolished Oliver
Goldsmith, whose tactlessness and fatuous inquisitiveness made him
a byword in the Streatham circle. 'Doctor Goldsmith', writes Mrs
Thrale, 'was certain a Man extremely odd: the first Time he dined
with us, he gravely asked Mr Thrale how much a Year he got by his
Business?' Henry Thrale was neither embarrassed nor ruffled. 'We
don't talk of those things much in company, Doctor,' he replied, 'but
I hope to have the honour of knowing you so well that I shall wonder
less at the question.'

For Johnson, Henry and Hester Thrale were soon 'my master' and
'my mistress'; and his affection rapidly extended to embrace the whole
family. Even his old disputes with Mrs Thrale's mother subsided
after the financial crisis of 1772, during which he had done such
valiant service; and, when she died in 1773, Johnson stood beside her
bed. Naturally, he loved the Thrales' children. Queeney, the eldest of
the brood, was an unaffectionate and self-willed child; stubborn to an
'uncommon degree', she showed a discretion that impressed and
alarmed her mother. Mrs Thrale would always find her particularly

difficult to understand; whatever Queeney's defects might be, she exclaimed at a later period, they had nothing in common with 'my faults, of Confidence, Loquacity and foolish Sensibility'. But, although she was not 'of a caressing or obliging Disposition', she had a well-equipped mind*; and Johnson watched over her adolescence. He told

Hester Maria Thrale (1764–1857), whom Johnson nicknamed 'Queeney', aged twenty months. A strong and intelligent child, she developed into a cool and stubborn young woman, at once her mother's pride and scourge. Portrait by Zoffany.

Mrs Thrale that she was his 'own dear girl', and addressed her as 'My lovely Dear', 'My dear Charmer' or 'My dear Sweeting', and, now and then, as 'Queen Hester', the title from which she took her nickname. In 1772 he also made her an expensive present – a charming little mahogany cabinet, intended to house her collection of 'natural curiosities'.**

Unlike Queeney, the Thrales' eldest son was a conspicuously attractive character. His innumerable friends, of course, included Johnson; 'he *does* love little Harry!' wrote Mrs Thrale; and both the Thrales shared Johnson's feelings:

* At the age of two years, Mrs Thrale records, she was not only 'perfectly healthy', 'eminently pretty' and strong enough 'to carry a Hound puppy two Months old quite across the Lawn', but was quickly learning to count and spell, and knew 'all the heathen Deities by their Attributes. . . .'

** This delightful piece of furniture, which shows no signs of having been much used, is now in the collection of Lord Lansdowne at Bowood.

A better or finer, a wiser or kinder Boy ... cannot be found; he goes to Jenning's free School here in Southwark, & is half adored by Master & Scholars, by Parents & Servants – by all the Clerks.... He has Charity, Piety, Benevolence; he has a desire of Knowledge far above his Years.... He always does his Exercise at Night in my Dressing room, and we always part after that is over pleased with each other – he is so rational, so attentive, so good; nobody can help being pleased with him.

Although slightly '*too forward* in *some* things' – he had once been caught by a pedagogue telling his schoolfellows improper stories – Harry was the best of children. On 15 February 1776, he celebrated his ninth birthday; and on 22 March, with a family-party and an Italian friend, he paid a festive visit to the Tower of London, where he 'continued in high spirits both among the Lyons & the Arms*: repeating Passages from the English History, examining the Artillery & getting into every Mortar till he was as black as the Ground ...'.

Next day, still cheerful and well, Harry breakfasted with the clerks at his father's brewery and returned home, carrying a couple of penny cakes, which he proceeded to divide among his sisters 'for Minuets that he made them dance'. Then the servants noticed that he was twisting in pain, 'making a Figure of 5 : 10' as 'we always called his manner of twisting about when anything ailed him'. Before long he grew sick; and Mrs Thrale, called by her household, saw 'his Countenance begin to alter'**. She gave him a warm bath; a physician was summoned, who administered in rapid succession draughts of hot wine, usquebaugh (or whisky) and a popular restorative known as Daffy's Elixir. Mrs Thrale wept, and was scolded by her husband; he bade her not cry, or she would certainly 'look like a Hag' when she went to Court tomorrow. For Mr Thrale 'apprehended no danger at all'. But Harry died that afternoon.

Apparently he had been killed by a ruptured appendix.[3] In eighteenth-century domestic life, such catastrophes were not uncommon; and Mrs Thrale had accepted the death of other children, although it always hurt her to lose a child she had borne, with a stoicism that did her credit. But, since the loss of Ralph, who had died at the age of two in 1775, Harry was her only son. He was, moreover, an exceptional human being, who seemed to inherit both his father's solid intelligence

---

*The Tower then contained a famous menagerie, besides its display of ancient and modern weapons.

**This account of Harry Thrale's character and of his last illness is derived from Mrs Thrale's unpublished 'Children's Book' now in the collection of Mrs Donald Hyde of New York, quoted by James L. Clifford *Op. cit.*

and his mother's liveliest qualities. On Mr Thrale the effect of Harry's death was particularly strange and terrible. While his wife broke down and succumbed to a nervous seizure, he remained 'stiffly erect', a ghastly smile on his face, sitting in a corner of the room, speechless and motionless as he stared into vacancy, his hands thrust into his waistcoat pockets[4]. He never quite recovered. Mrs Thrale would gradually regain her spirits; but her husband, who was perhaps the more vulnerable, despite his stern, authoritative manner, became enveloped in a slowly thickening cloud of sluggish, self-indulgent gloom.

'The Citizen at Vauxhall, 1784'. Vauxhall Gardens are described by Boswell as 'that excellent place of publick amusement . . . peculiarly adapted to the taste of the English nation . . .'

Always an epicure, he now ate so voraciously as to fill his friends with apprehension. Mrs Thrale was not an exacting wife; and Mr Thrale's amatory escapades had caused her very little sorrow. She knew, for example, that in 1773 the *Westminster Magazine* had published, first a graphic account of how a certain 'Miss H---t' had been carried off by an amorous London brewer, then the no less ribald story of his relationships with a publican's daughter, 'Mrs D--n', and with 'a new favourite, the celebrated Mrs R---'. Nor was she much perturbed when he contracted a venereal disease, merely noting in 1776, some nine months after Harry's death: 'Mr Thrale's Complaint *was* venereal at last – what need of so many Lyes about it! I'm sure I care not, so he recovers to hold us all together.' But his gluttony, and the passion with which he indulged it, soon presented a far more serious problem; and his physicians warned him that, unless he cut down his dinners, the result might be an apoplectic stroke.

These warnings he continued to disregard; gluttony and venery were now his only solace. Johnson, who had been visiting Lichfield when he learned of Harry's death, but who had immediately hastened to the Thrales' side, expressed deep concern for his unhappy 'master'. 'Is my master come to himself?' he demanded of Mrs Thrale in October 1778, 'Does he talk, and walk, and look about him, as if there were yet something in the world for which it is worth while to live? ... All sorrow that lasts longer than its cause is morbid.'

Thus Mrs Thrale came more and more to rely on Johnson's massive, reassuring presence. Often she implored him to intercede with Thrale. 'Conjure him not to fret so', she had written that April, 'when he really has every Reason to be thankful.... Oh Dear Me! But he is woeful cross; & glad at heart shall I be to have you with us – for we *grind* sadly else.' And, in June: 'Do huff my Master & comfort him by Turns according to your own Dear Discretion: he has ... given you a Right to talk to Him about his ill Tim'd Melancholy and do keep your Influence over him for all our sakes.' She herself was once again pregnant; and on 21 June, wearily but resignedly, she gave birth to a short-lived daughter.

Johnson also expostulated with Mr Thrale, seconding Mrs Thrale 'by earnest and pathetic entreaties', on the difficult subject of his business; for, although frequently apprehensive that he might be going bankrupt, Thrale was determined to brew a far greater number of barrels than the current market could absorb. Johnson, in short, was now an *ami de la maison*, who supported and advised the Thrales in nearly every department of their public and their private lives. He had assisted Thrale when he decided to stand as Member of Parliament for Southwark towards the end of 1765, and patiently corrected the address in which the candidate announced his claims. To a dozen other tasks, concerning the Thrales' household, their friend readily devoted no less skill and zealous care.

Most important, however, was the generally inspiriting and commanding effect of the great man's personality. In Johnson his 'master' and 'mistress' discovered an extraordinary array of attributes, blended into the puissant character of a single human being. He dreaded death;

he pretended to hate life. Yet few men have been so strongly attached to the simple pleasures of existence – riding in a post-chaise, teasing a pretty girl, meeting old friends and reviving old memories, eating peaches or piles of buttered muffins, playing with the favourite cat he liked to feed on oysters, or 'rambling' at night around the streets of London.

Nor were the pleasures in which he indulged himself always contemplative or sedentary. He frequently rode out hunting with Mr Thrale, either on the Sussex downs above Brighthelmstone or through the countryside near Streatham*. 'As an instance of his activity', Mrs Thrale describes a feat that, much to his friends' astonishment, he had once performed at Streatham Place, when he and her husband, who had ridden 'very hard for fifty Miles after Mr Thrales Foxhounds', had finished their dinner – no doubt a luxurious meal – and were sitting and talking in the Blue Room:

> ... I mentioned some Leap they spoke of as difficult; no more says Johnson than leaping over that Stool – it was a Cabriolet that stood between the Windows – which says I, would not be a very easy Operation ... I believe after fifty Miles Galloping – & in Boots too. He said no more, but jumped fairly over it, & so did Mr Thrale.... Johnson loved a Frolick or Joke well enough, tho he had strange serious Rules about them too, and very angry was he always at poor me for being merry at improper times and Places.

Like many other inveterate melancholics, Johnson possessed conspicuous physical courage.** He boxed proficiently; and from Garrick Mrs Thrale heard of an occasion when, at a country playhouse, 'a young Fellow took away Johnson's Chair which he had quitted for five minutes; & seated himself in it on the Stage. When the original Possessor returned, he desired him to leave his Chair which he refused, and claimed it as his own.' Johnson did not protest, 'but lifting Man and Chair ... took & threw them at one Jerk into the Pit'. Similarly, Topham Beauclerk related how, two large pointers having been brought into the room, they immediately began a fight and 'alarmed

---

*His mount was 'Mr Thrale's old hunter', which he managed 'with a good firmness'. But, at times, according to Mrs Thrale's *Anecdotes*, Johnson would abuse the sport. 'I have now learned (said he) ... to perceive that it is no diversion at all, nor ever takes a man out of himself for a moment: the dogs have less sagacity than I could have prevailed on myself to suppose.... It is very strange, and very melancholy, that the paucity of human pleasures should persuade us ever to call hunting one of them.'

**A recent example was the late Evelyn Waugh, like Johnson a courageous, though inexperienced hunting man, whose contempt for danger on the battlefield often astonished his commanding officers.

the People present not a little with their ferocity, till Johnson gravely laying hold on each Dog by the scruff of the Neck, held them asunder at Arms length, and said come Gentlemen where is your difficulty? put one of them out at one Door and t'other out of the other; & let us go on with our Conversation'.

Most of all, perhaps, it was Johnson's intuitive sympathy, his knowledge of human life, and his capacity of feeling for others, that the Thrales' had learned to value. He was often abrupt and rude; sometimes, if he were irritated and put out, his behaviour could be downright brutal; witness the famous story told in the *Anecdotes* of his brush with Henry Thrale's nephew:

On another occasion, when he was musing over the fire in our drawing-room at Streatham, a young gentleman* called to him suddenly, and I suppose he thought disrespectfully, in these words: 'Mr Johnson, Would you advise me to marry?' 'I would advise no man to marry, Sir (returns for answer in a very angry tone Dr Johnson), who is not likely to propagate understanding'; and so left the room. Our companion looked confounded, and I believe had scarce recovered the consciousness of his own existence, when Johnson came back, and drawing his chair among us, with altered looks and a softened voice .... insensibly led the conversation to the subject of marriage, where he laid himself out in a dissertation so useful, so elegant, so founded on the true knowledge of human life ... that no one ever recollected the offence, except, to rejoice in its consequences.

Clearly, it was the unfortunate enquirer's youth, and the youthful weakness he had revealed as he wilted and collapsed beneath the snub, that brought Johnson back into the room. He was naturally fond of young people; and both childhood and poverty were conditions that seldom failed to move his heart. His early memories, remarks Mrs Thrale, 'made Mr Johnson very solicitous to preserve the felicity of children'. And elsewhere, in *Thraliana*: 'As he was always on the side of the husband against the Wife, so he was always on the side of the Children against the Old ffolks – old People, says he, have no Honour, no Delicacy; the World has blunted their Sensibility & Appetite or Avarice governs the last stage.'

Towards the poor, among whom he had once been numbered, his attitude was no less sympathetic. What was to be gained, demanded an acquaintance, from giving halfpennies to common beggars; 'they only lay it out in gin and tobacco'. 'And why', responded Johnson, 'should they be denied such sweeteners of their existence? It is surely

---

*Sir John Lade, a particularly foolish young baronet; for a further account of his career, see pp. 195–6.

very savage to refuse them every possible avenue to pleasure.... Life is a pill which none of us can bear to swallow without gilding; yet for the poor we delight in stripping it still barer, and are not ashamed to shew even visible displeasure, if ever the bitter taste is taken from their mouths.'

Henry Thrale and his guests were habitually gluttonous; but they did not often talk of hunger. Johnson, on the other hand, had, in his poverty-stricken youth, known what it was to pass a tavern or a cookshop, and avidly sniff the food he could not buy. Thus, when Mrs Thrale complained to him about the pungent smell of roast goose, 'You, Madam, replies Johnson, have always had your hunger fore-stalled by Indulgence, and do not know the Pleasure of smelling one's Meat before hand :– a Pleasure answered I that is to be had in Perfection by all who walk through *Porridge Island** of a Morning! – come come says the Doctor gravely, let us have done laughing at what is serious to so many: Hundreds of your Fellow Creatures dear Lady, turn another way that they may not be tempted by the Luxuries of *Porridge Island* to hope for Gratifications they are not able to obtain.' Mrs Thrale was slightly displeased. These notions, she comments, just as they doubtless were, revealed his proletarian origins; they seemed 'the faeculancies of his low Birth....'

She was touched, however, by the invariable kindness he showed to his 'family' of starveling pensioners. 'Mr Johnson' she wrote, 'has more Tenderness for Poverty than any other Man I ever know'; and at 8 Bolt Court, the house to which, in 1776, after ten years' residence, he had removed from Johnson's Court, he supported 'whole Nests of People. ... A Blind Woman & her Maid, a Blackamoor & his Wife, a Scotch Wench who has her Case as a Pauper depending in some of the Law Courts; a Woman whose Father once lived at Lichfield ... and a superannuated Surgeon. ...' While he was at home, he also kept 'a sort of odd Levee for distress's Authors, breaking Booksellers, and in short every body that has even the lowest Pretensions to Literature in Distress'.

Among the elegance and luxury of Streatham Place, he did not forget his hungry lodgers; but, at the end of the week, he would punctually return home to ensure that they were provided with three decent meals, and would not travel back until the following Monday. Of the dependants whom Mrs Thrale lists, the blackamoor was his Jamaican body-servant, Francis Barber, a freed slave, whom Johnson had befriended, and who had entered his service in the year 1752.

---

*An alley in Covent Garden that contained 'numbers of ordinary Cooks Shops to supply the low working People with Meat at all hours': Mrs Thrale's note in *Thraliana*.

Johnson, Mrs Thrale noticed, would speak of Negroes as 'a race naturally inferior, and made few exceptions in favour of his own; yet whenever disputes arose in his household ... he always sided with Francis against the others, whom he suspected (not unjustly, I believe) of greater malignity'. He himself had paid for Barber's schooling, and had educated him in Christian faith and morals.

Apart from Francis, a warmly devoted servant, all Johnson's pensioners at Bolt Court were cantankerous, poor and ill-conditioned. But the blind woman, Anna Williams, had some slight pretensions to gentility and wit. Once Tetty's friend, she had been adopted by John-

Francis Barber (d. 1801), Johnson's negro servant; portrait attributed to Reynolds. Johnson spoke of negroes as 'a race naturally inferior'. But 'whenever disputes arose in his household', he always took the side of Francis.

Portrait of Johnson's blind hostess, Anna Williams (1706–83), by Sir Joshua Reynolds' sister, Frances.

son during the earliest days of his bereavement; and now she acted as his hostess. When he received guests at Bolt Court, it was Miss Williams' privilege to pour out their tea, which, since she had completely lost her sight, she was obliged to measure with her finger. She was an authoress, too, and generously assisted by Johnson, had published in 1766 a small collection of her own writings. She was, however, excessively irritable; and the maid she employed would long ago have given notice, had Johnson not secretly arranged to pay her an additional half-crown a week.

Of the Scotch wench, Poll Carmichael, a good deal less remains on record – except that her host declared she was 'a stupid slut', adding 'I had some hopes of her at first; but when I talked to her tightly and closely, I could make nothing of her; she was wiggle-waggle, and I could never persuade her to be categorical.' As for Mrs Desmoulins, she was the daughter of Johnson's god-father, and had 'the chief management of the kitchen; but our roasting (said Johnson) is not magnificent....'

Finally, there was the superannuated surgeon, that remarkable personage Robert Levett, an unlicensed physician, who, in his rough and ready way, had undertaken the care of Johnson's health. Levett had had an adventurous life, and had once been married to a prostitute. A clever, though 'brutal' and uneducated man, he practised among the poorest of the poor. 'Johnson would observe, he was, perhaps, the only man who ever became intoxicated through prudence'; for his patients often paid him in drink, which, as they were customarily penniless, he thought it uneconomical to refuse. When he died in 1782, the *Gentleman's Magazine* commemorated his passing with a lively portrait-sketch: 'His person was middle-sized and thin; his visage swarthy, adust and corrugated. His conversation, except on professional subjects, barren. When in dishabille, he might have been mistaken for an alchemist, whose complexion had been hurt by the fumes of the crucible, and whose clothes had suffered from the sparks of the furnace.' Levett remained with his protector until he died; and every morning, when Johnson was at Bolt Court, he and Levett, attended by the negro valet, would drink tea together in unbroken silence.

All his pensioners loved and respected their host; among themselves they waged incessant warfare. 'Williams hates everybody', he reported to Mrs Thrale. 'Levett hates Desmoulins and does not love Williams. Desmoulins hates them both. Poll loves none of them.' Sometimes he hesitated to return home, such was the flood of complaints and re-criminations that would assail him once he had crossed his threshold. Yet Johnson retained his good-humour; he had never been fastidious. Though he had young and brilliant friends whose companionship delighted him, he was just as much at his ease with his cross and unattractive hangers-on.

He relished luxury and social ceremony; but he had also a deep-rooted taste for what Mrs Thrale called 'the Tea and Bread and Butter of Life'; and from those he befriended he did not expect either commanding intellect or impressive virtues:

Heroic virtues (said he) are the *bon mots* of life; they do not appear often,

Drawing by C. Tomkins of Johnson's house in Bolt Court, with Johnson
approaching the steps and Francis Barber at the door.

and when they do appear are too much prized I think; like the aloe-tree, which shoots and flowers once in a hundred years. But life is made up of little things; and that character is the best which does little but repeated acts of beneficence; as that conversation is the best which consists in elegant and pleasing thoughts expressed in natural and pleasing terms. With regard to my own notions of virtue ... I hope I have not lost my sensibility of wrong; but I hope likewise that I have lived long enough in the world, to prevent me from expecting to find any action of which both the original motive and all the parts were good.

It was his understanding of the 'little things' of human existence, and his appreciation of their value, that made him not only so kind a guardian to his 'family' at Bolt Court, but so affectionate a friend and adviser to the well-bred inhabitants of Streatham Place. Nothing was beneath his notice, from 'my master's' conduct of his brewery to 'my mistress's' dealings with her household. They were always aware of him; and they had the comforting knowledge that he would never fail his friends. For this, naturally, they were obliged to pay a price. His odd habits sometimes became dangerous; and then Henry Thrale, with his solid common sense, thought it necessary to step in.

Chemistry had long been a subject that fascinated Johnson; and his good-natured hosts had therefore installed 'a sort of laboratory at Streatham', where the Thrales used to divert themselves 'with drawing essences and colouring liquors. But the danger Mr Thrale found his friend in one day when I was driven to London, and he had got the children and servants round him to see some experiments performed, put an end to all our entertainment; so well was the master of the house persuaded, that his short sight would have been his destruction in a moment, by bringing him close to a fierce and violent flame.' Future experiments were voted 'too dangerous' and Mr Thrale insisted that we 'should do no more towards finding the philosopher's stone'.

Meanwhile, Mrs Thrale, however exhausted she might be by a long day of nursing, teaching and household management, in order to please her exacting old friend was obliged to sit up late at night. Johnson feared and hated the hours of darkness; he dreaded the solitude that awaited him once he had retired to bed. Her function, therefore, was to remain beside him far into the small hours, listening, talking and pouring endless cups of tea from a gigantic pot. 'I love to hear ... my mistress talk', her grateful guest exclaimed, 'for when she talks, ye gods! how she will talk.' It was a task that demanded strength and stamina. But 'Mrs Thrale', she wrote, 'among her other Qualifications, had prodigious strong nerves – and that's an admirable Quality for a Friend of Dr Johnson's.'

Love and Friendship   3

In September 1776, when they had been married nearly thirteen years and Hester Thrale was thirty-five, Mr Thrale paid a somewhat belated tribute to his superior wife's intelligence. Perhaps he was a much more sensitive, and, at heart, a far gentler and kindlier person than she had ever chosen to imagine; and now, having learned that she enjoyed the kind of personal commonplace books that among the French were called *Ana*, he had decided to present her with six imposing quarto volumes. The pages were blank: the covers, of undressed calf; and each displayed the title *Thraliana* stamped in gold upon a red label.

She immediately started work. It was many years, she began, since Dr Samuel Johnson had recommended her to get a little book, and to write down in it all the anecdotes which might come to her knowledge, 'all the Observations I might make or hear; all the Verses never likely to be published, and in fine ev'rything which struck me at the time. Mr Thrale has now treated me with a Repository ... I must endeavour to fill it with Nonsense new and old.'

For over three decades she continued filling it; and the result was an extraordinary combination of autobiography and anecdotage, in parts trivial and slight enough, but, when she writes of herself, her family and her friends, extremely vivid and rewarding. The second volume, which opens just twelve months after she had begun the first, is by far the most valuable; for it contains a full-length portrait of Johnson as, through long experience of his gifts and oddities, she had come to know and love him. It is not an uncritical portrait; she makes it clear that, although the great man she had helped to domesticate was wise and virtuous and often kindly – his influence had transformed her whole life – being 'a Friend of Dr Johnson's' was now and then a painful privilege.

To her record we owe some curious sidelights on Johnson's sexual and emotional nature. There seems no doubt that he had fallen deeply in love with the woman he styled his *Thralia dulcis* – his 'dearest mistress', who, he declared, had 'a temper the most delightful' of any woman he had yet encountered – and that his attachment was passionate and possessive as well as romantic and paternal. Not only did he love her passionately; he also trusted her implicitly. It was 'about the years 1767 or 1768', she wrote, that he had confided to her 'a Secret far dearer to him than his life'; and such was his 'nobleness, & such his partiality, that I sincerely believe he has never since that Day regretted his Confidence, or ever looked with less kind Affection on her who had him in her Power'.

This was a secret she did her best to keep; and, long afterwards, when Johnson was dead and she heard that various *Lives* were being written, 'Poor Johnson!' she exclaimed, 'I see they will leave *nothing untold* that I laboured so long to keep secret; & I was so very delicate in trying to conceal his fancied Insanity, that I retained no proofs of it – or hardly any – nor ever mentioned it in these Books, lest by dying first *they* might be printed and the Secret (for such I thought it) discovered.'

Evidently, the secret he imparted to Mrs Thrale must have concerned not, as Boswell assumed, his previous enslavement by another mistress, but his belief that he was suffering from a mental disease that had already overthrown, or would one day overthrow his reason. There were moments, indeed, while he lived at Streatham, when it appeared to be on the point of foundering; and in 1788, having read a newspaper report about the sovereign's nervous breakdown, Mrs Thrale comments: 'I don't believe the King has ever been much worse than poor Dr Johnson was, when he fancied that eating an Apple would make him drunk', adding in footnote: 'he never was as *bad* for his Madness was chiefly Delirium.'

Still more significant than Johnson's dread of madness were the counter-measures he adopted. Believing that a madman required restraint and discipline – the current eighteenth-century view – he implored Mrs Thrale to act as his gaoler and, should she note the recurrence of dangerous symptoms, sternly confine him to his own room. Though she agreed, he would sometimes reproach her with having temporarily relaxed her supervision; and in 1773, when both were at Streatham Place, he wrote her a pathetic letter. Using bad French, he begs that she will spare him henceforward *'la necessité de me contraindre, en m'ôtant le pouvoir de sortir d'ou vou voulez que je sois. Ce que vous ne coûtera que la peine de tourner le clef dans la porte, deux fois par jour'.*[5]

Mrs Thrale despatched a protesting reply:

What Care can I promise my dear Mr Johnson that I have not already taken? ... You were saying but on Sunday that of all the unhappy you was the happiest, in consequence of my Attention to your Complaint; and today I have been reproached by you for neglect, and by myself for exciting but generous Confidence which prompts you to repose all Care on me ... and brood upon an Idea hateful in itself, but which your kind partiality to me has unhappily rendered pleasing. – If it be possible shake off these uneasy Weights, heavier to the Mind by far than Fetters to the body. Let not your fancy dwell thus upon Confinement and severity.... If we go on together your Confinement will be as strict as possible except when Company comes in....

Johnson, it seems, sometimes demanded of Mrs Thrale a degree of 'severity' that she found alarming and repulsive, and did not always care to grant. But since he insisted, and she loved and respected him, she had reluctantly let him have his way; and several references in the pages of *Thraliana* show that Johnson was not only confined to his room but, at his own request, was occasionally chained and beaten.* Theirs, she observes, had been a strange attachment, based on 'a dreadful and little suspected Reason ... but the Fetters and Padlocks will tell Posterity the truth'.

For Johnson, melancholy, and the solitude that accompanied it, had long been associated with sinful and luxurious fancies; and the melancholia that oppressed him all his life would appear to have brought out in his sexual temperament a profoundly masochistic strain. He was haunted, we learn from his secret diary, by crazy broodings about gyves and handcuffs, *'de pedicis et manicis insana cogitatio'*; and, although Mrs Thrale's nature was certainly not sadistic, she played the invidious part that he demanded. Their rôles were now reversed; temporarily at least, Mrs Thrale's master and counsellor became his pupil's abject slave. Hitherto, she had lived in modest submission, first to her selfish father, then to a cold and egocentric husband; and, as she reviewed her later life, she could not always resist some vain and self-complacent feelings.

'How many Times', she remarks, 'has this great, this formidable Doctor Johnson kissed my hand, ay & my foot too upon his knees!' Yet the fact that she had him in her power did not diminish her respect and gratitude. 'Uniformly great', she writes in May 1779, 'is the Mind of that incomparable mortal.' La Rochefoucauld had asserted that no man was a hero to the valet who attended him. But 'Johnson is more a

---

* 'Says Johnson a Woman has *such* power between the ages of twenty five and forty five that she may tye a man to a post and whip him if she will'. Mrs Thrale adds in a marginal role: 'This he knew of himself was *literally* and *strictly* true I am sure'.

Hero to me than to any one – & I have been more to him for Intimacy, than ever was any Man's Valet de Chambre.'

None of their friends suspected that Johnson's relationship with Mrs Thrale had a dark, and perhaps a tragic side; and her response to his pleas for greater severity – the promise she gave him that his imprisonment should be 'as strict as possible except when Company comes in' – suggests that, so far as she could, she was careful to conceal his plight. It was widely known, however, that Johnson dreaded madness; and Boswell refers to the 'diseased imagination' that so often overcast his spirits. But both the extent and the nature of his neurotic disturbances undoubtedly remained hidden; and what scandal the relationship provoked was confined to the gossip columns of the London press, where, as early as 1773, a report had appeared, alleging that 'an eminent Brewer was very jealous of a certain Authour in Folio, and perceived a strong resemblance to him in his eldest son'.

Scandal of this kind was easy enough to discount; and, in the eyes of the 'polite world', Johnson's association with Mrs Thrale was an altogether blameless friendship, derived from intellectual reverence on the one hand, and from chivalrous devotion on the other. Among the notabilities who frequented Streatham Place, Johnson was *primus inter pares*; but, although no rival dared to dispute his position, Mrs Thrale had many other courtiers, some of whom were as talkative and self-willed, and had perhaps as strong a claim to genius. Joshua Reynolds, for example, was a monarch in his own sphere. When he first made the journey to Streatham, he was already forty-three; and, two years later, he would be elected President of the newly-founded Royal Academy.

He was a fortunate man; none of the maddening reverses encountered by most young artists had impeded Reynolds' steady progress. Born near Plymouth, the son of a country schoolmaster, he had had a pleasant youth. His father seems to have been fond of drawings; and, so long as he could paint and draw, Joshua once declared, he was always the 'happiest creature alive'. His earliest subjects, the local gentry of Devon, quickly recognized his talents; and by the year 1750 he could afford to visit Rome, where he remained for over two years and, besides studying and copying the great Italian masters, executed some brilliant caricature-groups of his fellow English tourists. Next, he turned his attention to the urban *beau monde*; and, not long after his return from Italy, having set up at a London studio, he launched out into the long and successful career that, with few reverses or disappointments, he was to continue until 1789. He would then finally abandon his art – he was still at the height of his

Sir Joshua Reynolds (1723–92); an early self-portrait. Here he is shielding his eyes against the light; later, they were protected by square-rimmed spectacles. In all his self-portraits we notice Reynolds' slightly deformed upper lip.

powers – only because he had already lost the use of one eye*, and believed that he might be facing total blindness.

Meanwhile, he had escaped the temptations of fame. 'There goes a man not to be spoiled by prosperity', Mrs Thrale remembered Johnson saying; and, on another occasion: 'Everybody loves Reynolds except you.' For Mrs Thrale, in her odd, capricious way, had decided that, although he was 'a glorious Painter, a pleasing Companion & a

* For an expert analysis of Reynolds' malady, which appears to have been a retinal haemorrhage, see Patrick Trevor-Roper: *The World Through Blunted Sight*.

Sensible Man', she did not really like the artist. He 'was not much a Man to my natural Taste: he seems to have no Affections, and that won't do with me ...'.

Other observers, including Boswell, spoke of Reynolds' charm and amiability; and perhaps what Mrs Thrale disliked was his negligent attitude towards his sister, who had long managed, or mismanaged, his London household, and whom, it was clear, he sometimes found annoying. But then, so did most of the friends they entertained. Frances Reynolds was herself an amateur artist; and Mrs Thrale unkindly hinted that he might be a little jealous of her slight pictorial gifts; at least, he did not love her 'as one should expect a Man should love a Sister he has so much Reason to be proud of.... The poor Lady is always miserable, always fretful....' Whatever the cause, Frances Reynolds was an irritating, ill-balanced woman, and displayed, wrote Fanny Burney, 'an habitual perplexity of mind and irresolution of conduct, which to herself was restlessly tormenting, and to all around her ... teazingly wearisome'. At dinner-parties, observes Mrs Thrale, she affected 'an odd dry Manner, something between Malice and Simplicity'; and her naïve interpositions had the additional drawback of being often shrewd and sharply pointed.

During his last years, when his sister had left his house, Reynolds became warmly attached to his charming niece, 'Offy'; and apart from his alleged neglect of Frances (who might well have tried any brother's patience) there is nothing in the record of his private life to suggest that he may have lacked affection. Passion, however, he certainly did not show. Despite talk of a 'little Girl at Westminster' and some early 'dissipation', the privileged painter of beautiful women led a singularly chaste existence. He had 'grown callous', he said, 'by contact with beauty'; and, though he admired the seductive Kitty Fisher, then one of the chief luminaries of the London demi-monde, it seems unlikely that he shared her bed. Nor did he venture into marriage. For a time, while he was living in Rome, he had paid tentative court to Angelica Kauffman, and she evidently returned his feelings; but the marriage they were said to have agreed on somehow never took place. Afterwards he would explain his distrust of matrimony by saying that every woman he liked had ultimately grown indifferent to him, and 'he had no reason to suppose it would not be the same as to any other woman'. Having so long succeeded in his passionate pursuit of his art, in his personal life he could not have tolerated failure.

He was an immensely ambitious man; few eighteenth-century artists have had so wide an intellectual scope; and, reluctant to be regarded as a painter alone, Reynolds soon determined to become a literary critic and a master of the English language. Here he received some valuable assistance from Johnson, who had encouraged him to contribute to the *Rambler*, and generally supervised his education. Reynolds' *First Discourse*, addressed to the students of the Royal Academy, was delivered on 2 January 1769; the fifteenth and last, on 10 December 1790. Together, they set forth the author's philosophy of art, in which Raphael and Michelangelo occupy the most exalted positions, but room is found – albeit somewhat grudgingly – for the artists of the great Venetian school. Since Hogarth had published his *Analysis of Beauty*, no other English painter has provided so detailed

Portrait by Reynolds of Jack and Theresa Parker; the later eighteenth century saw the beginning of the Romantic cult of childhood.

and so original a survey of his own aesthetic views. But, whereas Hogarth's style is often eccentric and slapdash, Reynolds' is urbane and polished.

Some of his opponents pretended that the *Discourses* were very largely Johnson's work; and Johnson, it is true, as Reynolds freely confessed, in addition to forming his mind and brushing off 'a deal of rubbish', had advised him on points of grammar and occasionally improved his phrases. But he himself both planned and composed every lecture of the series, as he wrote – it was usually late at night – pacing to and fro across the floor, while he hammered out his periods.

The style he at length evolved, though distinctly Johnsonian, was also strongly individual. Michelangelo – an artist who spoke 'the language of the gods' – had provided the example of creative genius that Reynolds always held up; and it was Michelangelo's name that, with fine dramatic effect, at the end of his farewell *Discourse* he uttered as his last word. Simultaneously, he exalted the genius of Raphael; and, in his *Fifth Discourse*, he attempts to distinguish between their different types of greatness:

It is to Michael Angelo, that we owe even the existence of Raffaelle: it is to him Raffaelle owes the grandeur of his style. He was taught by him to elevate his thoughts, and to conceive his subjects with dignity. His genius, however formed to blaze and to shine, might, like fire in combustible matter, for ever have lain dormant, if it had not caught a spark by its contact with Michael Angelo: and though it never burst out with *his* extraordinary heat and vehemence, yet it must be acknowledged to be a more pure, regular, and chaste flame. Though our judgment must upon the whole decide in favour of Raffaelle, yet he never takes such a firm hold and entire possession of the mind as to make us desire nothing else, and to feel nothing wanting.

Although, when he read the *Discourses*, Johnson sometimes observed 'I think I might as well have said that myself', his prose-style, if more sonorous and moving, was often considerably less lucid. They were not Reynolds' only prose works; his unpublished productions are said to have amounted to some thousand pages of manuscript, among them being literary sketches of Johnson, Goldsmith and Garrick, together with a collection of notes on Shakespeare*. For Reynolds, the art of writing was closely connected to the art of painting. The latter, he believed was a universal language, in which the artist endeavoured to depict the characters and define the ethos of his own age.

Like Hilliard, Holbein, Van Dyck and Kneller, he created the composite image of a whole society. But Reynolds' view was broader

* First published in 1952, in the Yale Edition of the Private Paper of James Boswell, among which they were discovered.

Right Portrait by Reynolds of Colonel George Coussmaker, in the uniform of the Grenadier Guards. The picture illustrates Reynolds' gift of building up a majestic composition out of surprisingly simple elements. 'Damn him, how various he is!' exclaimed his rival, Thomas Gainsborough.

and more catholic than that of any previous English artist, extending
from aristocrats, statesmen and soldiers to musicians, actors, writers
and men of letters, and from patrician 'toasts' to famous actresses and
fashionable courtesans. There was nothing conventional or repetitious
about his presentation of his sitters, in each of whom he seems to have
recognized a separate aesthetic problem. 'Damn him, how various
he is!' exclaimed his admiring adversary, Thomas Gainsborough.*
If Reynolds cultivated the lyrical side of his art – for example, when
he produced his enchanting portrait of Lady Spencer and her little
girl** – he also dearly loved its rhetoric; and his huge group of the

The Duke of Marlborough and his family; this portrait by Reynolds, now at
Blenheim Palace, has been described as the 'most monumental achievement' in
the history of British portrait-painting.

*The two painters appreciated one another's talents, but were never close friends. After
1784, there was a serious estrangement; but, when Gainsborough died, Reynolds paid him a
noble, though not uncritical tribute, in his *Fourteenth Discourse*.

** Afterwards Georgiana, Duchess of Devonshire.

Johnson by Sir Joshua Reynolds; 'a tormented giant, whose spiritual struggles are reflected in the convulsive movement of his knotted hands . . .'

Marlborough family at Blenheim, a work both intimate and grandiose, is still, writes a modern art-historian, the 'most monumental achievement'[6] in the field of British portrait-painting.

Sometimes the artist's rhetorical idiom may appear a trifle pompous. But, should we begin to tire of so many high-born ladies striking solemn classic attitudes – impersonating the Comic Muse, sacrificing to the Graces, in the rôle of Juno receiving a girdle from Venus, or even, like Mrs Peter Beckford, 'Caliph' Beckford's unfortunate 'lost soul', paying sacrilegious homage to Hecate, Goddess of the Underworld – we need only turn to some of his smaller, less elaborate portraits. Here, undistracted by the flowing robes and massive architectural details that his assistants, his 'drapery-men' and 'landscape-men', often provided to fill up the canvas, we can enjoy his quick imaginative grasp of the character that he is studying – Samuel Johnson, seen as a tormented giant, whose spiritual struggles are reflected in the convulsive movement of his knotted hands; or an embittered scholar, the purblind Giuseppe Baretti, concentrated with fierce attention upon the page he reads.

At Streatham, thirteen portraits by Reynolds – they included pictures of Mrs Thrale and Queeney, Henry Thrale, Johnson, Garrick, Goldsmith, Burney, Murphy, Baretti and the artist himself – had been hung around the library walls*. It was Johnson's favourite room; perhaps it was also Reynolds'. He is said never much to have appreciated the company of his fellow painters, and 'preferred to set up as a sort of Patron of Literature', noted Mrs Thrale in 1777, 'so that no Book goes rapidly thro' a first Edition now, but the Author is at Reynolds' table in a Trice ...'. As a literary meeting-place, Boswell considered, Sir Joshua's table was superior even to that of the famous Dilly brothers; and his establishment of the Literary Club (otherwise 'The Club') under Dr Johnson's aegis, had confirmed his position among the literati. Of modern writers, Mrs Thrale records, Goldsmith was 'the Person Sir Joshua seemed to have most Friendship for'; indeed, he had often lent him money. Naturally, Reynolds had a profound respect for Johnson; but, being an amiable man himself, he was apt to criticize the sage's social roughness – his habit of 'entertaining prejudices on a very slight foundation', and turning 'the most light and airy dispute' into a ferocious gladiatorial duel. 'He fought upon every occasion as if his whole reputation depended upon the victory of the minute.[7]

Goldsmith's manners, though almost equally bad, were a good

---

* With the sole exception of Murphy's, all these portraits were sold by Mrs Thrale in 1815.

Oliver Goldsmith (1728–74); 'his person was short, his countenance coarse and vulgar, his deportment was that of a scholar awkwardly affecting the easy gentleman'. Engraving after a portrait by Reynolds.

deal less disturbing. For Goldsmith seemed never to have grown up. The ebullient Irishman, who combined an invincible conceit with an inextinguishable loquacity, on his first appearance at Streatham Place had bewildered both the Thrales. Not only did he impertinently question Henry Thrale about the profits of his trade; but he also begged Johnson to help him pick the lock of a chest that happened to have caught his eye.

The Doctor's Curiosity was as drole as his Vanity: [comments Mrs Thrale in *Thraliana*] He saw a great Cedar Chest in my House once – & nothing would serve him but to know what was within: I was from home ... his

Visit was to Johnson. What makes you so uneasy says Mr Johnson – why says he I long to pick the Lock of that Chest so – do dear Mr Johnson look if none of your keys will undo it.

His hostess' opinion – 'a Man extremely odd' – was shared by all who knew him well. Endless stories were told of his infantile behaviour; and many anecdotes, regarding his follies and vanities, are preserved in Boswell's *Life*:

He was much [according to Boswell] what the French call *un étourdi*, and from vanity and an eager desire of being conspicuous ... he frequently talked carelessly without knowledge of the subject.... His person was short, his countenance coarse and vulgar, his deportment was that of a scholar awkwardly affecting the easy gentleman. Those who were in any way distinguished, excited envy in him to so ridiculous an excess, that the instances of it are hardly credible. When accompanying two beautiful young ladies with their mother on a tour in France, he was seriously angry that more attention was paid to them than to him....

Garrick, who teased him about his 'bloom-coloured coat' of which he was inordinately proud – just as Topham Beauclerk had teased Boswell about his lavish gold-laced suits – declared that, although he 'wrote like an angel', he was apt to talk 'like poor Poll', while Horace Walpole, who had a high respect for his gifts, dubbed him as 'inspired ideot'. Reynolds, however, once suggested to Boswell that Goldsmith's apparent idiocy might be a form of affectation. He had 'frequently heard Goldsmith talk warmly of the pleasure of being liked, and observe how hard it would be if literary excellence should preclude a man from that satisfaction, which he perceived if often did, from the envy which attended it; and therefore Sir Joshua was convinced that he was intentionally more absurd, in order to lessen himself in social intercourse, trusting that his character would be sufficiently supported by his works'.

This was an explanation that Boswell thought over-subtle. But there is no doubt that his reputation for childish simplicity tended to strengthen Goldsmith's hold upon his readers. Since the word 'sentimental' had first been popularized by Sterne, it had slowly changed the literary climate. Simplicity, modesty, innocence were now qualities to which writers and critics attached a special value; and Sir Joshua himself would paint a succession of pretty pictures that idealized the state of childhood. The Noble Savage had begun to raise his head; and Goldsmith, as the 'inspired ideot', a direct descendant of his ingenuous Vicar of Wakefield, became a doubly attractive figure.

Goldsmith had a simple and easy style – an attribute that early critics of his novel immediately seized upon. 'This author', observed the *Critical Review*, 'seems to us to possess a manner peculiar to himself; it is what the French would term *naïté*. ... Simplicity is his characteristic excellence. He appears to tell his story with so much ease and artlessness, that one is almost tempted to think, one could have told it every bit as well without the least study; yet so difficult is it to hit off this mode of composition with any degree of mastery, that he who should try would probably find himself deceived.... We find nothing in this performance to turn the attention upon the writer, or to inflame the passions of the reader.... Genuine touches of nature, easy strokes of humour, pathetic pictures of domestic happiness and domestic distress ... are some of the methods he has made use of to interest and move us.'

Goldsmith's style, however, like the hero himself, is perhaps a little too conscious of its own modest, unassuming virtues; and the story the Vicar relates is both simple and, at times, extremely silly. The theme of 'domestic happiness' provides some charming pictures – for example, a vignette of the Primrose family eating their midday meal among the haycocks:

Our family dined in the field, and we sat, or rather reclined, round a temperate repast, our cloth spread upon the hay.... To heighten our satisfaction, two blackbirds answered each other from opposite hedges....

– having their portraits painted by an ambitious journeyman artist, or 'burning nuts' and joining in a rowdy game of hunt-the-slipper at a nearby farm-house. But the scenes of 'domestic distress' – when Wealth and Fashion invade their earthly paradise, the wicked squire betrays Olivia Primrose and, thanks to his machinations, the unfortunate Vicar is cast into a common gaol – are a good deal less accomplished; and improbability is piled on improbability to enable the novelist to reach a happy end.

Meanwhile, a series of chapter-headings underline the story's moral message. Thus Chapter IV is said to enclose '*A proof that even the humblest fortune may grant happiness, which depends not on circumstances, but constitution*'; Chapter XIV, that '*seeming calamities may be real blessings*'; and Chapter XXIII, that '*None but the guilty can be long and completely miserable*'. The book's main subject is the struggle between virtue and vice; but, alas, virtue, as personified by Dr Primrose, is represented as a state of almost continuous self-complacency. That 'great monogamist', author of a learned pamphlet denying the widowed clergyman's right to remarry,* appears firmly persuaded,

* Here Dr Primrose was a follower of William Whiston (1667–1752), whose Arian views had

Illustrations to an edition of *The Vicar of Wakefield* published in 1793.
Left His daughters visit Dr Primrose in gaol. *Right* Olivia rejects with disdain the money offered her by Squire Thornhill.

throughout the whole narrative, of his own superior merits; and, during the last chapter, his 'former benevolence' is 'repaid with unexpected interest'. Mr Burchell, the 'harmless amusing companion', whom he has previously befriended as a 'poor forlorn creature', proves to be Sir William Thornhill, 'a man of large fortune' and an important politician, uncle, moreover, to the wicked squire; and, through his good offices, both 'affluence and innocence' descend once more upon the Primrose household.

The Vicar of Wakefield, which Johnson claimed to have read and carried off and, though he did not think that the book would succeed, sold to an enterprising publisher, John Newbery*, all within the space of a few hours, was written at Wine Office Court between 1761 and

caused him to be expelled from his professorship at Cambridge.

*Newbery, whom Goldsmith brings into *The Vicar of Wakefield*, was also the first English publisher to produce a long series of successful children's books.

1762, and finally reached the public, after an inexplicable delay, in March 1766. Goldsmith's two long poems, *The Traveller* and *The Deserted Village*, appeared in 1764 and 1770; and his most successful comedy, *She Stoops to Conquer*, in 1773, not very long before his death. By 1764, when he became a founder member of Sir Joshua Reynolds' Literary Club, he was generally acclaimed as 'one of the brightest members of the Johnsonian school'.

Goldsmith, declared Anthony Chamier, a fellow member of The Club, 'was a man, who, whatever he wrote, did it better than any other man …'. 'Dr Goldsmith', said Johnson himself, 'is one of the first men we now have as an authour and he is a very worthy man too.' Boswell, however, though he considered *The Vicar* 'a fascinating performance', was decidedly critical of Goldsmith's talents. No modern author, he wrote, 'had the art of displaying with more advantage … whatever literary acquisitions he made'. Yet 'his mind resembled a fertile, but thin soil. There was a quick but not a strong vegetation of whatever chanced to be thrown upon it.'

Of the two judgments, it is undoubtedly Boswell's that now strikes us as the better-balanced. Goldsmith's famous novel is not a book that, once we have emerged from the schoolroom, we very often re-read; while *The Traveller* (warmly praised by Johnson) seems no more than a nicely accomplished piece of late-Augustan verse-spinning. It contains some memorable passage – for example, the first line, in which Goldsmith recalls the mood of his own vagrant and unhappy youth:

> Remote, unfriended, melancholy, slow…

and his dramatic evocation of the landscape of the Netherlands:

> To men of other minds my fancy flies,
> Embosom'd in the deep where Holland lies,
> Methinks her patient sons before me stand,
> Where the broad ocean leans against the land …

But, alas, Goldsmith, like the author of *Cooper's Hill* – a poet whom, in *Windsor Forest*, Pope himself had gladly followed – feels that he must generalize and moralize his own sensations. Here the poet closely resembles Rasselas. He explores the world, merely to discover that no country and no form of government provides the refuge he is seeking:

> Vain, very vain, my weary search to find
> That bliss which only centers on the mind …

The Deserted Village is based on a theme already set forth in *The*

Traveller – the triumph of wealth over innocence, and of urban luxury over simple rustic pleasures:

> Have we not seen, round Britain's peopled shore, —
> Her useful sons exchanged for useless ore ...
> Seen opulence, her grandeur to maintain,
> Lead stern depopulation in her train? ...

The 'stern depopulation', of which Goldsmith writes, has sometimes been attributed to the pernicious effects of the Industrial Revolution. In 1770, however, the southern counties of England were still comparatively unscarred; and Goldsmith's real subject, as he himself makes clear, was the havoc caused by rich landlords – frequently members of the mercantile middle class, anxious to join the ranks of the feudal landed gentry – who, while they were 'improving' their new estates and opening up impressive prospects, would light-heartedly clear away a whole village.

Such a catastrophe, at the whim of an immensely prosperous London merchant, had overtaken 'a little village, distant about fifty miles from town', where the poet happened to have spent the summer months. But he does not add that these destructive landlords were not entirely unenlightened, and that many 'model villages', far more spacious and less insanitary than the old, were built to accommodate the villagers whom their improvements displaced.

Goldsmith's generous lament for 'sweet Auburn' –

> Along thy glades, a solitary guest,
> The hollow sounding bittern guards its nest;
> Amidst thy desert walks the lapwing flies
> And tires their ecchoes with unvaried cries,
> Sunk are thy bowers in shapeless ruin all,
> And the long grass o'ertops the mouldering wall ...

was very far from realistic; and, even on its first appearance, the social message of *The Deserted Village* did not go uncriticized. 'A fine poem', observed a contributor to the *Critical Review*, 'may be written upon a false hypothesis'; few ruined villages were then to be met with; and 'England wears now a more smiling aspect than she ever did ...'. Criticism was also levelled at Goldsmith's roseate picture of the joys of rustic life, which would afterwards provoke the young George Crabbe to compose a very different poem. In 1783, Johnson, who had been shown the manuscript, consented to revise *The Village*, finding 'its sentiments', writes Boswell, 'as to the false notions of rustick happiness and rustick virtue quite congenial with his own ...'. Both the ageing Johnson and the young Crabbe were practical, hard-headed men; Goldsmith, the literary sentimentalist, existed in an atmosphere of dreams and legends. So long as he lived, he never escaped from childhood, though the cares of the adult would prove increasingly difficult to shake off. He died at the age of forty-six, in June 1774, 'of a fever,' reported Johnson to Boswell, 'made, I am afraid more violent by uneasiness. His debts began to be heavy, and all his resources were exhausted. Sir Joshua is of opinion that he owed not less than two thousand pounds.' Had ever poet, Johnson wondered, been so much trusted before, or received such ample credit?

It was David Garrick who had remarked at the St James' Coffee House, while Goldsmith was amusing the company in his noisiest, most foolish vein, that, until he was safely dead and buried, nobody could hope to draw his portrait, since the splendid impression that a reading of his works created was bound to vanish after one had listened for half-an-hour to the poet's conversation. Garrick himself was also a ready talker; but he exerted his powers of charming with exemplary tact and skill. Not that he was ever modest; Garrick knew that he was a man of genius, the greatest actor on the English stage, who, by means of a single word or gesture, even by the way he raised his hand, could produce a sudden breathless hush in any audience he confronted.

The quality that makes an actor great frequently defies either description or analysis; but, among Garrick's innumerable admirers were two or three accomplished writers, including Goldsmith, who portrayed him at length in a set of verses he called *The Retaliation*; Fanny Burney, whom he had known from her school-days; and an ingenious German traveller, Georg Christoph Lichtenberg. Chronicling Evelina's momentous visit to London, the novelist Fanny Burney had naturally arranged for her heroine to visit the Drury Lane Theatre.

A model village, built at Milton Abbas, Dorset, by the Earl of Dorchester in 1752, to replace cottages he had pulled down.

Top left David Garrick; print from a portrait by Gainsborough; 'Garrick was pure gold, but beat out to thin leaf'.

Top right 'The principal entry to the Theatre Royal, Drury Lane'; from Robert and James Adam's *The Works in Architecture*. Garrick had become a joint patentee of the Theatre, scene of his greatest triumphs, as early as 1747.

Above The Theatre Royal, Drury Lane, after its alteration in 1774; from Robert and James Adam's *The Works in Architecture*.

There she watches Garrick as Ranger in a modern comedy, *The Suspicious Husband**, and is immediately dazzled and delighted:

Such ease! such vivacity in his manner! Such grace in his motions! such fire and meaning in his eyes! – I could hardly believe he had studied a written part, for every word seemed spoke from the impulse of the moment. His action at once so graceful and so free! – his voice – so clear, so melodious, yet so wonderfully various in its tones – such animation – every look *speaks*!

Lichtenberg gives us a no less enthusiastic, but far more detailed description of some of Garrick's performances at Drury Lane – how, for instance, as the Prince of Denmark, he encountered his father's ghost upon the battlements; and how, with a thrilling intonation, he pronounced the words 'To be or not to be ...'. It seemed to matter little whether he impersonated a tragic or a comic personage, Hamlet or Vanbrugh's Sir John Brute. What counted was the fire that he lent to his rôle, and his extraordinarily subtle delineation of the varying aspects of a human character – a star-crossed hero, a drunken elderly man, a conceited dandy or a crafty servant.

Garrick never made a false move; everything about him appeared to be perfectly adjusted to the part that he was playing, from the manner in which he crossed the boards to the angle at which he cocked his hat, 'sometimes pulling it down over his eyes, sometimes pushing it side-ways off his forehead.... One gets a sense of ease oneself as one observes the power and assurance of his movements....' Among his fellow actors, Lichtenberg remarked, Garrick appeared to walk 'like a man among puppets'. Physically, he was rather small, 'if anything, below the average', and his body was somewhat thick-set; but his limbs were 'wonderfully proportioned', and his whole frame was 'most gracefully knit together'. His hands were small; and his shapely legs tapered down into 'the neatest feet you can imagine'. Evidently, he had great reserves of strength; nothing he did was 'wasted, slurred or dragged, and where other actors, in their arm and leg movements, permit themselves a latitude of six inches or more on either side of what looks well', Garrick, 'with admirable assurance and decision', judged it to a nicety.[8] Both Lichtenberg and Fanny noted the piercing brilliance of Garrick's eyes. 'When I have chanced to meet them', wrote Fanny Burney, 'I have really not been able to bear their lustre.'

Perhaps the most important feature of his acting was its consummate naturalness. Only in private life, said his unkinder friends, did he reveal the histrionic touch. In society, he was to apt to organize his life as if he were managing a new play, dividing his time and his

---

*By Benjamin Hoadley (1706–1757).

conversational talents between the numerous friends he visited. 'It was difficult to get him ... and as difficult to keep him. He never came into company', pronounced Joshua Reynolds, 'but with a plot how to get out of it.' Messengers would constantly arrive to remind him that he was 'wanted in another place. It was a rule with him never to leave any company saturated.'[9]

There were moments when his dearest friends grew restive; and Johnson, who had been often a little exasperated by his former pupil's endless triumphs, once, when he was dining with Topham Beauclerk a short while after Garrick's death, summed up his character in Boswell's hearing: 'He had friends, but no friend. Garrick was so diffused, he had no man to whom he wished unbosom himself.' Boswell agreed: 'Garrick was pure gold, but beat out to thin leaf.' Johnson felt he must admit, however, that 'Garrick was a very good man, the cheerfullest man of his age; a decent liver in a profession which is supposed to give indulgence to licentiousness; and a man who gave away, freely, money acquired by himself. He began the world with a great hunger for money; the son of a half-pay officer, bred in a family whose study was to make four-pence do as much as others made four-pence halfpenny do. But, when he had got money, he was very liberal.'

Here Johnson did not exaggerate either Garrick's generosity or the innocence of his domestic life. As a young man he had had a stormy love-affair with the Irish actress, Peg Woffington; but, no sooner had he married the Viennese *danseuse* Eva-Maria Veigel, better known as 'Violetta' or 'La Violette', than he became a whole-heartedly devoted husband. The couple were childless; and, although, on his deathbed, Garrick pretended that he had never wished for offspring – 'he knew the quickness of his feeling was so great', he said, 'that, in case it had been his misfortune to have had disobedient children, he could not have supported such an affliction' – he was at his happiest with children near. Letitia Hawkins, daughter of Johnson's biographer, always recollected, when she looked back on her own childhood, the exhilarating effect of Garrick's presence:

'I see him now in a dark blue coat, the button-holes bound with gold, a small cocked hat laced with gold, his waistcoat very open.... In the relaxation of the country he gave way to all his natural volatility, and with my father was perfectly at ease, sometimes sitting on a table, and then, if he saw my brothers at a distance on the lawn, shooting off like an arrow out of a bow in a spirited chase of them round the garden.'

As an immensely successful actor-manager, Garrick lived upon a splendid scale, through his own dignity emphasizing the dignified position to which, since he first appeared at an obscure London theatre on 19 October 1741, he had gradually raised the English stage. For the country house he had bought near Hampton, he employed Robert Adam to redesign the frontage and construct a new orangery; while in 'Shakespeare's Temple,' with its elegant Ionic portico, he stored his

Below The Garricks on the lawn of their villa at Hampton. David Garrick is offering his brother, George, a cup of tea. The large figure at Mrs Garrick's side, though sometimes assumed to be Johnson, is, in fact, a certain Mr Bowden; by Zoffany. *Bottom* Mr and Mrs Garrick before 'Shakespeare's Temple'; picture by Zoffany.

Left The Burney family; silhouette on glass.
Right Charles Burney (1725–1814); portrait by Sir Joshua Reynolds. 'Dr Burney' said Johnson, 'is a man for all the world to love.'

large collection of Shakespearian relics. Thomas Chippendale provided much of his furniture, from a book-case and tapestry-covered chairs to the curtains and a mahogany breakfast-tray.

None of these embellishments can have much appealed to Johnson, who took little interest in his domestic surroundings, and generally affected to despise the arts. He accepted artists only if he were convinced of their moral or their social value. Thus, Dr Charles Burney, the eminent musicologist, he appreciated first and foremost as a thoroughly good man and a fluent, entertaining talker. 'I love Burney', he proclaimed: 'my heart goes out to meet him! ... Dr Burney is a man for all the world to love.' Indeed, Burney's lovable qualities were as conspicuous as his astonishing professional industry. Arthur Murphy voted him 'extraordinary' and 'wonderful'; and Mrs Thrale praised 'the Goodness of his heart', the Suavity of his Manners', his fascinating conversational gifts and 'the grace of the dear Creatures style'. Men who are popular in society are sometimes, like Topham Beauclerk, not quite so popular among their families. Burney's children, however, adored him and, though they detested his cross-grained second wife, formed a remarkably harmonious household. 'We were as merry', writes Fanny Burney on the subject of a family gathering, 'and laughed as loud as the Burneys always do, when they are together.'

Nor were his talents confined to social and domestic life. His enormous *History of Music* long remained a standard volume; and

A Sunday-evening concert at Dr Burney's;
a caricature of 1782.

his slighter literary works ranged from a *Musical Entertainment*,
published in 1766, to a biography of Metastasio and an ambitious
poem on astronomy. Some passages of this poem, where he is describing a scientific voyage to Lapland, certainly deserve quotation:

> Another expedition, near the Pole,
> Was thought expedient to complete the whole ...
> When sage Le Monnier, Clairaut, Camus join
> With ardent Maupertuis in this design,
> All geometricians of superior class
> All eager expectation to surpass.
> Paris they quit, to icy regions steer
> More late than southern brethren just one year.

The good Doctor's only apparent vice seems to have been his social
snobbery, which was accompanied, now and then, by a certain narrow-
mindedness. It was the 'almost religious respect' he entertained for
royal personages that would one day make him condemn his beloved
daughter, Fanny, though he acknowledged and admired her literary
talents, to five miserable years of courtly servitude; and, when Boswell
published his *Life of Johnson*, he found the volume strangely shocking.
'Among all the good qualities of our friend Boswell ...' he wrote,
'delicacy had no admission. He was equally careless what he said of
himself, or what he said of others.' Yet he agreed that the *Life* 'will

Charles Burney in later life; drawing by George Dance.

merit the gratitude of posterity so long as the language of our country shall be intelligible'.

Burney, nevertheless, had a deep devotion to his art. Throughout his life he had worked prodigiously hard – sometimes from seven in the morning until eleven o'clock at night – and thus accumulated a small fortune that enabled him to keep his own carriage. But, although he enjoyed his comforts, the motives that inspired him were by no means altogether selfish. During the eighteenth century, professional musicians often ranked with upper servants; and Charles Burney did as much to raise their standing, and advance the cause of English music, as David Garrick was doing simultaneously to improve the reputation of contemporary drama.

His success had not come easily. Burney was the offspring of a 'witty and accomplished' father, but of a 'niggardly ... nearly un-natural mother'; and his apprenticeship to the composer, Thomas Arne, an 'avaricious ... sordid and tyrannical' man, whose face was once compared to a plate of beetroot, with a couple of oysters in lieu of the eyes, had caused him many early sufferings. Moreover, he was a life-long manic-depressive. For all his gaiety and industry, he experienced bouts of appalling nervous depression, when he would declare how much he dreaded the autumn – 'to me a constant momento mori ... its withered leaves tumbling about my ears' – or speak of a 'listless and irresolute disposition' that left his intelligence 'as flimsy as a dish-clout ...'.

In 1784, the year of Johnson's death, Burney was elected to The

Club; and no doubt he would have entered much earlier, had not Johnson, Reynolds and Burke lacked either the slightest taste for his art, or 'the smallest knowledge upon its subject', and 'esteemed and loved him solely for the qualities that he possessed in common with themselves'. But Burney had been a visitor at Streatham Place at least since 1776, when Mrs Thrale had engaged him to teach her daughter music; and there he must often have seen Burke, who, in 1783, secured him a useful post as organist at Chelsea College.

In Johnson's immediate circle, Edmund Burke held an almost un-challenged record – he had dared to differ from the sage on a major political issue, and yet had come off scot-free. Burke's championship of the rights of the American Colonists had gravely displeased the author of that notorious pamphlet *Taxation No Tyranny*; and Mrs Thrale afterwards published, among her *Anecdotes*, what she claimed was an unkind Johnsonian parody 'of a fine poetical passage in one of Mr Burke's speeches ...'. But neither antagonist ever forgot his manners; 'Mr Burke uniformly showed Johnson the greatest respect'; and Johnson delivered a series of resounding eulogia on the strength and variety of Burke's intelligence. 'Yes; Burke is an extraordinary man,' he told Boswell in 1776. 'His stream of mind is perpetual.' And, in 1784: 'Yes, Sir; if a man were to go by chance at the same time with

Edmund Burke (1729–97) by Sir Joshua Reynolds. 'His stream of mind is perpetual', Johnson declared. But he was the first man Mrs Thrale 'had ever seen drunk, or heard talk Obscaenly'.

Burke under a shed to shun a shower, he would say – "this is an extraordinary man". If Burke should go into a stable to see his horse drest, the ostler would say – "we have had an extraordinary man here".'

Burke's *Philosophical Enquiry into the Origin of Our Ideas of the Sublime and Beautiful*, published as long ago as 1756, he considered 'an example of true criticism'; and, with occasional reservations, he applauded Burke's oratory. In private intercourse all that Johnson disliked was a certain ribald strain: 'When Burke does not descend to be merry, his conversation is very superiour indeed. There is no proportion between the powers which he shows in serious talk and in jocularity. When he lets himself down to that, he is in the kennel'. Burke, said Boswell, had 'orderly and amiable habits'. He had been dubbed 'the Demosthenes of England', just as Sir Joshua Reynolds was its 'Apelles'. But there were moments when Demosthenes forgot his dignity, and the effect that he produced was less imposing. Burke, recorded Mrs Thrale, who had once spent a good deal of time among her outlandish Welsh neighbours, was the first man she 'had ever seen drunk, or heard talk Obscaenely'. In his house at Beaconsfield, the scene was apt to be squalid; 'Mrs Burke drinks as well as her Husband, and ... their Black a moor carries Tea about with a cut finger wrapt in Rags....'

The most agreeable side of Burke's character is revealed by the generous help he gave Giuseppe Baretti. In October 1769, a procession of distinguished witnesses, Burke, Garrick, Beauclerk and Johnson, appeared at the Old Bailey to give evidence on behalf of that unhappy and ill-natured man. When a prostitute accosted him in a London street, he had roughly brushed the girl aside. Her attendant bully had assaulted him; and Baretti, producing a penknife, had dealt his adversary a fatal blow. The favourable testimony of his friends, writes Boswell, 'had due weight with the Court and Jury'; and Johnson had given 'his evidence in a slow, deliberate, and distinct manner, which was uncommonly impressive'.

Baretti was acquitted. In 1773, probably on Johnson's advice, Mrs Thrale had engaged him to teach her eldest daughter modern languages; and he had then made his home at Streatham Place, where he lived for three years 'as at an inn', and soon proved an odd and difficult companion. The author of a *Dissertation on Italian Poetry* and a *Dictionary and Grammar of the Italian Language*, he had reached London from his native Turin more than two decades earlier. But he could not settle down; he disliked and mistrusted the English; and for his hostess he presently developed a peculiar detestation. True, he had a 'Soul above Disguise'; but he was also arrogant and fiercely proud. Though he accepted everything the Thrales could offer, he bitterly resented his subjection; with the result, Mrs Thrale noted, that he breathed 'defiance against all Mankind', and exhibited his aversions, which were 'numerous and strong', in a variety of savage sayings.

'His Powers of Mind', admitted Mrs Thrale, 'exceed most people's. ... But his Powers of Purse are so slight that they leave him dependent on all, – Baretti is forever in the State of a Stream dam'd up.' Could he but 'once get loose – he would bear down all before him.' Even Johnson, who had known and befriended Baretti since he first arrived in England, often found him hard to tolerate, and 'used to oppose and battle him'; yet 'the moment he was cool he would always condemn himself for exerting his superiority over a man who was his Friend, a Foreigner and poor'.

Many of the Thrale's guests considered him pleasant company; and everyone respected his extensive knowledge of the world and his genuine love of literature. But he could not refrain from repeatedly meddling in the domestic problems of the Streatham household, and enfuriated Mrs Thrale by 'openly urging Mr Thrale ... to cut down

Giuseppe Baretti (1719–89), Queeney's purblind and ill-tempered tutor, painted for the Thrales by Reynolds.

some little Fruit trees my mother had planted', threatening to beat the younger children if he thought them disobedient, and calling his hostess an 'unnatural mother' because, when Queeney was 'grievously tormented with worms', she had presumed to administer 'tin pills'.

Worse, he conceived a 'violent attachment' for Queeney, whom he urged – though she needed no urging – to assert her independence. But Queeney's far more attractive brother Baretti never learned to love. During Harry's last illness, he asserted that the boy should be whipped for causing his mother unnecessary alarm; and, after Harry's death, he continued to argue that Mr and Mrs Thrale must not postpone a projected foreign holiday, on which he had hoped to accompany them in the rôle of guide and courier. Nevertheless, Baretti remained at Streatham until 6 July 1776. His departure was sudden. The previous evening, Mrs Thrale informs us, though she had just invited him to dinner 'with great particularity of Attention', he was said to have announced that Streatham Place was pandemonium, and to have 'grown very odd and very Cross'. Next day, having sent his 'Clokebag' ahead, 'without taking leave of any one person, except it may be the girl', he had left the house and walked to London. Mrs Thrale never saw him again; but she occasionally suffered from his brooding hatred. In 1788, when she published Johnson's correspondence, he issued a series of journalistic 'Strictures', describing his one-time benefactor as a 'frontless female, who goes now by the mean appelation of Piozzi'.

It was his learning that had recommended Baretti and, beside excusing his savage temper, had earned him a position among the portraits that hung around the Streatham library. Once he had abandoned his early bohemian habits, all the members of Johnson's intimate circle, except for the 'family' he harboured at Bolt Court, were, in some degree, learned; and none was more erudite than the celebrated orientalist Sir William Jones. He seems not to have frequented Streatham Place; but, when the literary politician John Courtenay, composed his eulogistic verses on the *Moral and Literary Character of Dr Johnson* and the great man's 'brilliant school', he reserved a special niche for Jones, both as a scholarly translator and as an accomplished modern poet:

> Here early parts accomplish'd Jones sublimes,
> And science blends with Asia's lofty rhymes:
> Harmonious JONES! who in his splendid strains
> Sings Camdeo's sports, on Agra's flowery plains:
> In Hindu fiction while we fondly trace
> Love and the Muses, deck'd with Attick grace.

The eighteenth century liked to attach some distinguishing epithet to the names of famous persons; besides 'Dictionary Johnson', we read of 'Corsica Boswell', 'Demosthenes Taylor', 'Microscope Baker', 'Pliny Melmoth' and 'Abyssinian Bruce'. The translator, of course, was 'Persian Jones'; but 'Harmonious', one cannot help thinking, would have been an even more appropriate epithet. The adjective suited Jones admirably, not only in his public career but also in his private life.

A promising youth, whose immensely long poem, *an Ode in honour of St Caecilia's Day Descriptive of the Effects of Musick*, was much admired by Mrs Thrale, he had soon embarked on a studious investigation of Eastern languages and literatures. Jones, Johnson told Beauclerk, was 'the most enlightened of the sons of men'; and he seems to have deserved – or very nearly deserved – that tremendous panegyric. For Jones was a polymath, or came as near to being a polymath, a universally cultured and erudite person, as anyone could have hoped to make himself after the year 1700. He was said to have mastered thirteen languages, and to have acquired a working knowledge of some twenty-eight. The first English scholar to unravel the mysteries of Sanskrit, in which he discerned astonishing resemblances both to Latin and to Greek, he translated the Persian lyricist, Hafiz, and the Indian dramatist, Kálidása. At the same time, he compiled a Persian dictionary, produced a considerable number of euphonious

Sir William Jones (1747–94), 'the most enlightened of the sons of men'.

English and many ingenious Latin verses, studied astronomy and botany, and became a successful advocate at the London Bar.

Johnson he loved, though, like Burke, he did not share his politics. Jones was an impassioned Whig; and, as a politician, he championed the rights of the American Colonists, attacked the press-gang system and the oppressive feudal game-laws, valiantly supported John Wilkes, and was the associate and admirer of Benjamin Franklin. None of their political differences, however, appears to have clouded his friendship with the great Tory. A member of the Literary Club, he was present at the famous meeting, held on 30 April 1773, where Boswell, who had passed the earlier part of the evening 'in a state of anxiety which even the charming conversation of Lady Di Beauclerk could not entirely dissipate', was first admitted as a member.

Few of his contemporaries were inclined to criticize Jones, except for his old school friend, Dr Samuel Parr, who once tartly observed that, 'when Jones dabbled in metaphysics he forgot his logic; and when he meddled with oriental literature he lost his taste'. Otherwise, 'Harmonious Jones' was generally liked and esteemed, thanks not only to his remarkable store of learning, but to 'the affability of his conversation', his 'modest unassuming manners' and his refreshing lack of pedantry. In 1783, at the sensible age of thirty-six, he wedded the eldest daughter of the Bishop of St Asaph, and began a contented married life. He had no offspring; but Lady Jones, a no less amiable character, was herself an ardent botanist and sympathized with her kindly husband in his solicitude for beasts and birds. During their voyage to India, we learn, they adopted 'two large English sheep which came with us from Spithead, and, having narrowly escaped the knife, are to live as long and as happily with us as they can; they follow us for bread, and are perfectly domestic'.

In 1783, Jones had been appointed puisne judge of the Bengal Supreme Court; and he was to remain abroad, translating, botanizing and examining the Hindu and Moslem legal systems, for his last eleven years. By codifying Indian laws, he proposed, we are told, 'to be the Justinian of India'. But he did not survive to complete this undertaking – an inflammation of the liver carried him off, nearly ten years after Johnson's death, on 27 April 1794. Meanwhile, he released a flood of letters[10], which, if never definitely sparkling, are almost always brisk and pointed. While some – particularly when his correspondent was his former pupil, Lord Althorp – reveal, above all else, his instinctive desire to please, others display a bolder and a fiercer spirit.

Although he liked and respected Edmund Burke, he refused to

allow the great orator to browbeat him or put him down. The issue was the impeachment of Warren Hastings, for whom, personally, he had a deep regard 'as a man of taste and a friend to letters'; and he felt that, until Hastings' conduct had been scrutinized in Parliament, he was fully entitled to the benefit of the doubt:

You have declared, I find, that 'if you *hear* of my siding with Hastings, you will do everything in your power to get me recalled'. What! if you hear it only! without examination, without evidence! ... Ought you not to know, from your long experience of my principles, that, whilst I am a judge, I would rather perish than *side* with any man!

HE FORMED A DIGEST OF HINDU AND MOHAMMEDAN LAWS

Sir William Jones, 'the Justinian of India'; relief from his monument in the Chapel of University College, Oxford.

Johnson himself, whatever he thought of the cause – between 1774 and 1781, he had written the Governor three courtly letters, recommending various friends – would surely have approved such spirit. Jones, in fact, was a fine example of the late-eighteenth-century *honnête homme* – a man who blended learning with good sense, and enlightened intellectual views with 'affability of conversation'; a man of the world who understood the world, but did not necessarily subscribe to its more outrageous social standards. In *Thraliana* Jones is seldom mentioned. But, on 11 January 1795, Mrs Thrale notes that she and 'our Philosopher Mr Lloyd of Wygfawr'* had 'lamented

* John Lloyds's grandmother and her own Salusbury grandmother had been close friends. Lloyd himself was an astronomer and a scientific writer.

together the Death of *Sir William Jones the Orientalist*, Selim Jones
as they called him, – an irreparable loss – likewise the Death of poor
Josiah Wedgwood ...'.

Many birds of passage also arrived at Streatham, and remained for
a few weeks or a few months, to enjoy their full share both of Henry
Thrale's opulent hospitality and of memorable Johnsonian talk. One,
for instance, was a travelling Irish clergyman, Dr James Campbell,
himself a minor man of letters, who reached London in 1775, with
the express purpose, it was said, of interviewing Dr Johnson. But
Johnson 'seemed angry' when Boswell repeated this tale; though Tom
Davies quickly reminded him that a man had come from Spain to see
Livy; and that an Italian admirer, the musician Arcangelo Corelli,
had crossed Europe merely to catch a glimpse of Purcell and, on
learning that he was dead, had immediately gone back again. 'I should
not have wished to be dead' Johnson responded, 'to disappoint
Campbell, had he been so foolish as you represent him; but I should
have wished to be a hundred miles off'. He was not, however, entirely
displeased, and 'laughed with some complacency', Boswell informs us,
'when I told him Campbell's odd expression concerning him. "That
having seen such a man, was a thing to talk of a century hence".'

Campbell was a bold, attractive person, tall and handsome, and
(Mrs Thrale noted) 'a fine showy talking man. Johnson liked him
of all things in a year or two.' Campbell's own impressions were
slightly less agreeable; he was at first horrified by Johnson's appear-

The Adams Brothers' Adelphi in process of construction, 1771–2. Here both the
Garricks and the Beauclerks were to occupy houses looking across the Thames.
Picture by William Marlow.

ance and by the series of nervous tics that convulsed his face and body. 'Johnson', he exclaimed in his diary[11], 'you are the very man Lord Chesterfield describes: a Hottentot indeed.....' The great writer, he declared, had 'the aspect of an idiot, without the faintest ray of sense gleaming from any one feature – with the most awkward garb, and unpowdered grey wig, on one side only of his head – he is forever dancing the devil's jig, and sometimes he makes the most driveling effort to whistle some thought in his awkward paroxysms'.

Campbell had originally called at the Thrales' London house on 14 March 1775, and had been 'received with all respect.... She is a very learned lady, and joins to the charms of her own sex, the manly understanding of ours. The immensity of the brewery astonished me.' He dined at Deadman's Place on the 16th and 25th. On the 16th, there was a small gathering, his host and hostess, Dr Johnson and Baretti, 'a plain sensible man, who seems to know the world well'. But on the 25th, he found 'ten or more gentlemen' – Johnson apologized for his absence – and his hostess was the only lady:

The dinner was excellent: first course, soups at head and foot, removed by fish and a saddle of mutton; second course, a fowl they call a galena* at head, and a capon larger than some of our Irish turkeys, at foot; third course, four different sorts of ices, pine-apple, grape, raspberry and a fourth; in each remove there were I think fourteen dishes. The first two courses were served in massy plate. I sat beside Baretti....

On Saturday, 8 May, Campbell also dined at the brewers'; and on this

*A guinea fowl.

Sketch of a London coffee-house during the later decades of the eighteenth century; by an unknown artist. Note the convenient curtains drawn between the boxes. Newspapers were provided *gratis*.

occasion, he encountered Boswell, and heard Johnson affectionately teasing Mrs Thrale:

Johnson [Boswell relates] had supped the night before at Mrs Abington's* with some fashionable people whom he named; and he seemed much pleased with having made one in so elegant a circle. Nor did he omit to pique his *mistress* a little with jealousy of her housewifery; for he said, (with a smile,) 'Mrs Abington's jelly, my dear lady, was better than yours.'

In *Thraliana*, there are further references to Dr Campbell – during the summer of 1771, when he was again upon a London visit, and for the last time, as Goldsmith's prospective biographer, in the earlier part of 1792. By the 1770s, he had become if not a close friend, at least an accredited member of the Streatham circle. It was a singularly homogeneous world that Johnson and his friends shared. Through

*The well-known actress, whom Lichtenberg admired and Reynolds painted in the character of Roxalana, from Bickerstaffe's play, *The Sultan*.

any one of half-a-dozen societies they were always free to come and go. London was a small place; in 1750, the whole London area had less than 700,000 inhabitants; and though the population had now begun to increase* and would have doubled before 1820, it was still nearly as compact and self-sufficient as a modern market-town.

Here every person of social importance was well acquainted with his fellows – at least, by name and reputation; and a reputation, once established, very seldom lost its lustre. In polite society, everybody knew of Johnson, and was proud to have encountered him, even to have exasperated the great man and perhaps provoked a knock-down snub. Johnson, of course, had numerous adversaries – Whigs, deists and enemies of the Christian faith – whom we shall be describing on another page. But few literary men, either ancient or modern, have received such general recognition, or have been connected at so many different points with the existence of the century in which they lived. He may not have particularly valued the art of Reynolds and Garrick, or shared the musical taste of Dr Burney. But each was a close friend; and it was the strength of Johnson's private affections, almost as much as his learning and eloquence, that had helped him found his 'brilliant school'.

Eighteenth-century Englishmen had a deep regard for friendship, which was reflected by their social customs; and, though they appreciated the elegant domestic interiors that we admire in conversation pieces, a good deal of their time was spent away from home, dining with friends, drinking and talking at a club, or enjoying the solid masculine comforts of a tavern or a coffee-house. It was an intensely gregarious age; Johnson's contemporaries, like those of Samuel Pepys, were perpetually arranging parties, or long 'rambles' that took them out of London in search of the historic or the picturesque. William Hickey, son of an Irish lawyer known both to Johnson and to Goldsmith, as soon as he had got into the country would hasten to arrange an alfresco concert. But Johnson was tone-deaf, and only moderately interested in romantic landscapes or historic buildings. What he needed was the presence of his friends and the noble stimulus of conversation, where mind struck against mind, and the controversial sparks flew far and wide. Then his heart warmed, and his imagination kindled; and he could forget the dreadful pangs of solitude that, accompanied by a hideous sense of his own unworthiness, very often descended on him if he sat alone at Bolt Court.

---

*Between 1700 and 1750, the population had remained nearly static; and in the 1740s parish registers had recorded twice as many burials as baptisms. The passing of laws that controlled the sale of gin seems gradually to have curbed the death-rate.

4 The World of Women

Johnson was a man who loved women; and, unlike many Englishmen, not only did he love them; he also much enjoyed their company. Intelligence, at least in those he loved, had never been a quality he found essential. But, should it appear, it seldom came amiss; and a number of his female friends were drawn from a little group of learned women then famous as 'The *Bas Bleu* Ladies'. The *Bas Bleu* were an oddly-assorted group; they lacked a concerted aim and, although they were undoubtedly feminists, determined, so far as they could, to improve the position of their own sex, they can hardly be said to have founded any kind of 'liberation movement'. What they shared was a contempt for card-playing, which was still the chief diversion of polite society, and a belief that it was better to exchange ideas than endlessly shuffle slips of coloured pasteboard. Nor is it certain how they got their title. The name is supposed to have had something to do either with the odd garb of Mr Benjamin Stillingfleet, an amiable dilettante, author of a well-known *Essay on Conversation*, who frequented *Bas Bleu* soirées, or with the azure stockings worn by Madame de Polignac when she visited Mrs Montagu's drawing-room.*

The Bluestockings had no single leader. Mrs Delany, often regarded as their *doyenne*, was not an active *Bas Bleu*. Born in the year 1700, a member of the patrician Granville family, she was both too old and too retiring; but she provided an example of feminine distinction that the other ladies were content to follow. Hers was a more powerful character; and, whereas the majority of her admiring associates had led placid and well-sheltered lives, Mrs Delany, during her difficult girlhood, had had some real experience of male tyranny. Before she was eighteen, her imperious uncle, Lord Lansdown, had dragooned

---

*The former explanation seems the more probable. Mr Stillingfleet's dress, writes Boswell, was 'remarkably grave, and in particular it was observed that he wore blue stockings. Such was the excellence of his conversation . . . that it used to be said, "We can do nothing without the *blue stockings*"; and thus by degrees the title was established.'

Mrs Delany (1700–88). 'She reads to improve her mind, not to make an appearance of being learned.' But she resolutely refused to meet either Mrs Thrale or Samuel Johnson.

her into an unhappy marriage; and the husband he obliged her to accept was a dissipated country gentleman named Pendarves.

'I expected', she wrote in her memoirs, 'to have seen somebody with the appearance of a gentleman, when poor old dripping, almost drowned Gromis was brought into the room. . . . His wig, his coat, his dirty boots, his large unwieldy person, and his crimson countenance were all subjects of great mirth and observation to me. . . . Gromis was then nearly sixty, and I seventeen years of age.' He was also fat and 'much afflicted with gout'; and she had rejected him out of hand; but Pendarves had appealed to her uncle, and Lord Lansdown had insisted. On her way to the altar, 'I wished from my soul that I had been led, as Iphigeneia was, to be sacrificed. I lost not life, indeed, but all that makes life desirable – joy and peace of mind.'

In 1724 the hateful Pendarves died, suddenly carried off by an apoplectic stroke; and her second marriage, to Dr Delany, a cultivated Irish clergyman, once the friend of Swift, proved singularly happy and successful. Much of her middle age was spent at her husband's deanery, quietly occupied with good works; and not until 1769, after the Doctor's death, did she begin to set up as a London hostess. It was modestly done; Mrs Delany, whom Edmund Burke considered 'the highest-bred woman' he knew, 'the woman of fashion in all ages', avoided any form of ostentation. For her, the essence of good breeding was to be delicately unobtrusive. 'There is nothing I wish so much for Mary', she wrote to her sister on the subject of her niece's education, 'as a proper knowledge of the polite world. It is the only means of giving that sensible kind of reserve which great retirement converts . . . into awkward sheepishness or forward pertness.'

Among those who appreciated her social virtues were the British royal pair; and such was the esteem they felt for their 'dearest Mrs Delany' that, when she visited them at Windsor, they would often abandon protocol and positively order her to sit down. On one memorable occasion, the King himself pulled up a chair; and as, 'with some confusion', she hesitated to accept the privilege, 'Mrs Delany, sit down, sit down', exclaimed Queen Charlotte in her gutteral, commanding voice; 'it is not every lady has a chair brought her by a King.'

Soon she had become so great a favourite that the King and Queen granted her the use of a pleasant house at Windsor, which they furnished 'with everything themselves . . . not only plate, china, glass and linen, but even all sorts of stores – wine, sweetmeats, pickles, etc., etc.'; and here she frequently received her young adorer, Fanny Burney. The novelist considered her irresistible; and, during her latter years, she was generally recognized as the noblest type of educated woman. Though her gifts were diverse and numerous, she chose to carry them lightly and display them modestly. While she was still Mrs Pendarves, the future Mrs Montagu, having first catalogued her personal charms – the bloom of her skin, 'the shining delicacy of her hair' and 'the sweetness of her smile' – added an impressive list of her accomplishments:

She reads to improve her mind, not to make an appearance of being learned; she writes with all the delicacy and ease of a woman, and the strength and exactness of a man; she paints and takes views of what is beautiful or whimsical in nature with a surprising genius and art. She is mistress of the harpsichord and a brilliancy in playing peculiar to herself; she does a number of works, and of many of them is the inventor.

Mrs Delany had invented, for example – or so her friends believed – a particularly ingenious method of portraying flowers and plants,

'*Alcea rosea*, the Yellow Hollyhock'; a page from Mrs Delany's herbal.

which she delineated, not with pencil and brush, but with the help
of tiny scraps of coloured paper, giving her mosaic patterns an
exquisite 'richness and consistence, by laying one piece over another,
and often a transparent piece over part of a shade.... She pastes
them as she works upon a black ground.... These flowers have both
the beauty of painting and the exactness of botany....' She had begun
work in 1776, when, 'having a piece of Chinese paper on the table of
bright scarlet, a scarlet geranium of the same colour caught Mrs

Delany's eye; and, taking out her scissors, she amused herself with cutting out each flower in the paper which resembled its hue'. Before she died, in her eighty-ninth year, she had completed a Herbal that included nearly a thousand illustrations. It was a fitting monument, an arduous labour of love, which had demanded taste and skill and knowledge, yet was sufficiently frivolous and ladylike to dispel the smallest suspicion of vulgar pedantry. Mrs Delany could never forget her rank; she was a 'high-bred' woman first and foremost. If she elected to draw a social line, she drew it with extreme decision; and she had firmly refused to make the acquaintance either of Samuel Johnson or of Hester Thrale.

Elizabeth Montagu, so-called 'Queen of the Bluestockings', was a considerably more eclectic hostess, who regarded both Johnson and Mrs Thrale as suitable additions to her crowded gatherings; and Johnson, who (writes Boswell) 'certainly was vain of the society of ladies' and sure that he was well-equipped to please, paid her some resounding tributes. Mrs Montagu, he remarked, had 'a constant stream of conversation', and it was 'always impregnated; it has always meaning'. She did not 'make a trade of her wit; but Mrs Montagu is a very extraordinary woman'. He noted the masculine turn of her intellect: 'that lady', he said, 'exerts more mind than any person I ever met with; Sir, she displays such powers of ratiocination such radiations of intellectual eminence, as are amazing'. But he seems to have preferred her conversational qualities to her critical and literary talents; and of her celebrated *Essay on the Writings of Shakespeare* he had a rather poor opinion.

In October, 1769, when Reynolds presumed to suggest that the *Essay* did her honour, he retorted with his customary vehemence:

JOHNSON: 'Yes, Sir; it does *her* honour, but it would do nobody else honour. I have, indeed, not read it all. But when I take up the end of a web, and find it pack-thread, I do not expect, by looking further,· to find embroidery. Sir, I will venture to say, there is not one sentence of true criticism in her book'. GARRICK: 'But, Sir, surely it shews how much Voltaire has mistaken Shakespeare, which nobody else has done'. JOHNSON: 'Sir, nobody else has thought it worthwhile'.

Nevertheless, he usually enjoyed her parties:

Left Mrs Montagu (1720–1800); from a portrait by Reynolds. 'Sir, she displays such powers of ratiocination, such radiations of intellectual eminence, as are amazing.'

One evening (reports a 'social friend'*) at Mrs Montagu's, where a splendid company was assembled, consisting of the most eminent literary characters, I thought he seemed highly pleased with the respect and attention that were shewn him, and asked him on our return home if he was not highly *gratified* by his visit: 'No, Sir, (said he,) not highly *gratified*; yet I do not recollect to have passed many evenings *with fewer objections.*'

Subsequently, he refused to allow Boswell to praise Mrs Montagu, 'observing "She does not gain upon me, Sir; I think her empty-headed".' Their friendly association, however, lasted until 1781, when Mrs Montagu took umbrage at a reference, published by Johnson in *The Lives of the Poets,* to her ancient crony Lord Lyttelton; and she decided she would cast him off. Johnson was nettled; his social pride was hurt. 'Mrs Montagu has dropt me', he said. 'Now, Sir, there are people whom one should like very well to drop, but would not wish to be dropped by.'

Mrs Thrale, too, had once admired the hostess. Mrs Montagu, she records in *Thraliana* during the summer months of 1777, had recently 'made many polite advances, and desired my friendship in a Way that flattered my Vanity. She is ... a very conspicuous Character in the World, and her Conversation flows very freely from a very full Mind.' Mrs Montagu was then almost sixty; and three years later, at the zenith of her social career, she moved into a new house, built for her by the famous 'Athenian' Stewart, the great arbiter of neo-classic taste, on the north-western side of Portman Square. Thanks to her marriage with a good-natured mine-owner, she had become a very rich woman**; and Montagu House contained, besides her dressing-room, which was embellished with scores of wanton cupids sporting amid jasmine bushes, a drawing-room hung with an irridescent feather-tapestry*** that enraptured William Cowper, who made it the subject of a charming occasional poem:

> The birds put off their every hue
> To dress a room for Montagu.

*The Reverend Dr Maxwell, 'sometime assistant preacher at the Temple', who obligingly allowed Boswell to make use of some notes he had compiled.

**In 1808, eight years after her death, Mrs Thrale complained that her great wealth had latterly made her arrogant and snobbish: 'Mrs Montagu was prouder of her Coalpits than of her Knowledge; & vainer of the Quality Friends gracing her Apartment, than of the Wits who followed humbly in her Train . . .'.

***The only surviving examples of late-eighteenth-century featherwork, as a form of mural decoration, are to be found in the drawing-room and gallery of La Ronde, the home of the Parminster family, built near Exmouth in 1798, where, along the walls of the gallery, it is combined with equally elaborate shellwork.

'Abelard and Eloisa'; Mrs Montagu and her admirer, the Reverend William
Mason, once Horace Walpole's literary correspondent. A caricature of 1778.

> The peacock sends his heavenly dyes,
> His rainbows and his starry eyes!
> The pheasant, plumes which round enfold
> His mantling neck with downy gold . . .
> All tribes beside of Indian name,
> That glossy shine, or vivid flame . . .
> Contribute to the gorgeous plan,
> Proud to advance it all they can.

Horace Walpole, too, approved of her 'new palace'. It was noble
and simple, he declared, 'not larded, and embroidered, and pom-
ponned with shreds and remnants', like the meretricious 'harlequinades of Adam'.

Mrs Montagu's entertainments were very largely conversational; and, to facilitate conversation, the chairs were arranged across the room in a ceremonious crescent:

At Mrs Montagu's, [Fanny Burney tells us] the semi-circle that faced the fire retained during the whole evening its unbroken form, with a precision that it seemed described by a Brobdignagian compass. The lady ... commonly placed herself at the upper end, near the commencement of the curve, so as to be courteously visible to all her guests; having the person of the highest rank or consequence, properly on one side, and the person the most eminent for talents, sagaciously, on the other side, or as near to her chair and her converse as her favouring eye and a complacent bow of the head could invite him to that distinction.

Such social artifices were despised by Mrs Vesey, whom her fellow Bluestockings had nicknamed 'The Sylph' because her nature was so gay and volatile, and who, abhorring a formal arrangement of seats, 'was wont to push all the small sofas, as well as chairs, pell mell about the apartments', and even placed 'the seats back to back, so

Left Robert Adam (1728–92); medallion by Tassie. Horace Walpole preferred the chaste decorations of Mrs Montagu's house to the gaudy 'harlequinades of Adam'. *Right* Elizabeth Vesey (1715?–91) nicknamed 'The Sylph', who, at her soirées, pushed the sofas around the room, and even placed chairs back to back, 'so that individuals could or could not, converse as they pleased . . .'

Mrs Chapone (1727–1801) from whose character Richardson was said to have drawn some of his most attractive heroines.

that individuals could or could not, converse as they pleased*, whilst she herself flitted from party to party, armed with an ear-trumpet ... catching an occasional sentence here, or a word there ...'. Her deafness had merely served to whet her insatiable appetite for conversation.

She was habitually encumbered, writes Fanny Burney, 'with two or three or more ear-trumpets hanging to her wrists or slung about her neck, or tost upon the chimney-piece or table. The instant that any earnestness of countenance or animation of gesture struck her eye, she darted forward, trumpet in hand, to inquire what was going on, but almost always arrived at the speaker at the moment when he was become, in his turn, the hearer.' Her husband, Agmondesham Vesey, Member of Parliament and Accountant-General of Ireland, was as friendly and good-natured as his wife. Johnson praised his 'gentle manners', but found him tiresome when he joined The Club. Hearing Vesey discourse at length on Cataline, he preferred to absent himself 'and thought of Tom Thumb'.

*See VESEY's plastic genius make
A circle every figure take;
Nay, shapes and forms, which would defy
All science of Geometry ...
Th'enchantress wav's her wand; and spoke!
Her potent wand the Circle broke ...
Hannah More: *The Bas Bleu, or Conversation.* 1786.

All the *Bas Bleus* were ardent Richardsonians; but Mrs Chapone's**
link with the great novelist had been particularly intimate. Before her
marriage, she had had the luck to belong to his 'flower garden' of
adoring ladies; and upon her, it was said, he had based some of his
most attractive female characters; which explained, according to one
of her friends – the remark was repeated by Mrs Delany with a touch
of gentle malice – why Richardson's heroines were not always quite
'so polished as he takes them to be'.

During later life, Mrs Chapone herself adventured into literature;
and, in 1773, she published a volume entitled *Letters on the Improvement of the Mind addressed to a young lady*. Dedicated to Mrs Montagu,
it brought her 'a great harvest of fame'; and for her next book,
Miscellanies in Prose and Verse, the publisher paid her over two
hundred guineas. Johnson himself thought well enough of her talents
to allow her to contribute essays to *The Rambler*; and in 1783 he sent
her a judicious criticism of a poetic tragedy she had had privately
printed, describing an image he particularly approved of as 'new,
just and delightful'; though the diction, he admitted, was sometimes
imperfect, and the dialogue struck him as a trifle laggard.

One of Mrs Chapone's dearest friends was the learned and versatile
Elizabeth Carter, who, besides being an accomplished modern poetess,
had produced a translation of Arrian's second-century *Discourses of
Epictetus and Encheirdion*. But she was not the kind of dishevelled
blue-stocking who neglects her households duties. 'My old friend
Mrs Carter', claimed Johnson, 'could make a pudding as well as
translate Epictetus from the Greek and work a handkerchief as well
as compose a poem'. She had been a friend of his youth; in 1732
he had suggested that she should undertake an English version of a
treatise by Boethius; and, like Mrs Chapone, she was privileged to
provide material for *The Rambler*. Meanwhile, in addition to Greek
and Latin, she had mastered Italian, German, Spanish and Hebrew –
a feat, he said, that entitled her 'to be celebrated in as many different
languages as Lewis le Grand'.

She was also a moralist, whose views closely resembled those of
Mrs Delany. She did not believe that a woman, however learned,
should abstain from social life. 'Society', she had announced in *The
Rambler*, 'is the true sphere of human virtue'; suffering was 'no duty,
but where it is necessary to avoid guilt or to do good'. Cheerfulness
was a quality she always insisted on: 'Be cheerfully prudent', she

**In *Vanity Fair*, the elder Miss Pinkerton, 'the Semiramis of Hammersmith', is said to
have been 'the correspondent of Mrs Chapone herself', and to have owed 'her reputation and
her fortune' to a visit once paid her by 'the late reverend Doctor Samuel Johnson'.

advised, 'and decently agreeable; as for your opinions, be consistent in all and obstinate in none...'.

Miss Carter was the child of a country clergyman, from whom she had inherited her thirst for knowledge; and, although she lived a somewhat fashionable life – rambling around England with Lord Lyttelton and his cronies, and visiting Paris and Spa with the Montagus and Lord Bath – she remained a modest, self-effacing character, and is reported to have entered and left the room with an almost feline stealth and speed. In her old age – she survived until 1806 – she was observed at a crowded Bluestocking party; rather stout, she

Elizabeth Carter (1717–1806); by Sir Thomas Lawrence. 'My old friend Mrs Carter', Johnson claimed, 'could make a pudding as well as translate Epictetus from the Greek . . .'

wore a 'scarlet gown and petticoat, with a plain undress cap and a perfectly flat head'. When she had seated herself, she immediately pulled out her knitting from the small work-bag hanging on her arm – 'but with no fuss or airs' – and joined in the conversation 'with that ease which persons have when both their thoughts and words are at command . . .'. She talked fluently, but smoothly and pleasantly, 'with no toss of the head, no sneer, no emphatic look...'. In *Thraliana*, where she is given high marks – seventeen for 'Worth of Heart', fifteen for 'Conversation Powers', eight for 'Good Humour' and eighteen for 'Ornamental Knowledge' – she is referred to as 'our venerable *Carter*', a glory of the present age.

Equally glorious, and no less learned, was the philanthropic Hannah More, who had the distinction of being liked and admired both by Samuel Johnson and by Horace Walpole. She had first reached London from the West Country, where her father kept a rustic school, early in the 1770s, bringing with her a letter of introduction, addressed to

Bath, a favourite gathering place of the Bas Bleu Ladies; the North Parade, by Thomas Malton.

Sir Joshua Reynolds' sister; and through Frances Reynolds she had presently been introduced, not only to Mrs Montagu, but to the Garricks, Edmund Burke and Johnson. Miss More evidently pleased Johnson; and when she and her sister Sally, accompanied by Miss Reynolds, paid him a visit at his own house, he received them with the greatest courtesy and, as they prepared to leave, called for his hat and escorted them, under a heavy shower of rain, 'down the very long entry to our coach'. Later, in Sir Joshua's drawing-room, Sally reports, 'Hannah ... was placed next to him, and they had the entire conversation to themselves.... It was certainly her lucky night. I never heard her say so many good things. The Old Genius was extremely jocular...'.

Among Miss More's earliest literary attempts had been poems in the fashionable 'Gothick' vein; and it was these, rather than her more solemnly improving works, that had attracted Horace Walpole. She is said first to have met him with Mrs Delany; but, once Miss More had become a social lioness, they soon had many other common friends, including Mrs Vesey and the formidable Mrs Montagu, at whose brilliant assemblies of wit and talent Walpole – a courtly antique figure, in a lavender-coloured silk suit, his *chapeau bras* clasped between his hands, walking on tip-toe, with slightly bent knees – very often made his bow.

Not only did Walpole applaud her imaginative gifts – the Strawberry Hill Press produced a small edition of her medieval ballad, *Bishop Bonner's Ghost*; while she would dedicate to him in 1786 a poetic tale entitled *Florio* – but he also advertised his deep regard for her conspicuous moral virtues. During their odd flirtation, which lasted as long as he lived, they continued gently bandying compliments. He styled her 'Saint Hannah', sometimes 'Holy Hannah', and declared that, 'even though there were no Sunday ... in the week', by dint of good works alone she was sure to go to Heaven. But his crowning tribute was a copy of the Scriptures, magnificently bound and printed.

Johnson was slightly-more critical. On 15 May 1784, having dined 'at Mrs Garrick's, with Mrs Carter, Miss Hannah More, and Miss Fanny Burney', he described them to Boswell as three incomparable women. But Miss More's habit of flattering him – too frequently and perhaps with insufficient subtlety – was apt, now and then, to try his patience. She remained, nevertheless, a welcome guest at Streatham. In *Thraliana*, her 'Worth of Heart', her 'Useful' and 'Ornamental Knowledge' receive exceptionally high marks; and elsewhere, on 5 December 1787, Mrs Thrale observes that Miss Hannah More was 'the cleverest of all of us Female Wits', and her *Florio*, 'a very excellent Piece of writing', despite the fact, she feels obliged to add, that 'we none of us much love the author...'.

By this time, Johnson himself was dead; but Miss More's triumphant literary career continued until 1819*, when she issued a

* She died, after a long decline, at the age of eighty, on 7 September 1833.

characteristically tendentious essay, *Moral Sketches of Prevailing Opinions and Manners.* In her youth, she had written poems and tragedies; but, later in life, she turned her hand to works of which 'usefulness', she announced, 'has been more invariably the object'. She had a varied range. *Percy* and *The Fatal Falsehood* were remarkably successful plays; and they were followed in 1782 by a series of four *Sacred Dramas. Thoughts on the Importance of the Manners of the*

Hannah More (1745–1833); portrait by H. Pickersgill, 1822. 'It is the educationalist, placid and stout and shrewd, rather than the Bas Bleu Lady and purveyor of medieval romance, who emerges in Pickersgill's nineteenth-century portrait.'

Great to General Society came out in 1788; and, during the same year, she produced a poem on *Slavery* that helped to encourage the movement for the abolition of the Slave Trade.

Then, with *Coelebs in Search of a Wife*, she expanded into moral fiction. Simultaneously, besides proselytizing the 'polite world', she undertook the education of the poor and, with her sisters, set up a girls' school near the country cottage she had bought in Somerset. As an educationalist, her views were patriarchal. Her purpose, she wrote, was 'not to make fanatics', but to teach her pupils 'such coarse works' as might fit them to become servants. Otherwise her aims were strictly limited: 'I allow of no writing for the poor.'

It is the educationalist, placid and stout and shrewd, rather than the *Bas Bleu* lady and purveyor of medieval romance, who emerges in Pickersgill's nineteenth-century portrait. But today, if we endeavour to read her books, it is the early verses that seem most attractive. By contemporary critics her poems were vastly admired. According to Miss Reynolds, 'the beauteous Bertha', heroine of her ballad, *Sir Eldred of the Bower*, 'had kindled a flame in the cold bosom of Dr Johnson'. *The Bleeding Rock*, exclaimed Mrs Montagu, was surely destined to 'stand unimpaired by ages'. 'A truly elegant and tender performance' were the terms that Richard Burke employed.

Though Sidney Smith would afterwards scoff at *Coelebs*, very few of her immediate contemporaries doubted Hannah More's genius. Of all that tremendous output, little now remains enjoyable. Her poems, however, have at least the merit of helping us to revise our attitude towards the later eighteenth century. In many of the arts of life, for example in architecture, decoration and gardening, the great executants of the period seldom made a false move. But in literature taste was more uneven; and both the cult of sensibility, popularized by Laurence Sterne, and the 'Gothick' craze, launched by Horace Walpole, as they sank into the literary mind had had a weakening and confusing influence.

Walpole's *Castle of Otranto*, the first and most brilliant of the 'Gothic Novels', appeared when Hannah More was nineteen; and she shared his consuming passion for the English Middle Ages. The ill-fated protagonists of *Sir Eldred* are an innocent maiden and her knightly brother. When Sir Eldred, who does not suspect their relationship, discovers the handsome pair embracing –

> Wild frenzy fires his frantic hand,
> Distracted at the sight,
> He flies where the lovers stand,
> And stabs the stranger knight.

> 'Die, traitor, die! thy guilty flames
> 'Demand th'avenging steel!' –
> 'It is my brother!' she exclaims,
> ''Tis EDWY – Oh, farewell!'

The Bleeding Rock, the poem that Mrs Montagu so much admired, has a similarly romantic and lugubrious subject. Seduced and abandoned by Polydore, Ianthe undergoes an appalling metamorphosis:

> Then, strange to tell! if rural folks say true,
> To harden'd Rock the stiff'ning damsel grew;
> No more her shapeless features can be known,
> Stone is her body, and her limbs are stone;
> The growing rock invades her beauteous face;
> And quickly petrifies each living grace . . .
> Yet – strange the marvels Poets can impart!
> Unchang'd, unchill'd, remained the glowing heart;
> Its vital spirits destin'd still to keep,
> It scorn'd to mingle with the marble heap.
>
> When babbling Fame the wondrous tidings bore,
> Grief seiz'd the soul of perjur'd Polydore . . .

Hannah More's remarkable fluency was only equalled by her versatility; she could also turn out richly embroidered verses, mock-heroic or serio-comic, in the correct Augustan manner. Such were *Sensibility*, addressed to 'the honourable Mrs Boscawen', a minor member of the *Bas Bleu* group, and *The Bas Bleu, or Conversation*, dedicated to Mrs Vesey. The Blue Stockings, it must be remembered, though they prided themselves upon their erudition, were no less delighted with their powers of feeling, their quick and delicate response to man and nature. In the former work, the poetess deals at considerable length with the quality they most valued:

> Sweet SENSIBILITY! thou keen delight!
> Unprompted moral! sudden sense of right!
> Perception exquisite! fair virtue's seed!
> Thou quick precursor of the lib'ral deed! . . .
> To those who know thee not no words can paint,
> And those who know thee, know all words are faint

Between true Sensibility, however, a quality that prompts to virtue, and mere Feeling, which, in its more exaggerated forms, may well be vain and self-complacent, the author draws a sharp distinction:

There are, who fill with brilliant plaints the page,
If a poor linnet meet the gunner's rage ...
Who boast, quick rapture trembling in their eye,
If from the spider's snare they snatch a fly ...

Sensibility, she insists, should begin at home:

... The sober comfort, all the peace which springs
From the large aggregate of little things;
On these small cares of daughter, wife, or friend,
The almost sacred joys of *Home* depend:
There, SENSIBILITY, thou best may'st reign,
HOME is thy true legitimate domain.

Hannah More, 1827; silhouette by Edouart.

The second line of the passage quoted above has a fine Johnsonian
weight and rhythm; and, believing, as he did, that 'life is made up of
little things', Johnson would certainly have approved the argument.
But his highest praise he reserved for *The Bas Bleu*, which, though it
did not appear in print until 1786, had been written a good deal earlier
and extensively circulated in manuscript. Miss More professed to
have been taken aback by his whole-hearted approbation: 'He said
there was no name in poetry that might not be glad to own it. You
cannot imagine how I stared at this from Johnson, that parsimonious
praiser. I told him that I was delighted.... He answered quite characteristically, "And so you may, for I give you the opinion of a man who
does not praise easily".' Walpole, too, once the poem had appeared in

book-form, acknowledged it with rapturous applause. He was suffering at the time from a horrible fit of the gout, which had swollen and inflamed his hand; and the music of the verse, he said, gliding along his fingers, had very soon lulled him into an exquisite tranquility.

Such are the strange revolutions of literary taste! But, although Johnson's praise – or, indeed, Horace Walpole's – may be difficult to understand, it was natural enough that the *Bas Bleu* ladies themselves should find the poem wholly captivating. Each of a series of eminent Blue-stockings – 'VESEY, of Verse the judge and friend', 'BOSCAWEN sage, bright MONTAGU' and the 'deeply wise' Mrs Carter – is awarded a poetic crown; and together they are said to have rescued society from the shades of formal dullness. Conversation is the heaven-sent art that has at length enabled them to bring life and spiritual gaiety into modern English drawing-rooms:

> Hail, CONVERSATION, soothing Power,
> Sweet Goddess of the social hour!
> Not with more heart-felt warmth, at least,
> Does LELIUS bend, thy true High Priest;
> Than I the lowest of thy train,
> These field-flowers bring to deck thy fane ...
> Long may thy polish'd altars Blaze
> With wax-lights undiminished rays!
> Still be thy nightly offerings paid,
> Libations large of Lemonade.
> On silver bases, loaded, rise
> The biscuits' ample sacrifice ...
> Rise, incense pure from fragrant Tea,
> Delicious incense, worthy Thee!

In *The Bas Bleu*, the authoress strongly denies that she and her friends bore any resemblance to the group of *Précieuses Ridicules* who had once assembled and conversed at the Hôtel de Rambouillet –

> Where point, and turn, and équivoque,
> Distorted every word they spoke!
> All so intolerably bright,
> Plain Common Sense was put to flight. ...

The 'Chaste Queen, divine Simplicity', was the tutelary goddess of the *Bas Bleu* gatherings. They were essentially modern women, they chose to think, and had asserted a refining and civilizing influence on the social age in which they lived. Nor were the claims that they

The Bas Bleu Ladies and some of their associates. The group includes
Miss Carter, Hannah More and Mrs Montagu.

made entirely ridiculous. In their small way, they helped to change
society, by showing that women could take their place among men,
and that intellect was not necessarily a masculine prerogative. But
they conducted their useful operations within a rather narrow compass.

None was a rebel. They belonged, even Miss Carter and Miss More
who had originated in the professional middle class, to an affluent
haute bourgeoisie, which respected, and did its best to support the
existing social order. Thus they condemned the 'equalizing notions'
that had recently begun to emerge in France; and each of them, so
far as we can now judge, was a zealous champion of the Christian faith.

Meanwhile, a genuine rebel, a young woman haunted both by her
own sufferings and the common miseries of her sex, may have observed
the *Bas Bleu* from a distance. In 1778, Mary Wollstonecraft, a handsome, impulsive young woman of nineteen who had not long ago
shaken off her servitude to a drunken, improvident father and a foolish,
feckless mother, was staying in Bath as the ill-paid companion of an
irritable rich old widow. There she deplored the frivolous round of

amusements and 'the dissipated lives led by women of quality', but, at the same time, probably glimpsed the Bluestockings, some of whom were then in residence, and admired their show of intellectual freedom. They belonged, however, to the old Augustan world; whereas Mary Wollstonecraft represented the rebellious aspirations of a new age; and, when, in 1792, she published her *Vindication of the Rights of Woman*, both Hannah More and Horace Walpole registered their deep abhorrence, comparing it to Tom Paine's infamous *Rights of Man*, of which the preliminary section had appeared a year earlier. 'The Paines, the Tookes*, and Wollstonecrafts', wrote Walpole, were all 'philosophizing serpents'.

Though Johnson himself did not survive to deliver judgment on Paine's greatest work, he declared that Horne Tooke, whom Boswell described as a 'seditious delinquent', should be obliged to stand in the public pillory, 'that he may be punished in a way that would disgrace him'. Shortly before his final collapse, however, he entertained their fellow serpent unawares; for, while Mary and her sister, Eliza, were conducting a school they had founded at Newington Green, she met, through a friend and neighbour, the Reverend Richard Price, a similarly enlightened clergyman named Hewlett; and Hewlett encouraged her to visit Johnson. She did so; 'the Doctor', writes William Godwin in his biography of his late wife, 'treated her with particular kindness and attention, had a long conversation with her and desired her to repeat her visit often'. Mary agreed, and would have returned to Bolt Court, but for the news that he had fallen seriously ill.

Thus, Mary Wollstonecraft was one of the last young women who entered Johnson's magic circle. She had had many forerunners. Some were favourite protégées and pupils, to be advised and teased and reprimanded. Others aroused a much more poignant emotion that made them romantic legends in his memory, images of grace and youth and charm, around which his thoughts were constantly revolving. Molly Aston, for example, was a beauty he could never quite forget. Nearly twenty years after her death, on 5 July 1782, Mrs Thrale notes that Johnson, as they talked of Fanny Burney's new novel, had said that he supposed that 'Miss Burney's book concludes by leaving her heroine in measureless delight', and had wondered 'when anybody ever experiences measureless delight: *I* never did I'm sure except the first Evening I spent Teste a Teste with Molly Aston....'

Later, in the *Anecdotes* which she had quarried from *Thraliana*, Mrs Thrale provides a somewhat different story. Mr Thrale having

* Horne Tooke, 1736–1812, author of *Epea Pteroenta; or, the Diversions of Purley*; radical reformer and champion of the American Colonists.

asked him which had been the happiest period of his life, he replied, 'it was that year in which he spent one whole evening with M---y As--n. "That indeed (said he) was not happiness, it was rapture ...". I must add, that the evening alluded to was not passed *tête-à-tête*, but in a select company. ... "Molly (says Dr Johnson) was a beauty and a scholar, and a wit and a Whig; and she talked all in praise of liberty: and so I made this epigram upon her – she was the loveliest creature I ever saw!!!"'

Liber ut esse velim, suasti pulchra Maria
*Ut maneam liber – pulchra Maria, vale!**

Left Molly Aston (1706?–65), by an unknown artist. To Miss Aston Johnson said that he had owed the happiest moments of his whole existence.
Right Mary Wollstonecraft (1759–97); 'one of the last women who entered Johnson's magic circle'. Portrait by John Opie.

The memorable encounter of which Johnson spoke appears to have taken place in 1739, at a moment, after his earliest assault on London, when he had temporarily retired to Lichfield. Miss Aston, daughter

*Mrs Thrale's extempore translation, which Johnson said would 'do well enough', runs as follows:

> Persuasions to freedom fall oddly from you;
> If freedom we seek – fair Maria, adieu!

of a North-Country baronet, was a star of the Lichfield *beau monde*, one of her sisters being married to Gilbert Walmsley, another to the Honourable and Reverend Henry Hervey, a man whom, despite his profligate existence, Johnson always greatly loved.* Her large aquiline nose now seems more impressive than attractive; but she had shining reddish hair, a long and elegant neck, and, according to her portrait, an air of feminine liveliness combined with intellectual self-assurance.

Said to be 'haughty', she was not particularly popular among members of her own sex. 'The ladies', admitted Johnson, had never really loved Miss Aston. Naturally, Johnson's cult remained platonic. Not only did he and Molly Aston belong to very different worlds, but, in 1739, Johnson was already a married man; and, as Hawkins reminds us, 'he was a man too strict in his morals to give any reasonable cause of jealousy to a wife'.

Tetty, however, was decidedly displeased; and, Mrs Thrale having been bold enough to enquire what his wife had thought of his attachment:

She was jealous to be sure (said he), and teized me sometimes when I would let her; and one day, as a fortune-telling gipsey passed us when we were walking out ... with two or three friends in the country, she made the wench look at my hand, but soon repented her curiosity; for (says the gipsey) Your heart is divided, Sir, between a Betty and a Molly: Betty loves you best, but you take most delight in Molly's company: When I turned about to laugh, I saw my wife was crying. Pretty charmer! she had no reason!

Otherwise, we know little enough of Molly, except that she married a naval officer, Captain David Brodie, in 1753, and died about 1765. Later, he transferred his affections to Mary Meynell, whose parents lived in Derbyshire near his school-friend, John Taylor, the occupant of the manor-house at Ashbourne. Miss Meynell had married William Fitzherbert.

'That woman (he remarked to Mrs Thrale) loved her husband as we hope and desire to be loved by our guardian angel. F-tz-h--b--t was a gay good-humoured fellow, generous of his money and of his meat, and desirous of nothing but cheerful society among people distinguished in *some* way, in *any* way I think; for Rousseau and St Austin would have been equally welcome to his table and to his kindness: his lady however was of another way of thinking; her first care was to preserve her husband's soul from corruption.

*Son of the first Earl of Bristol, brother of Pope's enemy, John Lord Hervey. 'Not very long before his death', Johnson described this friendship to Boswell: 'Harry Hervey ... was a vicious man, but very kind to me. If you call a dog HERVEY, I shall love him.'

... She stood at the door of her Paradise in Derbyshire, like the angel with the flaming sword. ... But she was not immortal, poor dear! She died, and her husband felt at once afflicted and released.' I inquired if she was handsome? 'She would have been handsome for a queen (replied the panegyrist); her beauty had more in it of majesty than of attraction, more of the dignity of virtue than of the vivacity of wit.'

Most of the women whom Johnson courted and admired – but cannot, in the more obvious sense, be said to have pursued – were unquestionably 'modest women'; their virtue was an essential part of their charm; he respected their position either as honest virgins or

Left Life in the Demi-Monde, 1780; from a picture by John Collet, an artist who appears to have specialised in transvestite subjects. The background of the scene is probably a Covent Garden bagnio; the travestied young man is a naval officer. *Right* 'A Man Trap'; from a picture by Collet painted about the same period.

as blameless wives and mothers. Yet, all his life, he had a sympathetic regard for women who laid no claims to virtue; and, now and then, he would amuse the virtuous with picturesque anecdotes about the vicious. Thus, at Streatham, in 1778, he began suddenly to describe an old friend.

Here Fanny Burney reports the conversation. He had known every wit, Johnson declared, from Mrs Montagu down to Bet Flint:

'Bet Flint!' cried Mrs Thrale; 'pray who is she?' 'Oh, a fine character, madam! She was habitually a slut and a drunkard, and occasionally a thief and a harlot.' 'And, for heaven's sake, how came you to know her?' 'Why, madam, she figured in the literary world, too! Bet Flint wrote her own life, and called herself Cassandra, and it was in verse; it began:

> When Nature first ordain'd my birth,
> A diminutive I was born on earth:
> And I came from a dark abode
> Into a gay and gaudy world.

So Bet brought me her verses to correct; but I gave her half a crown, and she liked it as well. Bet had a fine spirit; she advertised for a husband, for she told me no man aspired to her! Then she hired very handsome lodgings and a footboy; and she got a harpsichord, but Bet could not play; however, she put herself in fine attitudes, and drummed.'

Once, he continued, when she stole a quilt from her lodging, Bet was obliged to go to gaol, but set forth in a sedan chair, preceded by her shame-faced footboy. At her trial, the judge had acquitted her. '"So now", she said to me, "the quilt is my own and now I'll make a petticoat of it." Oh, I loved Bet Flint!' There were many other adventuresses, some more celebrated than Bet Flint, whom Johnson, for reasons that escaped Mrs Thrale, had often talked with and befriended. 'Bless me, sir!' she exclaimed, 'how can all these vagabonds contrive to get at *you*, of all people?' '"Oh, the dear creatures!" cried he, laughing heartily, "I can't but be glad to see them!"'

Mrs Thrale's next question had perhaps a double edge: 'Why I wonder, sir, you never went to see Mrs Rudd? ...' Five years earlier, the *Westminster Gazette* had published an account of Thrale's alleged liaison with 'the celebrated Mrs R---', who may well have been the same person.* Mrs Rudd had since increased her fame; for, in 1775, she and her 'benefactors', the twin brothers, Robert and Daniel Perreau, had been accused of passing forged bonds. Mrs Rudd was Daniel Perreau's mistress; but, when the brothers showed signs of betraying her, she had adroitly turned King's Evidence, and had conducted her case with such remarkable skill, and with such a beguiling air of helpless virtue, that she had been acquitted amid the loudest applause ever heard in an English court of law, while both her less skilful accomplices were found guilty and condemned to hang.

---

*Mrs Rudd, a native of northern Ireland, had been born in 1745, and had previously lived under a series of impressive *noms de guerre*, such as the Countess de Grosberg, Miss de la Rochelle and Miss Malfaisans. Later, she became the favourite of John Wilkes.

'The extraordinary address and insinuation' she displayed in court had made her a subject of universal interest; 'one must respect Mrs Rudde for her Parts', said Reynolds, 'tho' her Vices were so great'. Boswell, too, was inclined to take her side. Even his wife, he wrote, had heard him 'rave with a strange force of imagination about the celebrated Mrs Rudd'; and, in April 1776, he decided to pay her a clandestine visit. The description of this visit, which he drew up for his wife's benefit – but, wisely, perhaps, once he had written it, decided that he would not send – is a magnificent piece of Boswellian reportage. As he awaited her alone in her dusty upstairs room, lighted

Mrs Rudd pleading her cause at the Old Bailey, December 1775; thanks to her eloquence and air of helpless virtue, she was acquitted amid loud applause.

only by a pair of tallow candles, he feared that the ghosts of the Perreaus might rise at any moment from the shadows. But the arrival of Mrs Rudd herself – 'a little woman, delicately made, not at all a beauty, but with a very pleasing appearance' – immediately put his mind at rest.

She spoke of her case 'with wonderful ease and delicacy'; and Boswell, having assured her that she was 'reckoned quite a sorceress, possessed of enchantment', seized and kissed her 'silken hand'. He also admired her ankles, and presently 'wished her good night with a kiss which she received without affectation of any kind'. When he talked to Johnson of the meeting, and Miss Williams expressed her disapproval, Johnson hastened to his friend's defence: '"Nay, Madam, Boswell is in the right; I should have visited her myself, were it not that they have now a trick of putting everything into the newspapers". This evening he exclaimed, "I envy him his acquaintance with Mrs Rudd".'

Kitty Fisher (d. 1767); 'her eyes were intensely blue – the bluest Mrs Thrale had ever seen . . .' Portrait by Reynolds at Petworth.

Another notorious personage whom Johnson never met, but whose acquaintance he would certainly not have refused, was the great hetaira, Kitty Fisher. 'Bet Flint, it seems', writes Fanny Burney, 'once took Kitty Fisher to see him, but to his no little regret he was not at home'; and, in his biography, Hawkins agrees that 'she once left her card' at Johnson's house. The most fashionable courtesan of her day, Catherine Maria Fisher, is said to have had German blood, and, before she launched into the London demi-monde, to have earned her living as a milliner's apprentice. During the later 1750s, she had reached the height of her profession; and among her platonic admirers was Sir Joshua Reynolds, who became a close friend, and in several portraits dwelt with devoted care upon her languid, somewhat feline beauty.

Her eyes were intensely blue – the bluest Mrs Thrale had ever seen; 'the Colour was truly Celestial', a brilliant 'Sky Blue, like a Ribbon'. Casanova claims to have been offered her services at a London house of assignation in the year 1763; but he had declined the proposal, he explains, because she could only speak English, a language he had not yet mastered; and, 'accustomed to love with all my senses, I could not abandon myself to love unless I employed my sense of hearing'. Shortly afterwards, she married and settled down, as the second wife of John Norris, one-time Member of Parliament for Rye, and spent her last years managing her husband's affairs and helping him pay off his debts. Her married life was brief but happy; she died at Bath in 1767 – according to one story, poisoned by the white lead with which, like other eighteenth-century beauties, she sometimes used to blanch her skin.

Neither Kitty Fisher nor Bet Flint offended Johnson's moral sense. To such women, as to his profligate male companions – Savage, Hervey, Topham Beauclerk – he allowed the very widest latitude. But he was always merciless in the judgment he passed on women of a different kind – 'modest women' who, despite the advantages of a respectable upbringing, had wilfully deviated from the paths of virtue. Lady Diana Beauclerk, for example, had deliberately broken up her marriage. The daughter of the third Duke of Marlborough, she had been married at the age of twenty-three to the second Viscount Bolingbroke, nephew and heir of the erratic statesman so much admired by Pope and Swift. Lord Bolingbroke was a rake and a drunkard*; and, to obtain a Parliamentary divorce and marry her fascinating lover, Topham Beauclerk, when her case reached the

---

* He seems to have infected his wife with a venereal disease. Nonetheless, he would appear to have loved her deeply, and bitterly lamented her departure.

House of Lords she had made a public confession of adultery. It achieved its purpose; and, in August 1768, Lady Diana and Beauclerk had been duly wed.

Although her second marriage was evidently happier than the first, it proved a somewhat disappointing union. Topham Beauclerk, who had been born in 1739, was the great-grandson of Charles II, through his liaison with the actress Nell Gwyn; and he had inherited both Charles' volatile temperament and his heavy black eyebrows. Francis Cotes' pastel-portrait of the seventeen-year-old Beauclerk shows an impudent, humorous, expressive face, with brown hair, greenish hazel eyes and a small sensuous, half-smiling mouth, slightly turned up at

Lady Diana Beauclerk (1734–1808); loved by all her husband's friends, except Johnson. 'The woman's a whore', he instructed Boswell, 'and there's an end on't'. From a drawing by Bartolozzi.

the corners – the face of a young man who knows that he has been born to charm, and does not hesitate to exploit his gifts.

Beauclerk remained a charmer so long as he lived; among his other admirable qualities, he was a brilliant conversationalist. 'Everything', once observed Johnson, 'comes from Beauclerk so easily that it appears to me I labour if I say a good thing.' In an obituary tribute, Johnson would speak of 'his wit and his folly, his acuteness and maliciousness, his merriment and reasoning', which Beauclerk's friends were never to enjoy again. Some of them had dreaded his sharp tongue. But he always respected Johnson's moral prejudices, and was 'too polite', Boswell noted, 'and valued learning and wit too much to offend Johnson by sallies of infidelity or licentiousness, and Johnson delighted in Beauclerk's good qualities and hoped to correct the evil'.

Nor was his learning a form of social display. When her husband died in 1781, Lady Diana was obliged to sell his books, and a stout volume appeared under an imposing title, *A Catalogue of the Large & Valuable Library of the late Honourable Topham Beauclerk, F.R.S. . . . comprehending an excellent Choice of Books, to the Number of up to Thirty Thousand Volumes in most Languages, and upon almost any Branch of Science and Polite Literature**. There can be no doubt that he was unusually well-read; but Beauclerk combined his love of reading with a taste for much more vulgar pleasures. Reynolds' sharp-tongued sister, Frances, compared Johnson and his young disciple to Socrates and Alcibiades. He made a poor husband; and during the later part of his life, wrote Lady Louisa Stuart**, 'the man of pleasure grew morose and savage, and Lady Di had much to suffer from his temper; so had his children, to whom he was a selfish tyrant without indulgence or affection'. He had long been an invalid; and it was said the reckless use of opium had both hastened his end and soured his character.

Lady Diana was often pitied by their circle – for instance, when she gave a dinner-party, but Beauclerk chose to spend the night abroad. On such an occasion, Garrick, who, like all Beauclerk's friends, except for Johnson, was devoted to his wife, produced some neat consolatory verses. The absentee host had himself arranged the party; but 'the dice came between', and he had failed to turn up:

> Nor indeed did they want him, for sweet Lady Di
> Did more than the loss of ten Beauclerks supply.
> At nine of next morning I saw with these eyes
> His Honour sneak home, neither merry nor wise.

* Beauclerk's was sold by auction in April and May 1781, and realized £5,011.
** In a note on the correspondence of George Selwyn.

Five years older than Topham Beauclerk, Lady Diana, to judge from Bartolozzi's sketch, was a large and stately woman – perhaps the kind of large, submissive woman who is often enslaved by small attractive men. A talented amateur, she produced innumerable drawings of prettily-imagined subjects – nymphs dancing and children disporting themselves with goats and little goat-legged boys, affectionate cupids and romantic peasants. She also illustrated books, including Horace Walpole's blank-verse tragedy, *The Mysterious Mother*; and Walpole, a keen patron of amateur artists, announced that Lady Diana's illustrations 'would be fully worthy of the best of Shakespeare's plays', and that 'Salvator Rosa and Guido could not surpass their expression and beauty. I have built a closet on purpose for them here at Strawberry Hill. It is called the Beauclerk closet. . . .'

To her son and beautiful Beauclerk daughters, both of whom contracted 'good' marriages*, Lady Diana had a deep attachment; and after her divorce from her brutal first husband, she would appear to have led a serenely virtuous life**. Yet Johnson could never forgive the divorce, even in a woman who had been beloved by a dear friend, and had done her best to make him happy; and, on 7 May 1773, when they had breakfasted with Mr Thrale, Boswell informs us that:

I endeavoured as well as I could to apologise for a lady who had been divorced from her husband by act of Parliament. I said, that he had used her very ill ... and that she could not continue to live with him without having her delicacy contaminated ... that the essence of conjugal union being gone, there remained only a cold form, a mere civil obligation; that she was in the prime of life, with qualities to produce happiness ... and that the gentleman on whose account she was divorced had gained her heart while thus unhappily situated. Seduced, perhaps, by the charms of the lady in question, I thus attempted to palliate what I was sensible could not be justified; for, when I had finished my harangue, my venerable friend gave me a proper check: 'My dear Sir, never accustom your mind to mingle virtue and vice. The woman's a whore, and there's an end on't.'

Once the newspapers had begun to describe his doings, and he was safely domesticated at Streatham Place, Johnson had lost his affection for bohemian company. Virtuous women now afforded him all the entertainment he required; and, early in August 1778, Fanny

---

*She had borne her previous husband two sons. Elizabeth Beauclerk, who sat for Reynolds' picture of 'Una and the Lion', married Lord Herbert; her sister Mary, Count Jervison of Walworth.

**On Lady Diana's moral character, Baretti made a characteristic comment: 'I know She is a Strumpet; had She not been so, She would have sate in Heaven next Jesus Christ.' *Thraliana, 28 May, 1777.*

Burney, under the wing of her father, Dr Charles Burney, first appeared among the Thrales. She was already celebrated; that same year, 'at the latter end of February', her prentice novel, *Evelina, or, a Young Lady's Entrance into the World*, had been issued by a Fleet Street bookseller named Thomas Lowndes. The author was anonymous; but, after a good deal of public controversy and, on Miss Burney's own part, of embarrassment and trepidation, she had eventually given way and told her secret.

It was not the authoress' earliest attempt to write; she had been busily scribbling since her schooldays. The fourth of a family of nine

Elizabeth and Mary Beauclerk; water-colour portraits by their mother.

children, Miss Burney had received an extremely liberal education from her father's clever friends. True, she had begun badly; until she was eight years old, Dr Burney writes, Fanny 'did not know her letters', and was 'wholly unnoticed in the nursery for any talents, or quickness of study ...'. Yet, although 'silent, backward, and timid, even to sheepishness', the 'Old Lady', as her family had nicknamed her, was an extraordinarily observant girl; and, at her father's crowded London house, there was always much to see and hear.

David Garrick would suddenly enter the room, accompanied by Phil, his favourite spaniel, and amuse the children with a pyrotechnic performance of half-a-dozen different parts, even pretending to be a wire-drawn puppet, 'placing himself against a wall' and 'seeming to speak through a comb ...'. Fanny, too, would presently become a mime; and the great actor, who nicknamed Fanny either 'the Dumpling Queen' or 'Piety in Patterns', was no doubt one of the two chief influences that had helped to shape her gifts.

The other predominant influence was Samuel Crisp, an old friend of the Burney family and, to Fanny, while her talents were maturing, certainly 'the dearest thing on earth'. Crisp was her second father, a distinguished, scholarly personage, with fine manners, a fund of critical taste, 'bright, hazel, penetrating, yet arch eyes' and 'a noble Roman nose'. Now that he had lost his fortune, Crisp had retired to Chessington Hall, the Surrey manor-house that a Mr Christopher Hamilton, who had also experienced hard times, now let out in pleasant lodgings to a host of delapidated gentlemen and similarly impoverished ladies.

The Burneys called him 'Daddy Crisp'; and Fanny chose him both as her personal confidant and as her literary adviser. She adored her father; but Dr Burney, having fifty or sixty music-lessons to get through a week, was usually away from home on his professional errands; and Samuel Crisp, being lonely and unemployed, was able to give his beloved 'Fannikin' all the attention that she needed. There is clearly a link between her tender, solicitous 'Daddy' and Evelina's anxious guardian, the Reverend Mr Villars, into whose ear the heroine pours out a daily record of her youthful joys and sorrows.

When she launched out into the story of *Evelina*, Fanny Burney seems to have drawn some of her material from her recollections of an earlier book, *Caroline Evelyn*, which she is said to have burned upon her fifteenth birthday, amid a vast accumulation of juvenilia, including 'Elegies, Odes, Plays, Songs, Stories, Farces – nay, Tragedies and Epic Poems'. But *Evelina* was not a book that she could persuade herself to sacrifice; and, although still a timid and retiring character, she had determined that she would see it published.

Her brothers and sisters approved of this daring plan; and a domestic conspiracy was then hatched, with numerous subterfuges and disguises. Dodsley, the first publisher the conspirators approached, immediately turned their offer down; he must decline, he said, 'looking at anything that was anonymous'; but their next choice, Lowndes of Fleet Street, to whom Charles Burney, disguised 'in an old great coat, and very large old hat', carried the manuscript of the two preliminary volumes, at once accepted them for publication. Dr Burney remained in ignorance of the plot. Not until July, when he had already heard the book praised, did his daughter at last admit her authorship. He was immediately 'struck & astounded' by its merits, and concluded that the publisher had made *'a devilish good Bargain'*. In fact, on accepting the manuscript, Lowndes had offered the novelist twenty guineas.

Evelina enjoyed an immediate success – not only with the public at large, but with the most perceptive modern critics. Naturally, Mrs Thrale was determined to meet the celebrated Miss Burney, and Miss Burney no less ready to meet the famous Mrs Thrale. Early in August 1778, Dr Burney had called at Streatham as he returned from a visit to Samuel Crisp at Chessington; and Mrs Thrale, who had just been reading and warmly praising *Evelina* – she complained that it was far too short; 'there was a great deal of human life in it', she said; 'it was written by somebody who knows the top and the bottom, the highest and lowest of mankind' – begged that he would call on her again, and this time bring his gifted daughter. Miss Burney was taken aback; 'I have been' she confided to her diary, 'in a kind of twitter ever since, for there seems something very formidable in the idea of appearing as an authoress! ... Yet I am highly flattered by her invitation, and highly delighted in the prospect of being introduced to the Streatham society.'

It was a hot morning; and the journey to Streatham proved an uncomfortable adventure; 'for the roads were dreadfully dusty, and I was really in the fidgets from thinking what my reception might be, and from fearing they might expect a less awkward and backward kind of person. ...' But, having reached their goal – a white house, 'very pleasantly situated in a fine paddock' – she was quickly reassured. Mrs Thrale, who had been strolling about the garden, hastened to greet them as they left the chaise, 'taking both my hands' and welcoming her to Streatham 'with mixed politeness and cordiality ...'.

At the same time, she was sufficiently delicate not to mention *Evelina*, but led Miss Burney upstairs, took her around the house and, in the music-room, presented her eldest daughter, Queeney – 'a very fine girl, about fourteen years of age, but cold and reserved, though full of knowledge and intelligence'. Next, they moved on to the library; and there, at length, she spoke of Miss Burney's novel. Dr Johnson had liked it prodigiously:

'Yesterday at supper', said she, 'we talked it all over, and discussed all your characters; but Dr Johnson's favourite is Mr Smith. He declares the fine gentleman *manqué* was never better drawn, and he acted him all the evening.... He repeated whole scenes by heart. I declare I was astonished at him. Oh, you can't imagine how much he is pleased with the book; he "could not get rid of the rogue", he told me.'

Johnson himself was apparently still in his room – he seldom rose before midday; but, when the company was summoned to dinner, Miss Burney heard that she was to sit beside him:

Soon after we were seated, this great man entered. I have so true a veneration for him, that the very sight of him inspires me with delight and reverence, notwithstanding the cruel infirmities to which he is subject; for he has almost perpetual convulsive movements, either of his hands, lips, feet, or knees, and sometimes all together.... We had a noble dinner, and a most elegant dessert. Dr Johnson, in the middle of the dinner, asked Mrs Thrale what was in some little pies that were near him.

'Mutton', answered she, 'so I don't ask you to eat any, because I know you despise it.'

'No, madam, no', cried he; 'I despise nothing that is good of its sort; but I am too proud now to eat of it. Sitting by Miss Burney makes me very proud today.'

Dinner, of course, was then an afternoon meal; and the Burneys left Streatham about eight o'clock – but not before Fanny had promised to return and spend some days among her new friends. She kept her promise towards the end of August; and Johnson once again displayed 'the utmost good humour', unlike Mr Thrale, who was 'neither well nor in good spirits', and struck his guests as an unhappy man. Johnson, however, was clearly set on pleasing – 'so civil to me! – even admiring how I dressed myself! Indeed, it is well I have so much of his favour; for it seems he always speaks his mind concerning the dress of ladies, and all ladies who are here obey his instructions implicitly.'

This was an aspect of his character that Miss Burney noted with astonishment. Although he was 'sometimes so absent, and always so near-sighted, he scrutinizes into every part of almost everybody's appearance'. Some visitors were positively browbeaten:

They tell me of a Miss Brown ... who has a slovenly way of dressing. 'And when she comes down in a morning', says Mrs Thrale, 'her hair will be all loose, and her cap half off; and then Dr Johnson, who sees something is wrong, and does not know where the fault is, concludes it is in the cap, and says, "My dear, what do you wear such a cap for?" "I'll change it, sir", cries the poor girl.... "Aye, do", he says; and away runs poor Miss Brown; but when she gets on another, it's the same thing....'

It was the width of Johnson's interests, the elasticity of his imagination and 'his universal readiness upon all subjects', that particularly charmed Miss Burney, as it charmed so many of his friends. There was nothing he would not vigorously discuss – from David Garrick's latest prologue, 'the worst he had ever made', which he had denounced during Fanny's previous visit, and the exhausted expression on the veteran actor's face, to colours and 'the fantastic names given to them, and why the palest lilac should be called *soupir étouffé.** ...' On this point, Mrs Thrale had appealed to Dr Johnson. 'Why, madam', he promptly replied, 'it is called a stifled sigh because it is checked in its progress, and only half a colour.'

Meanwhile, Johnson's admiration for the young novelist – she had not yet reached her twenty-sixth birthday at the time she published *Evelina* – grew rapidly more and more effusive; and one evening, when they happened to meet in the house just after his return from a fleeting visit to London, he suddenly grasped her hands; 'then drawing me very unexpectedly towards him, he actually kissed me!' He had already compared her to Mrs Thrale. Having asserted that women, as a rule, were exclusively occupied with current fashions and, 'take them in general, have no idea of grace', he had hastened to add, 'I don't mean Mrs Thrale and Miss Burney.... They are goddesses! and therefore I accept them.'

It was the highest compliment Johnson could pay a woman; and a further proof of his regard was the possessive attitude he soon adopted:

I have had a thousand delightful conversations with Dr Johnson [she wrote on 21 September], who, whether he loves me or not, I am sure seems to have some opinion of my discretion, for he speaks of all this house to me with unbounded confidence, neither diminishing faults, nor exaggerating praise. Whenever he is below stairs he keeps me a prisoner, for he does not like I should quit the room a moment; if I rise he constantly calls out, 'Don't you go, little Burney!'

As usual, Johnson was prolific of advice. Noticing that Fanny had a timid and diffident nature, and was often overwhelmed – or pretended to be overwhelmed – by agonizing fits of shyness, he firmly recommended social courage. Thus, when Mrs Thrale announced that the tremendous Mrs Montagu was to dine at Streatham next day:

* French milliners of the eighteenth century often bestowed fantastic names upon the colours they employed – for instance, *cuisse de nymphe émue*; which, had he been asked to explain it, might have taxed even Johnson's ingenuity.

Dr Johnson began to see-saw, with a countenance strongly expressive of inward fun, and after enjoying it some time in silence, he suddenly and with great animation turned to me and cried, 'Down with her Burney! – down with her! – spare her not! attack her, fight her, and down with her at once! You are a rising wit, and she is at the top; and when I was beginning the world, and was nothing and nobody, the joy of my life was to fire at all the established wits.... To vanquish the great ones was all the delight of my poor little dear soul! So at her, Burney, – at her, and down with her!'

Although Fanny did not accept this advice – her method of attack was quietly critical rather than openly aggressive – no doubt she benefited by Johnson's help. Mrs Montagu's visit passed off smoothly. 'The conversation', Fanny reports, 'was not brilliant ... but Mrs Montagu behaved to me just as I could have wished, since she spoke to me very little, but spoke that little with the utmost politeness.' Later, 'when Mrs Montagu's new house was talked of', and Johnson, 'in a jocose manner, desired to know if he should be invited to see it', she issued a general invitation to the entire company. 'Everybody bowed and accepted the invite but me ... for I have no notion of snapping at invites from the eminent. But Dr Johnson ... was determined I should be of the party, for he suddenly clapped his hand on my shoulder, and called out aloud, "Little Burney, you and I will go together".'

At last, her recent novel was mentioned – a moment that the novelist had long been dreading. Mrs Montagu said that she hoped for the pleasure of seeing *Evelina*. '"*Evelina?*" repeated he; "has Mrs Montagu then found out *Evelina?*" "Yes", cried she, "and I am proud that a work so commended should be a woman's." Oh, how my face burnt!' And Johnson merely increased her dismay by remarking that he was sorry that Mrs Montagu should not have actually read the book, '"because you cannot speak of it with a full conviction of its merits: which, I believe ... you will find great pleasure in acknowledging." Some other things were said, but I remember them not, for I could hardly keep my place: but my sweet, naughty Mrs Thrale looked delighted....'

Henceforward, among the frequenters of Streatham Place, Fanny ranked as '*our* Miss Burney.... We were the first to catch her', Mrs Thrale reminded Johnson, 'and now we have got, we will keep her.

Right Fanny Burney, later Madame d'Arblay (1752–1840); 'a girl of prodigious parts'. Portrait by her cousin, Edward Burney.

And so she is all our own.' Simultaneously, in her shrewd and quiet way, Fanny was summing up the household. Queeney she gradually learned to appreciate – the cold and reserved Miss Thrale was less alarming than she had at first appeared; and her hostess she liked 'more and more.... I never before saw the person who so strongly resembles our dear father. ... She has the same natural liveliness, the same general benevolence, the same rare union of gaiety and of feeling in her disposition. ... Since the first morning she seeks me, sits with me, saunters with me in the park, or compare notes over books in the library....' Only the lethargic master of the household proved a trifle disappointing. Mr Thrale, she recorded, on 26 August, had come in late 'from giving an election dinner ... so tired, that he neither opened his eyes nor mouth, but fell fast asleep. Indeed, after tea he generally does.'

Mrs Thrale, on the other hand, though she evidently regarded Miss Burney as an attractive addition to her social circle, when she came to put down her thoughts in the commonplace-book, now her secret *liber veritatis*, was not quite sure she really liked her character. Possibly she was a little jealous of Johnson's affection for their new friend. But she also found her mannered and self-centred, much too concerned with the public impression that she felt obliged to make. Dr Burney, she wrote on 10 February 1779, was a man she loved well – if he had any fault, it was 'too much obsequiousness'; and his daughter, she admitted, was 'a graceful looking girl; but 'tis the Grace of an Actress', not that of a genuine woman of fashion. How could it be otherwise? The Burneys, she believed, were 'a very low Race of Mortals'; and Miss Burney's conversation would be 'more pleasing if she thought less about Herself...'. As it was, 'her early Reputation embarrasses her Talk, & clouds her Mind with scruples and Elegancies which either come uncalled for or will not come at all'.

Certainly, she was 'a Girl of prodigious Parts'; but, now and then, she became a tiresome housemate – 'so restlessly & apparently anxious lest I should give myself Airs of Patronage, or load her with the Shackles of Dependance...'. Such was Miss Burney's determination not to be imposed upon, that Mrs Thrale dared not 'ask her to buy me a Ribbon', or desire her to ring the bell, 'lest she should think herself injured...'

In her rôle as hostess, Mrs Thrale was delighted to praise '*our* Miss Burney's' famous book; but, privately, she had long ago decided that, compared with the masterpieces of Fielding and Smollett, *Evelina* was a 'flimzy' novel. Mrs Montagu, she heard, was another unfriendly critic, and had confessed that she could not bear the story, which revealed a damning lack of social insight; Miss Burney's silversmiths were pewterers, she claimed, and her captains vulgar boatswains.

Mrs Thrale was not alone in her criticisms; other members of the Streatham circle, though they were bound to admire the young woman's literary talents, considered her aloof and chilly. She was secretive, they felt; and her habit of remaining silent throughout the liveliest conversation naturally caused them to suspect that she might be taking surreptitious notes. Would they discover one day that she had put them into a novel? Under the sharp glance she occasionally directed towards them, prattlers and gossips began to grow uneasy. They complained that the presence of a 'silent observer' destroyed any hope of social freedom.

After the passage of nearly two centuries, Fanny Burney is still a somewhat baffling personage. Beneath her reserve and air of virtuous propriety, her social mannerisms and verbal airs and graces – the latter became particularly pronounced once she had encountered Johnson – lurked a very different character, fun-loving, caustic, disrespectful, gifted with an extraordinary memory and an avid taste for the ridiculous. No doubt, as Mrs. Thrale guessed, she had a passionately self-centred spirit; in all the fantasies concocted by her active mind, she herself must play the part of heroine.

Had she been prettier, she might have been more amiable; but hers was not a pretty face. At the best, it might be described as tolerably good-looking; and her cousin, Edward, presumably did his best when he sat down to paint her portrait. Beneath a huge, elaborately ribboned hat, her eyes are cool and shrewd and cautious; the nose and chin are rather too large for beauty; the mouth is sensible but not seductive. Men of her own age she seldom captivated; the admirers whom she preferred were always middle-aged or elderly. Thus, she would refrain from marriage until she was forty-one, and then give her hand to Alexandre-Jean-Baptiste Piochard d'Arblay, a distinguished forty-year-old exile.

5 Prose and Verse

The effect produced on a writer's contemporaries by a famous work of literature is very often just as interesting, and deserves at least as much scrutiny, as the merits of the book itself. From the modern point of view, *Evelina* is an awkward, ill-conducted story. Although some of its minor personages are lively caricatures, none of its protagonists seems to possess the smallest spark of individual life; the dialogue is often clumsy and stilted; and its heroine neither grows nor changes, but rushes through a series of absurd adventures towards the long-expected happy ending. Yet, when it first appeared under Lowndes' imprint, it fascinated innumerable English readers, among them many of the keenest and most critical intelligences of the later eighteenth century.

Johnson's enthusiastic appreciations have been quoted on a previous page. As for Sheridan, he publicly declared that *Evelina* was '*superior to Fielding*'; while Reynolds announced that, having opened the book and been obliged to lay it aside, he had found that he 'could think of nothing else' and, in order to finish it, had willingly sat up till dawn. Burke, too, it had deprived of a night's sleep; and even Mr Gibbon, her friends suggested to Fanny, feared that he might be put into her next novel. On the publication of her second book, *Cecilia*, a considerably less talented performance which came out in 1782, the historian said that, during the course of a single day, he had run through all five volumes.

Now and then, the novelist's distinguished admirers, struck by her audacious treatment of the social background, allowed themselves a good-natured joke at her expense. Thus, on 28 December 1782, she and Dr Burney dined with Reynolds, in a party that consisted of Miss Reynolds, Benjamin West (destined to succeed Reynolds as the President of the Royal Academy) and a lesser-known artist, Mr Jackson of Exeter, who was 'very handsome', she noted, 'and seems possessed of much of the ardent genius which distinguishes Mr Young*; for

his expressions, at times, are extremely violent, while at other times
he droops...'.

The occasion went well. Then, rather incautiously perhaps, im-
pelled by her usual sharp-eyed curiosity, Fanny enquired of their host
why, since he possessed two snuff-boxes, gold and tin, he so often
employed the 'vile and shabby' tin box. Sir Joshua laughed. Because,

Richard Brinsley Sheridan (1751–1816); pastel by J. Russell. He considered that
Fanny Burney's talents as a novelist were superior to those of Fielding.

he replied, 'I naturally love a little of the blackguard. Aye, and so
do you too (he added) little as if you look as you did, and all the people
all day long are saying, where can you have seen such company as you
treat us with?'

Reynolds, of course, was referring to the scenes of 'low life' that
Fanny had portrayed in *Evelina*; to the Branghtons, the vulgar
mercantile family, who live above a silversmith's shop on Snow Hill;
and to Madame Duval, the heroine's outrageous grandmother, and
the loud-voiced quarrels she is perpetually waging with the no less
outrageous Captain Mirvan. It was these passages that both amused
and astonished Fanny Burney's earliest readers; and today they strike

*Arthur Young (1741–1820), agriculturist and travel-writer, a family connection of the
Burneys.

us, certainly not as the most amusing, but as the oddest and most inexplicable part of the novelist's crowded narrative. Where, indeed, had she happened to meet such company; and whence sprang the sardonic gusto with which she set about depicting it? The novelist was shy and self-consciously well-bred. Yet, no sooner has Madame Duval made her appearance in the narrative, than its action, hitherto quiet and leisurely, takes a sudden shocking turn.

Captain Mirvan has spent the last few years abroad, beneath the broiling sun of India. But this scarcely explains why the husband of 'that kind and sweet-tempered woman, Mrs Mirvan', though apparently a gentleman by birth – had Mrs Mirvan married beneath her, the sensitive and snobbish novelist would surely have underlined the fact – should be so coarse and mean a character, so full of odious jibes and brutal pleasantries. Very different are the characters that emerge in Fanny's records of her own existence. Nor in the pages of Boswell and Mrs Thrale, although the eighteenth-century conception of

Middle-class junketing; a party bound for Vauxhall Gardens. The young woman awkwardly attempting to land might well be one of Fanny Burney's Branghtons.

humour – witness Mrs Thrale's treatment, at their first meeting, of the talented musician, Gabriel Piozzi – was sometimes rather heavy-handed, can we discover anything to equal the badinage that passes between the Captain and his favourite butt, or the hideous practical joke that Mirvan and Sir Clement Willoughby play upon the foolish old virago.

Yet the fun begins at once, when the Mirvans, returning from a visit to the Italian puppet-show, give a lift in their carriage to a 'tall elderly woman' who complains that she has lost her way. She and the Captain immediately pick a quarrel. She asserts that the English are 'a parcel of brutes'. He, in response to her claim that she has some connection with his mother-in-law, who, she impertinently suggests, may employ the Captain as her steward, retorts that Madame Duval might well be mistaken for the lady's washerwoman. She then calls him 'a low dirty fellow'.

'Dirty fellow' (exclaimed the Captain, seizing both her wrists) 'hark you, Mrs Frog, you'd best hold your tongue, for I must make bold to tell you, if you don't, that I shall make no ceremony of tripping you out of the window; and there you may lie in the mud till some of your Monsieurs come to help you out of it.'

Not long afterwards, on a visit to Ranelagh, Madame Duval does actually fall into the mud and ruins her 'new Lyons negligee'. At her recital of her woes, Captain Mirvan enjoys an ecstasy of merriment. Her French companion has suffered the same fate; and the Captain:

... went from the lady to the gentleman, and from the gentleman to the lady, to enjoy alternately the sight of their distress. He really shouted with pleasure; and, shaking Monsieur Du Bois by the hand, wished him joy of having *touched English ground*; and then he held a candle to Madame Duval, that he might have a more complete view of her disaster, declaring repeatedly, that he had never been better pleased in his life.

The rage of poor Madame Duval was unspeakable; she dashed the candle out of his hand, stamped upon the floor, and, at last, spat in his face.

For a scene of this kind, we cannot help asking, whence did Fanny derive her raw-material? Most of her previous life had been spent at home, in a sober, well-behaved family; and among her father's associates, as portrayed in her journal and letters, there was no one who remotely resembled either Madame Duval or Captain Mirvan. We must assume, therefore, they were largely the products of her own imagination, and corresponded to a strain of feeling that she otherwise kept out of sight.

The persecution of 'poor Madame Duval' continues some way into the second volume, where she is exposed to still more frightful sufferings. Evelina comes on the old woman crouching in a roadside ditch, her feet 'tied together with a strong rope, which was fastened to the upper branch of a tree.... Her feet were soon disentangled, and then though with great difficulty, I assisted her to rise. But what was my astonishment, when, the moment she was up, she hit me a violent slap on the face! I retreated from her with precipitation....'

Naturally, her chief tormentor has been Captain Mirvan, assisted, on this occasion, by Sir Clement Willoughby, a fashionable gentleman who is paying assiduous court to Evelina; and, once they have enjoyed the spectacle, they mount their horses and immediately disappear, while Evelina remains to do the best she can:

The ditch, happily, was almost quite dry ... yet, so forlorn, so miserable a figure, I never before saw. Her head-dress had fallen off; her linen was torn; her negligee had not a pin left in it; her petticoats she was obliged to hold on; and her shoes were perpetually slipping off. She was covered with dirt, weeds, and filth, and her face was really horrible, for the pomatum and powder from her head, and the dust from the road, were quite *pasted* on her skin by her tears, which, with her *rouge*, made so frightful a mixture, that she hardly looked human.

Evelina's comments on her plight seem curiously unemotional. Having rescued her grandmother from the ditch, she listens to her tale of misery; and, 'though this narrative almost compelled me to laugh, yet I was really irritated with the Captain, for carrying his love of tormenting, – *sport*, he calls it, – to such barbarous and un-justifiable extremes'. But there is more irritation than genuine indignation in Evelina's gentle protests; and it is difficult not to suspect that through the novelist's character may have run a secret vein of cruelty.

If not of cruelty, at least of stifled rage and resentment. The Burney family as a whole, despite the misdeeds of the younger Charles Burney, who, in 1771, had been convicted of stealing library books and expelled from Cambridge, was singularly happy and united. Yet one member of the family had always struck a jarring note. The Doctor's first wife, Esther Sleepe, said before her marriage to have been 'a young person of beauty, wit, captivating manners and prudent conduct', had died in 1762; and in 1767 he had married Mrs Allen, the widow of a rich merchant whom he had known at Kings Lynn.
' He was 'very seriously impassioned' with Mrs Allen; and, by dint of 'constant importunity', he had persuaded her to accept his hand.

Left Frontispiece to the first volume of *Evelina*, in the edition of 1779.
Right Evelina and a friend, clasped together in the background, see Captain
Mirvan set a fierce monkey on the foolish dandy, Mr Lovel: 'The creature darting
forward . . . fastened his teeth to one of his ears'.

But none of his six children subsequently approved his choice; and,
although, towards the end of her life, Fanny, then Madame d'Arblay,
obliterated many descriptions of her step-mother in the pages of her
journals[12], enough remain in the diary of her sister Susan, and in
other family records, to show the kind of woman Mrs Burney was.
The relationship, Susan declared, had been a 'long & bitter slavery'.
Their stepmother, the Burneys said, was cross and rude and argumen-
tative. Susan also refers to 'her tenaciousness of opinion, her inflam-
matory powers, & malignancy . . .'. At the same time, 'the Lady', as the
young Burneys called her among themselves, seeing that they had
their own domestic jokes and gossip, in which they did not encourage
her to take a share, grew deeply jealous and suspicious.

That the good Doctor should have married such a woman frequently
surprised his circle. '. . . To be sure there's something very disagreeable in her', declared an otherwise good-natured friend, 'Laughing so

loud, & hooting, & clapping her Hands, – I can't love her, a nasty old cat...'[13] Miss Cooke was ready to agree, however, that Mrs Burney was 'certainly a very sensible woman'; and the Doctor, from whom his children always hid their dislike, found her an affectionate and loyal wife. Perhaps it was loneliness and ill-health – her husband was often away on his travels; his clannish offspring could spare her little affection – that had gradually warped her spirit.

There is no doubt that Fanny despised and detested her; and it seems to have been this conflict, rather than, as is sometimes suggested, the boisterous literary influence of Tobias Smollett, that inspired her savage handling of the unfortunate Madame Duval. There are other brutal episodes, it is true, retailed with much the same relish, for example, the race that some tipsy gentlemen organize between a pair of decrepit old women; and the account of how Captain Mirvan sets a fierce monkey, 'full-dressed, and extravagantly *à-la-mode*', upon the harmless Mr Lovel:

Poor Mr Lovel ... turned hastily round, and, forgetful of consequences, vented his passion by giving a furious blow to the monkey.

The creature, darting forwards, sprung instantly upon him, and clinging round his neck, fastened his teeth to one of his ears.

I was really sorry for the poor man, who, though an egregious fop, had committed no offence that merited such chastisement....

Mr Lovel was now a dreadful object; his face besmeared with tears, the blood from his ear ran trickling down his cloaths, and he sunk upon the floor, crying out, 'Oh I shall die, I shall die! – Oh I'm bit to death.'

Elsewhere, the ladylike novelist reveals a very different aspect of her character. Evelina herself is the perpetual fugitive, constantly in tremulous flight from some real or half-imagined peril. She is born to flee; and the dangers that threaten her are usually occasioned by her own imprudence. Thus, at Ranelagh, she allows her vulgar companions to persuade her to set foot in the garden's ill-famed 'dark walks':

By the time we came near the end, a large party of gentlemen, apparently very riotous, and who were hallowing, leaning on one another, and laughing immoderately, seemed to rush suddenly from behind some trees and ... formed a kind of circle, that first stopped our proceeding, and then our retreating. ... For some minutes, we were kept prisoners, till, at last, one of them rudely seizing hold of me, said I was a pretty little creature.

Terrified to death, I struggled with such vehemence to disengage myself, that I succeeded ... and with a swiftness which fear only could have given me, I flew rather than ran up the walk....

At the same time, she is seldom free from exquisite agonies of
social chagrin – embarrassed by her awkward behaviour on the dance-
floor; no less perturbed because she is commanded to take up residence
above a bustling silversmith's shop near Holborn; and deeply mortified
when the elegant Lord Orville finds her domiciled among the shop-
keeper's noisy and ill-bred family, who hitherto, as their inquisitive
attitude demonstrates, have never been privileged to observe a genuine
product of the English upper classes. Evelina can only blush for the
Branghtons; and she continues to glow with blushes throughout the
narrative. She also frequently trembles, once 'so violently, that my
chair actually shook under me'. Meanwhile, the fear of tarnishing her
reputation causes her incessant trouble. Nothing is more delicate,
she is reminded by Mr Villars, than a woman's reputation; 'it is, at
once, the most beautiful and most brittle of all human things'.

Yet the novelist had an extraordinarily acute eye; and, much as she
resented the ridiculous Branghtons and valued her own superior
social poise, she had enough of the 'blackguard' in her composition
to enjoy describing them:

The dinner was ill-served, ill-cooked, and ill-managed. The maid who
waited had so often to go down stairs for something that was forgotten,
that the Branghtons were perpetually obliged to rise from table themselves,
to get plates, knives and forks, bread, or beer. Had they been without
pretensions, all this would have seemed of no consequence; but they aimed
at appearing to advantage, and even fancied they succeeded. However, the
most disagreeable part of our fare was, that the whole family continually
disputed whose turn it was to rise, and whose to be allowed to sit still.

Although Evelina herself and her well-born friends may never rise
above the rank of puppets, the London background, against which
they perform their manoeuvres, is depicted in the sharpest and the
liveliest detail. At first, Evelina finds contemporary London a somewhat disappointing place. She notes, for example, that she and the
Mirvans had strolled through the Mall, 'which by no means answered
my expectations: it is a long straight walk of dirty gravel, very uneasy
to the feet; and at each end, instead of an open prospect, nothing is to
be seen but houses built of brick. When Mrs Mirvan pointed out the
*Palace** to me, – I think I was never more suprised.'

Kensington Gardens provided better company; 'but really if you
had seen how much every body was dressed, you would not think
that possible'. She, too, had begun to take an interest in the current

---

*The original Buckingham House, built by the Duke of Buckingham, at the beginning of
the eighteenth century, on the site of the present Buckingham Palace.

Birdcage Walk, St James's Park, by John Chapman, about 1750.

London fashions. They had 'been *a shopping*, as Mrs Mirvan calls it . . .
to buy silks, caps, gauzes, and so forth'; and, naturally, Evelina
delighted in the brilliant London shops, which newcomers had always
admired since the days of Queen Elizabeth. The mercers were particularly entertaining:

> . . . There seem to be six or seven men belonging to each shop, and every
> one took care, by bowing and smirking, to be noticed. . . . I thought I should
> never have chosen a silk, for they produced so many, I knew not which to

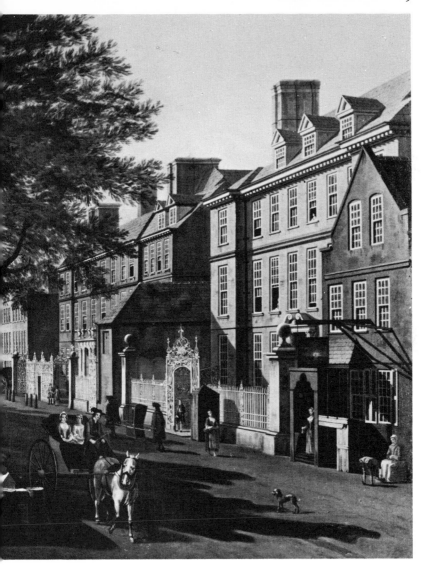

fix upon, and they recommended them all so strongly, that I fancy they
thought I only wanted persuasion to buy every thing they shewed me....
At the milliners ... what most diverted me was, that we were more frequently
served by men than by women; and such men! so finical, so affected! they
seemed to understand every part of a woman's dress better than we do our-
selves; and they recommended caps and ribbands with an air of such
importance, that I wished to ask them how long they had left off wearing
them!

That same day, she had her hair dressed; and, after she had been

The Queen's Palace, afterwards Buckingham Palace, in the first year of the nineteenth century. Its appearance disappointed Evelina; 'when Mrs Mirvan pointed out the Palace to me, – I think I was never more surprised'.

crowned with an enormous fashionable coiffure, 'you can't', she reported to Mr Villars, 'tell how oddly my head feels; full of powder and black pins, and a great *cushion* on the top of it. I believe you would hardly know me, for my face looks quite different . . .'. Thus accoutred, she goes to 'a *private* ball', where she first surveys a number of London gentlemen, who, 'as they passed and repassed, looked as if they thought that we were quite at their disposal . . . and . . . sauntered about, in a careless, indolent manner, as if with a view to keep us in suspense'; then accepts a stranger's invitation to take the floor and is almost immediately overtaken by a devastating bout of shyness. The discovery that her partner is a nobleman at once increases her alarm; 'how will he be provoked, thought I, when he finds what a simple rustic he has honoured with his choice!'

Before she has finally captured Lord Orville at the end of Volume III, Evelina's method of narration has grown considerably more elaborate.

'The New Fashioned Phaeton', 1776; high-flying head-dresses went with lofty, high-wheeled vehicles.

The 'great *cushion*', perched on the top of her head, has become an essential adjunct of her character; and, although she continues to blush and tremble and despond, she usually does so wearing full dress, and is often inclined (as Mr Coverley says of Sir Clement Willoughby) 'to tip us a touch of the heroicks'. When the novelist originally drafted her story, she was writing for her own amusement. At a later stage, when she felt that she had learned her craft, she gave her style a far more stately turn; and, when she was preparing to send her manuscript to the printer, she carefully revised her text*, suppressing vulgarisms, removing colloquialisms, and generally accommodating her use of the English language to the verbal prejudices of 'polite society'.

In the process of editing, she sacrificed many phrases that might perhaps have been considered 'low', and re-wrote certain paragraphs that appeared to exhibit her heroine as a little less than dignified. The result, if not positively disastrous, was certainly regrettable. Fanny's social pretensions were difficult to reconcile with the free employment of her native genius; and the book she published is an extraordinary mixture of contrasted and conflicting qualities, now sharply satirical,

Queen Charlotte and the Princess Royal; as the Queen's attendant, Fanny Burney was condemned to five long years of courtly servitude.

now lamentably sentimental, now shrewd to the point of cynicism, now heavily sententious or absurdly naïve.

Not until she had survived the popular success of *Evelina* and *Cecilia*, and been thrust into an entirely new world – the strange universe of an eighteenth-century Court – did she quite regain her

---

*A manuscript of one of the preliminary drafts of *Evelina* is preserved, among the Berg Collection, in the New York Public Library. For an extremely illuminating account of the changes it shows, see Joyce Hemlow: *Op. Cit.*

balance. In 1786, her father persuaded Fanny, much against her better judgment, to accept a supposedly flattering post as Queen Charlotte's Second Keeper of the Robes – a place, she was assured, already 'solicited by thousands and thousands of Fashion and Rank'; and, during her five years' servitude, she composed the fascinating chronicle – the diary she kept from 1786 to 1791 – that is undoubtedly her masterpiece.

The novelist was wretched at Windsor and Kew; and, like Evelina on her first arrival in London, she suffered numerous mishaps. Like her heroine, she was often put to flight – once by the poor mad King himself, once by her importunate acquaintance James Boswell. He accosted her outside St George's Chapel – 'his comic-serious face and manner', she observed, had 'lost nothing of their wonted singularity' – and, having begged her to give up Court-life, and threatened, if she refused, to adopt 'some violent measures' and organize a joint petition to her father, he added that his biography of Dr Johnson would very soon be coming out.

Meanwhile, he said, he required her help. 'My help?' his victim quavered anxiously:

'Yes, madam; you must give me some of your choice little notes of the Doctor's; we have seen him long enough upon stilts; I want to show him in a new light. Grave Sam, and great Sam, and solemn Sam, and learned Sam – all these he has appeared over and over. Now I want to entwine a wreath of the graces across his brow; I want to show him as gay Sam, agreeable Sam, pleasant Sam: so you must help me with some of his beautiful billets to yourself.'

Fanny evaded his pleas as best she could; and, though Boswell persisted, and 'proposed a thousand curious expedients' to convey Johnson's letters, which she explained that she had not 'at hand', from their present resting-place, she remained 'invincible'. But he was not to be put off, and, at the same time, repeated his demands that she should resign her post at Court:

He then told me his *Life of Dr Johnson* was nearly printed, and took a proof sheet out of his pocket to show me, with crowds passing and repassing, knowing me well, and staring well at him: for we were now at the iron rails of the Queen's Lodge.... He uttered again and again stronger and stronger exhortations for my retreat, accompanied by expressions which I was obliged to check in their bud. But finding he had no chance for entering, he stopped me again at the gate, and said he would read me a part of his work.... He began, with a letter of Dr Johnson to himself. He read it in strong imitation of the Doctor's manner.... But Mrs Schwellenberg* was at her window, a crowd was gathering to stand round the rails, and the King and Queen and Royal Family now approached from the Terrace. I made a rather quick apology, and, with a step as quick as my now weakened limbs had left in my power, I hurried to my apartment.

Fanny's portrait of Boswell, with his eagerness, noisiness and good-natured impudence, has seldom been improved on; it is in her diaries, rather than in her famous novel, that she reveals her most important gifts. But, for the student of eighteenth-century prose, *Evelina* has a double interest. Not only does it illustrate the condition of the English novel during Samuel Johnson's later life, but it displays the influence that Johnson exercised upon a young and highly gifted woman. Fielding had died in 1754; Richardson, in 1761; Tobias Smollett, ten years later. No adventurous modern novelist had yet arisen to replace them. Novels were many; but they were neither treated, nor deserved to be treated, as a serious form of reading. Some were 'Gothick' romances, of the kind popularized by Horace Walpole, whose *Castle of Otranto* had appeared in 1764; others, often the work of prolific woman writers, were sentimental modern tales, little superior to the products of the industrious Eliza Haywood (once pilloried by Alexander Pope) who still retained her popularity, and whose *History of Miss Betsy Thoughtless*, originally published in 1751 was reprinted, with a series of delightful vignettes by Thomas Stothard as late as 1783.

Hence the success of Fanny Burney's novel, both among contemporary fiction-addicts and in the loftiest circles of the literary world, where it fascinated readers as distinguished and as sharply critical as Johnson, Gibbon, Burke and Sheridan. Although Johnson first encountered the novelist some weeks after he had read her book, the influence of 'solemn Sam' is already apparent in the evolution of her prose-style. At her worst, when her style is most ponderous, she seems to be following Johnson's weighty footsteps; and the aspects of his style she imitated – what Boswell, before he met Johnson, had dared to describe as his 'inflated Rotundity and tumified Latinity of Diction' – are usually those we least admire today.

Pope was believed by the Romantics to have laid an icy hand on English verse. Similarly, Johnson may be said to have set an example that impeded the free development of English prose; an ability to turn sentences in the resounding Johnsonian manner soon became an

* An elderly German lady, Mrs Schwellenberg was Fanny Burney's immediate superior at Court, and one of the most censorious and ill-tempered members of the Royal household.

An illustration by Thomas Stothard to the reprint of *The History of Miss Betsy Thoughtless*, published in 1783. Eliza Haywood's romance, which had originally appeared in 1751, was the kind of popular novel that held the field before the publication of *Evelina*, and that Fanny Burney's masterpiece did not entirely supersede.

infallible index of the writer's good taste. It was Johnson the moralist whom his contemporaries most respected – the eloquent judge of life who presided over the pages of the *Rambler* and the *Idler*. In April 1760, he had closed the *Idler* with a characteristic farewell to his public:

> Much of the Pain and Pleasure of mankind arises from the conjectures which every one makes of the thoughts of others; we all enjoy praise which we do not hear, and resent contempt which we do not see. The *Idler* may therefore be forgiven, if he suffers his Imagination to represent to him what his readers will say or think when they are informed that they now have his last paper in their hands.
>
> Value is more frequently raised by scarcity than by use. That which lay neglected when it was common, rises in estimation as its quantity becomes less. We seldom learn the true want of what we have till it is discovered that we can have no more.

Here an array of weighty generalizations, each cleverly balanced one against another, the whole combined into a rhythmic march of words, are used to convey a fairly simple message: the author is giving up his task; and he hopes that his readers will be sorry to see him go. He himself, he admits, 'is not wholly unaffected by the thought that his last essay is now before him'. Hitherto, Johnson has carefully refused to dwell upon his own feelings. But now he introduces the terrible theme that had always darkened his imagination: 'This secret horrour of the last is inseparable from a thinking being whose life is limited, and to whom death is dreadful. . . . When we have done anything for the last time, we involuntarily reflect that a part of the days allotted to us is past, and that as more is past there is less remaining.'

Such flashes of personal emotion are rare; Johnson prefers to move away from the particular towards the general; and his habit of generalizing he indulges to the full throughout the *Rambler* and the *Idler*, the first begun in 1750 and brought to an end in 1752, the second launched in 1758 and concluded in the year 1760. The *Rambler* essays, which were published by Cave, who paid him a weekly salary of four guineas, though he once admitted that they might be 'too wordy', would appear to have satisfied his own taste and Samuel Rogers reports him as having said that, whereas his other works were wine and water, 'my *Rambler* is pure wine'.

Not until they appeared in book-form did they attract a large public. But then his essays became the solid basis of his literary reputation. Today, his biographer[14] admits, 'despite striking sentences' and a few complete essays that deserve especial study, they are 'not likely . . . to be much read again'. Yet, 'if he had written nothing except *The*

'A Lady coming from the Circulating Library', 1781. The growth of circulating libraries encouraged the development of the sentimental modern novel.

Rambler, his contemporaries would have regarded him as a very important literary figure'.

In the *Idler*, which proved slightly less popular, he was somewhat less ponderous. But both collections seem to justify Macaulay's taunt that Johnson was a false stylist who had translated the English language into 'Johnsonese', and Taine's remark that the truths he announces are a little 'too true'; the English, said Taine, had always enjoyed sermons; and it is usually some kind of sermon – often, of course, an extremely fine sermon, such as his splendid attack upon the existing penal laws – that the novelist sets out to preach.

Johnson himself, when, in a perceptibly lighter vein, he embarked upon the *Idler*, refers to a mode of style 'by which the most evident truths are so obscured that they can no longer be perceived'. Believing that the main facts of human existence had already been discovered, and that everything worth saying had already been said, he seldom troubled to avoid the obvious. What he contributed was a stately frame of words that gave his truisms an added weight. Even his personal sketches – of men and women whom he had observed at close quarters, the country housewife, the idle young dandy, the blustering squire and the harrassed woman of fashion – are no more than recognizable impressions of contemporary human types.

As a novelist, Johnson did not shine; he lacked the gift of invention and, at least when he was attempting to tell a fictitious tale, the knack of condensing his subject-matter into a lively and dramatic form. In his *Lives of the Poets*, he would afterwards provide an excuse:

It is indeed [he writes] much more easy to form dialogues than to contrive adventures. Every position makes way for an argument, and every objection dictates an answer. When two disputants are engaged upon a complicated and extensive question, the difficulty is not to continue, but to end the controversy. But whether it be that we comprehend but few of the possibilities of life, or that life itself affords very little variety, every man who has tried knows how much labour it will cost to form such a combination of circumstances, as shall have at once the grace of novelty and credibility, and delight fancy without violence to reason.

Rasselas, the novel that he had written in 1759, and used to declare that he had never re-read, was much admired by eighteenth-century readers. Boswell tells us that he re-read it every year; and that, at every perusal, as, 'with all the charms of oriental imagery, and all the force and beauty of which the English language is capable', the author condenscended to lead us 'through the most important scenes of human life', he felt his admiration grow, till he could 'scarcely believe that I had the honour of enjoying the intimacy of such a man'.*

Voltaire's *Candide*, he adds, is 'wonderfully similar in its plan and conduct to Johnson's *Rasselas*; insomuch, that I have heard Johnson say, that if they had not been published so closely one after the other that there was not time for imitation, it would have been vain to deny that the scheme of that which came latest was taken from the other'. In fact, *Candide* was the older by some two or three months; and

---

* Sir John Hawkins shared Boswell's enthusiasm for *Rasselas*. 'Considered as a specimen of our Language', he wrote in his *Life*, 'it is scarcely to be paralleled; it is written in a style refined to a degree of immaculate purity, and displays the whole force of turgid eloquence.'

Boswell points out that, although both these works seem designed to illustrate the same idea, 'the intention of the writers was very different'. Each exemplified the vanity of human wishes; but, whereas Voltaire 'meant only by wanton profaneness to obtain a sportive victory over religion ... Johnson meant, by shewing the unsatisfactory nature of things temporal, to direct the hopes of man to things eternal'.

Candide and *Rasselas* also differ in the authors' conduct of their stories. A child could read and enjoy *Candide* merely for the sake of its delightful narrative, without the smallest inkling that what he read was a ferocious attack on the philosophy of Gottfried Leibniz, and on Leibniz's conception of God as 'the Supreme Monad', who had produced 'the best of all possible worlds' to accommodate the human race. Beside *Candide*, the story that Johnson tells seems singularly slight and feeble.

Among his source-books was *Purchas his Pilgrimage*, the early-seventeenth-century volume of travellers' tales, which describes how Abyssinian princes of the blood were carefully segregated by their relation, the Emperor, from the rest of mankind, and condemned to a life of magnificent solitude, where they were permitted every pleasure except the joys of liberty*. Such has been the miserable fate of Rasselas; until, tiring of existence in a luxurious permissive society that was organized to gratify all the senses, but left the heart and mind untouched, he and his sister, Nekayah, his philosophic friend, Imlac, and Nekayah's lady-in-waiting, Pekuah, manage at last to penetrate the mountain barriers that surround this terrestrial paradise, and descend into the outer world.

Naturally, they are disappointed. Once they have left their permissive prison and established themselves in the great metropolis of Cairo, they meet a variety of free men, ranging from 'young men of spirit and gaiety' to a holy hermit and a powerful minister, but discover on each occasion that some secret flaw has marred the individual's happiness. Johnson's last chapter is entitled *The conclusion in which nothing is concluded*. Here Nekayah, having decided 'that of all sublunary things, knowledge was the best', determines to found a college of Abyssinian *Bas Bleu*; and Rasselas dreams of 'a little kingdom, in which he might administer justice ... and see all the parts of government with his own eyes; but he could never fix the limits of his dominion, and was always adding to the number of his subjects'.

As for the philosophic Imlac and his learned companion, the

---

*When James Bruce returned from Abyssinia, bearing evidence to confirm this tale, which he afterwards incorporated in *Travels to Discover the Source of the Nile, 1768–1773*, Johnson himself was the first to disbelieve his reports, and dubbed Bruce 'the Abyssinian Liar'.

astronomer, they were content 'to be driven along the stream of life without directing their course to any port'. But happiness eludes the travellers; 'of these wishes that they had formed they well knew that none could be obtained'. At that moment the flood-waters of the Nile make it difficult to leave Cairo. 'They deliberated a while what was to be done, and resolved, when the inundation should cease, to return to Abissinia.'

How different from Candide's magnificent last words, '*Il faut cultiver nôtre jardin*', are Johnson's dismal closing lines! Rasselas admits defeat; Candide continues to hope, despite the hideous experiences he has already lived through; and, of their contrasted histories, Voltaire's enchanting tale, though Boswell might deplore its wanton attacks on faith, is unquestionably the less subversive. Johnson himself felt obliged to praise its 'power'; whereas Voltaire merely remarked of *Rasselas*, '*Il m'a paru d'une philosophie aimable, et très-bien écrit.*' In this context, his use of the word '*aimable*' – there was little amiability about the hero's view of life – must, no doubt, have been ironic.

On the other hand, when he asserted that the book was well-written, he may have been paying it a genuine tribute. For Johnson, the business of arranging his characters' escape and transporting them to Cairo, was evidently a somewhat irksome task; it was not the kind of undertaking that suited his peculiar literary gifts. But, as soon as they begin to talk, and engage in elaborate dialogues, where 'every position makes way for an argument, and every objection dictates an answer', his style at once acquires an easy, rapid flow; with the result that *Rasselas* consists of a series of dissertations – on the use of learning, poetry, solitude, the natural life, social amusements, marriage versus celibacy, even on 'the art of flying' – rather loosely and vaguely stitched together by means of a series of fictitious episodes.

In these dissertations, either Rasselas or Imlac is almost always Johnson's mouthpiece. They express, for example, the author's dread of solitude, and of the terrifying thoughts it conjures up; his fear of the supernatural and reluctant belief that ghosts may really walk the earth; his contempt for those who study the past, when their chief concern should be with living men; his horror of madness; his devotion to poetry; his theory that human grief was very often hypocritical; and the conviction he had arrived at after many years of widowhood, that, if 'marriage has many pains ... celibacy has no pleasures'. Rasselas also observes, while admiring – or failing to admire – the pyramids, that they seemed 'to have been erected only in compliance with that hunger of imagination which preys incessantly

Thrale, 1770

DICTIONARY

OF THE

ENGLISH LANGUAGE:

IN WHICH

The WORDS are deduced from their ORIGINALS,

Explained in their DIFFERENT MEANINGS,

AND

Authorized by the NAMES of the WRITERS
in whofe Works they are found.

Abftracted from the FOLIO EDITION,

By the AUTHOR
SAMUEL JOHNSON, A. M.

To which is prefixed,
A GRAMMAR of the ENGLISH LANGUAGE.

In TWO VOLUMES.

VOL. I.

The THIRD EDITION, correćted.

LONDON,
A. MILLAR; W. STRAHAN; J. RIVINGTON; J. HIN-
BALDWIN; J. DODSLEY; L. HAWES, W. CLARKE
INS; R. HORSFIELD; W. JOHNSTON; T. LOWNDES;
N; B. LAW; and M. RICHARDSON.
MDCCLXVI.

Mrs Thrale's copy of Johnson's *Dictionary* in its third edition; 'compiled . . . for
the use of such as aspire to exactness of criticism or elegance of style'.

upon life, and must be always appeased by some employment'. Like Rasselas, Johnson was an unsatisfied man; and, like Imlac, content to 'drift along the stream', filling up the vacuity of human existence with any occupation that might come his way. *The History of Rasselas, Prince of Abissinia*, for all its conventional moralizing, is a profoundly pessimistic book.

It was never a book in which he had taken much pride – he had thrown it off, he said, hurriedly and casually, to earn the thirty pounds he then needed*; and a far more serious work was, of course, the *Dictionary*, which he had completed four years earlier. If the *History of Rasselas* reveals him as an accomplished master of the English language, this may have been partly due to the experience he had gained while he was building up the *Dictionary*, reviewing his material word by word, and compiling 'almost 2300 pages of definitions and examples'.[15] Johnson's only eighteenth-century predecessor was Nathaniel Bailey, whose *Universal Etymological English Dictionary* appeared in 1721, and was reissued with improvements and additions in 1736. Johnson set himself a considerably higher aim – to produce 'a dictionary like those compiled by the academies of Italy and France, for the use of such as aspire to exactness of criticism or elegance of style'.

The two-volume work that he published in 1755 was over twice as large as Bailey's, and possessed, moreover, the tremendous advantage of bearing the grandiose imprint of a single, highly-gifted mind. Though he employed half-a-dozen assistants, he was perpetually hovering at their elbows, and brought to the work the accumulated experience of a man 'long employed in the study and cultivation of the English language'. The scope of his private reading was extraordinarily wide; and from it he was able to draw a wonderful variety of apt quotations.** The search for definitions, besides taxing his scholarship and his knowledge of the world, also exercised his wit. He did not hesitate, if the occasion offered, to slip in some pointed satirical pleasantry; and certain unwarranted expressions of spite and prejudice – 'oats', runs a notorious entry: 'A grain, which in England is generally

---

*Johnson was paid an advance of thirty pounds on delivery of the manuscript, which, no doubt, paid the expenses of his mother's funeral; 'seventy five pounds (or guineas)' for each of the two volumes; 'and twenty-five pounds for the second edition'.

**Some delightful fragments of verse have survived only because Johnson quoted, or mis-quoted them. Thus, against the word 'wheel', he prints a quatrain, slightly improved, from the little-known poet, Richard Giffard:

> 'Verse sweetens care, however rude the sound,
> All at her work the village maiden sings;
> Nor as she turns the giddy wheel around,
> Revolves the sad vicissitude of things'.

given to horses, but in Scotland supports the people' – are artfully dispersed across his pages.

Johnson was not – nor did he pretend to be – a classical scholar who could have ranked with Richard Bentley or, afterwards, with Richard Porson. But, in modern literature, he was among the best-read men of his day, and probably knew more of human life, which he studied more intensely, from a greater variety of angles, than any of his fellow writers. By the age of twenty-six, when he added a majestic preface to his translation of *Father Lobo's Voyage**, he had already developed a remarkably individual prose style; and for nearly half a century he continued to employ it upon an extensive range of different subjects, as essayist, novelist, sermonist, travel-writer, literary bio-grapher and bellicose contemporary pamphleteer. Style, Gibbon declared, was an image of the writer's mind; and Johnson's style reveals both the strength of his character and his personal and intellec-tual failings. An admittedly lazy writer, who once remarked that 'no man but a blockhead wrote except for money', at times he seems to have permitted his style to function almost undirected and to have sat back, complacently surveying the result, as the flood of 'Johnson-ese' rolled on and on.

Style may also be a method of defence or concealment; and Johnson, a life-long melancholic, believed that he had much to hide. His grand manner was, in part, a defensive system thrown up around his secret self – a self that, during his periods of deepest gloom, he judged irremediably weak and worthless. It is when Johnson retreats behind his style that his mannerisms grow most oppressive; and, when his own emotions are suddenly allowed to appear, that we begin to recognize the great magician. Every true stylist has a distinctive form of music; and the music of Johnson's prose, besides ennobling even his dullest periodical essays, frequently overflows into his private letters. Indeed, his letters contain a series of splendid passages that, if one were asked to define the special Johnsonian quality, would be among the first one quoted.

For example, the letter that, in February 1755, he addressed to Lord Chesterfield. Eight years earlier, he had dedicated to Chesterfield a lengthy pamphlet, announcing his *Plan of an English Dictionary*, with the usual complimentary flourishes; but his prospective patron was then 'one of his Majesty's principal Secretaries of State', and, although he duly contributed £10, far too busy to be able to give Johnson all the assistance that he thought he needed. Not long before the *Dictionary* had appeared and proved immediately successful,

* *Father Lobo's Voyage to Abyssinia*, 1735.

exasperated by a report that favourable preliminary notices of his work had been contributed to a magazine by Chesterfield, he framed his scathing letter of reproach:

... Seven years, my Lord, have now past, since I waited in your outward rooms, or was repulsed from your door; during which time I have been pushing on my work through difficulties, of which it is useless to complain, and have brought it, at last, to the verge of publication, without one act of assistance, one word of encouragement, or one smile of favour. Such treatment I did not expect, for I never had a Patron before.

The shepherd in Virgil grew at last acquainted with Love, and found him a native of the rocks.

... The notice which you have been pleased to take of my labours, had it been early, had been kind; but it has been delayed till I am indifferent, and cannot enjoy it; till I am solitary*, and cannot impart it; till I am known, and do not want it. I hope it is no very cynical asperity not to confess obligations where no benefit has been received, or to be unwilling that the publick should consider me as owing that to a Patron which Providence has enabled me to do for myself.

This may not be strictly just – and there is no doubt that it hurt the victim, who protested that, far from shutting his doors against Johnson, 'he would have turned off the best servant he ever had, if he had known that he had denied him to a man who would have been always more than welcome'; but, as even Chesterfield admitted, it was supremely well-expressed – one of those pieces of prose that rise and fall like music, where every phrase and every turn of the argument are combined to form a single harmony.

The tone of Olympian indignation is sustained throughout the letter; this is predominantly the voice of 'solemn Sam'. But Johnson was, at the same time, a master of dramatic pathos; and, on more informal occasions, in letters intended only for a friend's eye, he is sometimes no less eloquent:

Last winter [he wrote to Giuseppe Baretti on 20 July 1762] I went down to my native town, where I found the streets much narrower and shorter than I thought I had left them, inhabited by a new race of people, to whom I was very little known. My play-fellows were grown old, and forced me to suspect that I was no longer young. My only remaining friend has changed his principles.... My daughter-in-law, from whom I expected most, and whom I met with sincere benevolence, has lost the beauty and gaiety of youth, without having gained much of the wisdom of age. I wandered about for five days, and took the first convenient opportunity of returning to a place, where, if there is not much happiness, there is, at least, such a

* During the preparation of the *Dictionary*, Johnson here reminds us, he had lost his wife.

diversity of good and evil, that slight vexations do not fix upon the heart.

Johnson's *Lives of the Poets*, the book, commissioned by a trio of London publishers, that he produced, in his 'usual way, dilatorily

Philip Dormer Stanhope, 4th Earl of Chesterfield (1694–1773); rebuked for his failure to encourage the progress of the *Dictionary* in one of Johnson's most resounding letters. Portrait by Allan Ramsay, 1765.

and hastily, unwilling to work, and working with vigour and haste', between Easter 1777 and Easter 1781*, exhibits his whole range of gifts. Though he pretended never to enjoy writing, the *Lives*, which were addressed, he said, 'not ... only to poets and philosophers', but to the educated Common Reader, seem to have given him far more real enjoyment than any of his previous efforts; and Fanny Burney describes how, at Streatham, 'while this charming work was in progress ... Dr Johnson would frequently produce one of its proof-sheets to embellish the breakfast-table.... These proof-sheets Mrs Thrale was permitted to read aloud; and the discussions to which they led were in the highest degree entertaining.' Sometimes, when the printer returned them, Johnson would give the sheets away; and Dr Burney, who had 'wistfully desired to possess one of them', was presented with the 'Life of Pope'.

The choice was fortunate. Johnson's study of Pope is the portrait of a literary hero, a man of genius who was also a good man, concerning whose 'social qualities, if an estimate be made from his Letters, an opinion too favourable cannot easily be formed; they exhibit a perpetual and unclouded effulgence of general benevolence, and particular fondness'. Johnson's moral views and his interest in human nature constantly reappear throughout the volumes. He does not spare us displays of political prejudice. Although, in *Paradise Lost*, 'every line breathes sanctity of thought, and purity of manners', Milton's 'political notions were those of an acrimonious and surly republican', his republicanism, the biographer feared, being 'founded in an envious hatred of greatness, and a sullen desire of independence; in petulance impatient of controul, and pride disdainful of authority.... It has been observed, that they who most loudly clamour for liberty do not most liberally grant it. What we know of Milton's character in domestick relations, is, that he was severe and arbitrary.... He thought woman made only for obedience, and man only for rebellion.'

Impartiality, whether in life or in literature, was not a virtue Johnson cultivated; and, if his *Lives* can be regarded as an historical and critical survey of English verse from Cowley and Denham down to the present day – Chaucer and the Elizabethans**have been firmly excluded – they are a singularly ill-proportioned piece of writing. Many of his subjects – particularly some of his later subjects – evidently annoyed or bored the writer, who soon sweeps them off into oblivion with the help of a few perfunctory pages. On Lyttleton, for example,

---

*The first instalment of the *Lives* appeared in 1779; the second in 1781.

**He had already, of course, paid a noble tribute to Shakespeare in the preface he wrote for his edition of Shakespeare's works, published in 1765.

Alexander Pope (1668–1744); bust by Michael Rysbrack, executed in 1730. Concerning Pope's social qualities, Johnson wrote, too high an opinion could not easily be formed. His letters 'exhibit a perpetual and unclouded effulgence of general benevolence, and particular fondness'.

Mrs Montagu's gallant old friend, he merely remarks that 'Lord Lyttelton's Poems are the works of a man of literature and judgement, devoting part of his time to versification. They have nothing to be despised, and little to be admired.' Far stranger, he questioned the genius of Gray, dismissing all his more 'Gothic' poems as examples of the 'false sublime', and at least one passage in the *Prospect of Eton College* as otiose and 'puerile'. Gray's *Elegy*, on the other hand, is allowed to possess considerable poetic value; for it 'abounds with images which find a mirrour in every mind, and with sentiments to which every bosom returns an echo.... Had Gray written often thus, it had been vain to blame, and useless to praise him.'

Johnson's views on poetry were essentially those of his age; it was 'the art', he declared, 'of uniting pleasure with truth by calling imagination to the aid of reason'. Like Pope, he had always asserted that it should have a moral purpose. And the truth that the poet sought to reveal must be assiduously generalized*; 'all appropriated terms of art', he wrote, while criticizing a poem by Dryden, 'should be sunk in general expressions, because poetry is to speak an universal language'; and the poet who descended to detail would necessarily lose half his strength. Yet, again like Pope, he was seldom quite consistent. Some of Dryden's finest works, he was obliged to confess, were among the most amoral – for instance, *Absalom and Achitophel*, a poem that includes 'irreligiously licentious' lines, yet 'will be found to comprise all the excellencies of which the subject is susceptible'; or the Shakespearian play that the poet had 'founded upon the story of Antony and Cleopatra**, *'the only play'*, he had announced, *'which he wrote for himself'*, and in which (according to Johnson) he had included 'the fewest improprieties of style and character'; though 'by admitting the romantick omnipotence of Love, he has recommended as laudable and worthy of imitation that conduct which, through the ages, the good have censured as vicious, and the bad despised as foolish'.

Johnson was also deeply concerned with the purification of the language and the reform of English prosody, both of which during the earlier part of the seventeenth century, the period of the so-called 'Metaphysical Poets', had fallen into sad confusion. 'After about half a century of forced thoughts, and rugged metre, some advances towards nature and harmony had been already made by Waller and Denham.' But it was Dryden who had 'refined the language, improved the sentiments, and tuned the numbers of English poetry'. As to Dryden's critical essays, they were 'the criticism of a poet; not a dull collection of theorems, nor a rude detection of faults ... but a gay and vigorous dissertation, where delight is mingled with instruction, and where the author proves his right of judgement, by his power of performance'.

---

* See *Rasselas*, Chapter X: 'The business of a poet, said Imlac, is to examine, not the individual, but the species; to remark general properties and large appearances: he does not number the streaks of the tulip, or describe the different shades in the verdure of the forest.'

** *All For Love*, 1677.

'Apollo and the Muses, inflicting Penance on Dr Pomposo round Parnassus';
caricature by Gillray of 1783.

Though his own detection of faults is not infrequently rude,
Johnson's *Lives of the Poets* are no less vigorous and no less entertaining. His approach was rarely systematic. He breaks off a
catalogue of Dryden's plays to record his vociferous dispute with the
rival dramatist, Elkanah Settle, and, many pages before he has reached
the end of his essay, describes the drunken riot said to have postponed
the great man's funeral. Elsewhere, Johnson deals at some length with
many of his subjects' private lives. Of Dryden's private character he
provides a vivid sketch; but of his domestic career he tells us very
little, except that 'he married the lady Elizabeth Howard ... with
circumstances, according to the satire imputed to lord Somers, not
very honourable to either party', and had three sons, of whom
Charles, 'usher of the palace to pope Clement the xith', was drowned,
while on holiday in England, during an ill-advised attempt 'to swim

across the Thames at Windsor'.

If, from a critical point of view, Johnson's noblest achievements are the essays he composed on Pope and Dryden, his most memorable attempt to draw a character was his life of Richard Savage, which he had originally published in 1744, but reprinted in 1781. Particularly moving is his picture of his old friend's death, then a prisoner, but still courageous and aggressive, behind the walls of Bristol Gaol:

> The last time that the Keeper saw him was on 31 July 1743; when Savage, seeing him at his bed-side, said, with an uncommon earnestness, 'I have something to say to you, Sir'; but, after a pause, moved his hand in a melancholy manner; and, finding himself unable to recollect what he was going to communicate, said, ''Tis gone!' The keeper soon after left him; and the next morning he died...
>
> Such were the life and death of Richard Savage, a man equally distinguished by his virtues and vices; and at once remarkable for his weaknesses and abilities.
>
> He was of a middle stature, of a thin habit of body, a long visage, coarse features, and melancholy aspect; of a grave and manly deportment, a solemn dignity of mien; but which, upon a nearer acquaintance, softened into an engaging easiness of manners. His walk was slow, and his voice tremulous and mournful. He was easily excited to smiles, but very seldom provoked to laughter.

The imaginative side of Johnson's nature – his ability to convey his vision of life through imagery and verbal music – is, as a rule, very much more apparent in his prose than in his verse. He seems to have made no very clear distinction between the poet and the prose-writer. Nor did he believe that men were born to be poets, and sometimes asserted, indeed, that he himself, if he had given it adequate thought, could have mastered, without much difficulty, any avocation that he chose to practice. 'The true genius', he asserted, 'is a mind of large general powers, accidentally determined to some particular direction'; and, during his youth, as a person of large mind, he had tried his hand first at a Juvenalian satire, then at an ambitious blank-verse tragedy, since each was a type of literary exercise that had brought earlier poets fame and fortune.

London, a Poem, in Imitation of the Third Satire of Juvenal, had appeared in 1738, just before he reached the age of thirty. Pope, now at the zenith of his reputation, was to live another six years; and *London* imitates not only Juvenal but the author of the *Moral Essays*. As a castigator of modern morals and manners, Johnson closely follows Pope – for example, in his habit of joining two apparently incongruous images to form a single pointed couplet:

Here Malice, Rapine, Accident, conspire,
And now a Rabble rages, now a Fire;
Their Ambush here relentless Ruffians lay,
And here the fell Attorney prowls for prey;
Here falling Houses thunder on your Head,*
And here a female Atheist talks you dead.

London was a poem that, of course, delighted Boswell, who remarks that, although 'in this justly-celebrated poem may be found a few rhymes which the critical precision of English prosody at this day would disallow', such imperfections are scarcely perceived 'in the general blaze of its excellence...'. Certainly, it had so much interested Pope that he caused enquiries to be made about the author and, learning 'that he was some obscure man', observed that 'he will soon be *déterré*'; which he followed up by recommending the poet, though unsuccessfully, to the attention of a literary peer.

For Johnson, like Pope, had directed his satire against the Whig administration, and against the wide-spread abuses said to flourish under Sir Robert Walpole's venal government. London itself was a sink of corruption that now resembled ancient Rome, infested with designing foreign adventurers and a horde of ferocious native criminals:

Prepare for Death, if here at Night you roam,
And sign your will before you sup from Home,
Some fiery Fop, with new Commission vain,
Who sleeps on Brambles till he kills his Man;
Some frolick Drunkard, reeling from a Feast,
Provokes a Broil, and stabs you for a Jest....

In vain, these Dangers past, your Doors you close,
And hope the balmy Blessings of Repose:
Cruel with Guilt, and daring with Despair,
The midnight Murd'rer bursts the faithless Bar....

Yet, for all its obvious merits – what Boswell calls its 'manly force, bold spirit, and masterly versification' – Johnson's earliest satire was essentially derivative, a young man's determined attempt to establish his own grasp of a familiar form of modern writing. Not until eleven years later did he publish a poem that, although he was still a disciple of Pope, possessed some genuine originality. It was again a satire, but a satire that often transcends its immediate object. *The Vanity of Human Wishes* deals, not so much with the 'horrours of London' or the

* According to contemporary newspapers, one of the dangers of eighteenth-century London life was the sudden collapse of some antiquated tenement.

vices of a corrupt society, as with human life in general; with the
sorrows of old age –

> In Life's last Scene what Prodigies surprise,
> Fears of the Brave, and Follies of the Wise?
> From *Marlb'rough's* Eyes the Streams of Dotage flow,
> And *Swift* expires a Driv'ler and a Show

– the sufferings of neglected genius –

> There mark what Ills the Scholar's Life assail,
> Toil, Envy, Want, the Garret, and the Jail

– the downfall of nations and sovereigns, and the decay of innocence
and youth and beauty.

If Johnson is at his worst in his absurdly tautologous opening
couplet –

> Let Observation with extensive View,
> Survey Mankind, from China to Peru –

in the long passage devoted to *Swedish Charles*, the ill-fated Charles XII
of Sweden, he achieved a height that, as an imaginative poet, he
would never touch again. After his attack on Russia and defeat at
Poltava, Charles had precipitately retired to Turkey, whence the
Sultan had expelled him:*

> The vanquish'd Hero leaves his broken Bands,
> And shews his Miseries in distant Lands;
> Condemn'd a needy Supplicant to wait,
> While Ladies interpose, and Slaves debate.
> But did not Chance at length her Error mend?
> Did no subverted Empire mark his End?
> Did rival Monarchs give the fatal Wound?
> Or hostile Millions press him to the Ground?
> His Fall was destin'd to a barren Strand,
> A petty Fortress, and a dubious Hand;
> He left a Name, at which the World grew pale,
> To point a Moral, or adorn a Tale.

The last two couplets are more often quoted than the eight preceding

*Charles XII (r. 1697–1718) had finally returned to Sweden, and died, in mysterious circum-
stances, while besieging the 'petty fortress' of Fredrikssten, during an invasion of Norway. See
'The death of Charles XII of Sweden' by Michael Srigley; *History Today*, December 1963.

lines; and thus we are apt to lose sight of the immensely dramatic effect produced by the rapid succession of contrasted paragraphs. Though the King's exile had been ignominious, we might have expected that for so great a hero Chance would have reserved an appropriately noble end. There is a brief pause between lines 4 and 5; a longer pause divides lines 8 and 9; and it is there that Johnson embarks upon his solemn closing strophe. Today the record, that once had terrified Europe, has dwindled to the proportions of a cautionary tale. Charles had died under the wall of a petty Norwegian fortress, picked off by an unknown marksman.

The passage cited above suggests that Johnson had a keen dramatic sense. Yet there is little sign in his blank-verse play, *Irene*, produced during the course of the same year, that he had any talents as a play-wright. Even Boswell reluctantly admits that it is not a very good play. Although, if 'analysed into parts, it will furnish a rich store of noble sentiments, fine imagery, and beautiful language', *Irene*, he confesses, is 'deficient in pathos, in that delicate power of touching the human feelings, which is the principal end of the drama. Indeed Garrick has complained to me, that Johnson not only had not the faculty of producing the impressions of tragedy, but that he had not the sensibility to perceive them.'

When Garrick produced *Irene* with a distinguished theatrical cast, after a 'violent dispute' between the producer and the dramatist, who first refused to make any of the alterations that Garrick was convinced it needed, it had a somewhat rough reception. 'The play went off tolerably', said Dr Adams, 'till it came to the conclusion', and 'Mrs Pritchard, the heroine of the piece, was to be strangled upon the stage, and was to speak two lines with the bow-string round her neck. The audience cried out *"Murder! Murder!"*. She several times attempted to speak; but in vain. At last she was obliged to go off the stage alive.'

This passage was afterwards removed, and the heroine put to death behind the scenes. But, 'although Mr Garrick's zeal carried it through for nine nights, so that the author had his three nights' profits', *Irene* proved a total failure. Johnson took his disappointment well; and, 'asked how he felt upon the ill success of his tragedy, he replied, "Like the Monument".' In later life, hearing an over-zealous admirer begin to read it aloud, he rose from his chair and quietly walked away.

Today, most readers will be prepared to sympathize with Garrick's unappreciative audience; *Irene* certainly lacks both dramatic interest and poetic value. One after another the ponderous lines are hammered out; there is no melodic connection between them; each forms a separate lumpish unit:

> Unhappy Fair! Compassion calls upon me
> To check this Torrent of imperious Rage.
> While unavailing Anger crouds thy Tongue
> With idle Threats and fruitless Exclamation,
> The fraudful Moments ply their silent Wings,
> And steal thy Life away. Death's horrid Angel
> Already shakes his bloody Sabre o'er thee.

Johnson, however, though he may not have relished the difficult job of writing for the modern stage, enjoyed his glimpses of the stage itself. He always welcomed the privilege of appearing in an unfamilar rôle, whether it be that of sportsman, efficient businessman or popular dramatic author; and, for the first night of *Irene*, Boswell heard, he 'had a fancy that ... his dress should be more gay than what he ordinarily wore', and 'appeared behind the scenes, and even in one of the side boxes, in a scarlet waistcoat, with rich gold lace, and a gold-laced hat'.

Once his tragedy had failed, he continued 'to frequent the *Green Room*, and seemed to take delight in dissipating his gloom, by mixing in the sprightly chit-chat of the motley circle then to be found there'. But Johnson was still a married man, whose wife, it is said, being now a neurotic invalid, frequently refused him her embraces; 'and Mr David Hume', Boswell adds, 'related to me from Mr Garrick, that Johnson at last denied himself this amusement, from considerations of rigid virtue; saying, "I'll come no more behind your scenes, David; for the silk stockings and white bosoms of your actresses excite my amorous propensities".'

One of the explanations of Johnson's failure as a dramatist, and of his inability to manage blank verse, may have been that, like most other eighteenth-century poets, he needed the incentive that he found in rhyme, which gave his finest occasional poems their peculiar blend of strength and fluency. Among such poems, written to commemorate some event that had stirred his imagination, three, at least, deserve especial notice. Johnson was very fond of composing epitaphs, sometimes Latin, sometimes English; and his inscription for the tomb of William Hogarth –

> The Hand of Art here torpid lies
> That traced the essential form of grace*:
> Here Death has closed the curious eyes
> That saw the manners in the face

*Hogarth's *Analysis of Beauty*, in which he attempts to establish the essential 'Line of Beauty', had appeared in 1753.

– is immeasurably superior to the far longer and more pompous lines, written by David Garrick, that can still be read upon the artist's monument.

The idea of death, too, inspired the poem with which he celebrated the passing of his old friend, Robert Levett. It is also an imaginative echo of Johnson's firm conviction that 'heroic virtues' were often 'too much prized', and that 'that character is the best which does little but repeated acts of beneficence...'. Levett had had few personal graces; but, 'obscurely wise, and coarsely kind', he had gone where none of the poet's more elegant and better-educated companions would have ever dared to go, and penetrated 'misery's darkest caverns' amid the filthiest alleyways of modern London.

It had been an inglorious, yet not an unhappy life; and Levett's death, in 1782, filled Johnson with a sense of irreparable loss:

> Condemn'd to hope's delusive mine,
> As on we toil from day to day,
> By sudden blasts, or slow decline,
> Our social comforts drop away.
>
> Well tried through many a varying year,
> See LEVET to the grave descend;
> Officious, innocent, sincere,
> Of ev'ry friendless name the friend ...
>
> His virtues walk'd their narrow round,
> Nor made a pause, nor left a void;
> And sure th'Eternal Master found
> The single talent well employ'd.

Johnson rarely attempted lyric verse, and then, seldom with any great success; yet the *Short Song of Congratulation* that he wrote to amuse Mrs Thrale, when he was already in his seventy-second year, upon hearing that Henry Thrale's foolish and extravagant young nephew, Sir John Lade, had just inherited his father's fortune, includes some of the poet's best-remembered and, today, most often-quoted lines. Sir John had had a long minority; and, earlier, Johnson had informed Bennet Langton that the young man's present occupation, he heard, 'was running about town shooting cats'; after which, 'in a sort of kindly reverie', he bethought himself of his own beloved cat, Hodge, remarking, 'But Hodge shan't be shot; no, no, Hodge shall not be shot.'

As a rich man, a notorious rake and dissolute crony of the Prince
of Wales, Sir John would presently waste his large heritage; and
Johnson's prophetic *Song* was written, and at once transcribed into
Thraliana, early in August 1780:

> Long-expected one and Twenty
> Lingring year at last is flown;
> Pomp and Pleasure, Pride & Plenty,
> Great Sir John, are now your own.
>
> Loosen'd from the Minor's Tether,
> Free to mortgage or to sell,
> Wild as Wind, and light as Feather,
> Bid the Slaves of Thrift farewell.
>
> Call the Betsys, Kates, and Jennys,
> All the Names that laugh at Care;
> Lavish of your Grandsire's Guineas,
> Show the Spirit of an Heir....
>
> Wealth, Sir John, was made to wander,
> Let it wander as it will:
> See the Jockey, see the Pander,
> Bid them come, and take their fill....

The *Song* had a curious subsequent history; it exercised a decisive
influence upon a very different lyric poet. A well-known modern
historian, the late G. M. Young, described how, one Sunday morning,
in the garden of All Souls, he joined the literary scholar, William
Paton Ker, and Ker's guest at the college, A. E. Housman. They were
talking of Johnson's verse; and Housman, speaking of the famous
Song, remarked – Young had forgotten his exact words – either 'That
poem started the *Shropshire Lad*', or, more probably, that the *Song*
had been 'in his mind' when he started to produce the series[16].

If pointed out, the resemblance is clear enough. Not only has
Housman adapted Johnson's peculiar lilting rhythm; but he has also
taken on something of Johnson's attitude, half derisive, yet half
romantic and nostalgic, towards the tragi-comedy of desperate youth.
It is odd to reflect that the ridiculous Sir John Lade, who, having
ruined himself and passed through the King's Bench Prison (whence
the Prince Regent, with his customary meanness, had refused to
rescue him) died, still bankrupt, in 1838, long after his death should
have helped to inspire the production of Housman's troop of star-
crossed rustic heroes.

A Great Infidel   6

It was on 7 June 1780, while she was staying with the Thrales at Bath,
that Fanny Burney enjoyed one of the most curious of her many
remarkable adventures. She confronted a feminine agnostic – during
the second half of the eighteenth century, a comparatively rare species –
who not only denied the immortality of the soul but spoke in rapturous
terms of free love. The novelist made this 'extraordinary new acquaintance' when she was visiting a Mrs Lambart. Amid a large company,
which included 'Lord Huntingdon, a very deaf old lord; Sir Robert
Pigot, a very thin old baronet; Mr Tyson, a very civil master of
ceremonies; Mr and Mrs White, a very insignificant couple; Sir
James C——, a bawling old man ... Mrs and Miss Byron*' and 'a pair
of tonish misses', she was introduced by her hostess to a certain
Miss W——.

At first sight, there seemed nothing to distinguish Miss W——
from any other young woman. She was 'young and pleasing in her
appearance, not pretty, but agreeable in her face, and soft, gentle,
and well-bred in her manners'; and their conversation, for some time,
revolved round 'the common Bath topics'. As soon as their hostess
had left them, however, Miss W—— gradually changed her tone and
plunged into subjects of a far more dangerous kind.

She began by abusing the human race in general. Her own sex, it
is true, 'she rather excused than defended, laying to the door of the
men their faults and imperfections; but the men, she said, were all bad –
all, in one word, and without exception, sensualists!, Miss Burney,
she tells us, 'stared much at a severity of speech for which her softness
of manner had so ill prepared me'; but Miss W——, having briefly
apologized, 'then led on to discoursing of happiness and misery: the
latter she held to be the invariable lot of us all ...'. She was sorry, she
declared, that she lacked 'an amorous disposition', as she believed that
'the reason the men are happier than us, is because they are more

* The wife and daughter of Admiral Byron, 'Foulweather Jack', the poet's grandfather.

sensual'. But she had not entirely given up hope; one might still, she felt, taste a moment of happiness, 'which must be the finding one worthy of exciting a passion' that she need not scruple to avow. 'That would, indeed, be a moment worth living for!' But such a happiness would never come her way; 'the men are so low, so vicious, so worthless!' 'What a strange girl!' commented Miss Burney. It was some time before she could recover from her astonishment, and produce a phrase or two of sober counsel.

She did little good. Poor Miss W——, besides being a determined misanthrope, was an habitual day-dreamer, only at peace when she was living in the country and could give free rein to her imagination, 'quite out of the world ... surrounded with sylphs', and oblivious to all else. 'Well, you are a most extraordinary character', Miss Burney replied, 'I must confess I have seen nothing like you!' That a celebrated novelist should think her extraordinary no doubt enchanted Miss W——, whose declamations on happiness and love and death grew increasingly enthusiastic. She trusted, she said, that, as she moved through the world, she might yet discover 'something like myself'. Here her interlocutor, still struggling to regain control of the dialogue, attempted to introduce a quiet joke. Miss W——, she said, had unquestionably the gift of attraction –

'But if you wait to be happy for a friend resembling yourself, I shall no longer wonder at your despondency.'

'Oh!' cried she, raising her eyes in ecstasy, 'could I find such a one! – male or female – for sex would be indifferent to me. With such a one I would go to live directly.'

There was worse to come. While Miss Burney was still debating whether she should laugh or frown, Miss W—— hurried wildly forward. Were she to form the friendship she dreamed of, she would not survive the beloved object's death.

'Not survive?' repeated I, 'what can you mean?'

She looked down, but said nothing.

'Surely you cannot mean', said I, very gravely indeed, 'to put a violent end to your life?'

'I should not', she said, again looking up, 'hesitate a moment.'

I was quite thunderstruck, and for some time could not say a word....'

When words returned, as usually they did – despite Miss Burney's diffidence, she was a forceful young woman – she addressed Miss W—— in so 'serious and earnest' a style that she herself feared, were she to write them down, her admonitions might sound a shade excessive.

By what right, she asked, did Miss W—— assume that she was entitled 'to rush unlicensed on eternity', and was startled to hear Miss W—— answer: 'By right of believing I shall be extinct.' Now she 'really felt horror-struck', and demanded where the young enthusiast could have picked up such appalling notions. '"In Hume", said she, "I have read his essays repeatedly".' Bolingbroke, she added, 'the divinest of all writers', was another infidel philosopher in whose works she often found comfort; after which Miss Burney could only recommend James Beattie on *The Immutability of Truth*.

At this point, the 'poor misguided girl' disappears from Fanny Burney's record. Did she desert her unsympathetic family for some male or female love, commit suicide, or perhaps retire into the seclusion of a gloomy private madhouse? The significant fact is that she had read David Hume, in Dr Johnson's world 'the Great Infidel', and by doing so had lost her faith and, before long, would probably lose her virtue. Johnson's detestation of Hume was well-known, and formed the basis of many interesting exchanges between the old man and his chief disciple. Though he had a personal regard for the philosopher-historian, whom he considered 'plain, obliging, kind-hearted', Boswell had always detested Hume's 'ostentatious infidelity', and, as often as the philosopher's name turned up, would sit back, rapt in admiration, while dark clouds gathered on Johnson's brow and he prepared to deliver solemn judgment.

Sometimes Boswell would contribute his own strictures – for example, on 20 March 1776, when he and Johnson were at Oxford, visiting Johnson's good friend Dr Adams. 'A most polite, pleasing, communicative man', the Doctor 'had distinguished himself by an able answer to David Hume's notorious *Essay on Miracles*; but he admitted that, having once dined in Hume's company, he had not refused to shake his hand:

I took the liberty [Boswell informs us] to object to treating an infidel writer with smooth civility. Where there is a controversy concerning a passage in a classick author, or concerning a question in antiquities, or any other subject in which human happiness is not deeply interested, a man may treat his antagonist with politeness and even respect. But where the controversy is concerning the truth of religion, it is of such vast importance to him who maintains it ... that the person of an opponent ought not to be spared. If a man firmly believes that religion is an invaluable treasure, he will consider a writer who endeavours to deprive mankind of it as a *robber*. ... An abandoned profligate may think that it is not wrong to debauch my wife, but shall I, therefore, not detest him? ... No, I will kick him down stairs, or run him through the body....

Here Johnson agreed. 'When a man', he said, 'voluntarily engages in an important controversy, he is to do all he can to lessen his antagonist, because authority from personal respect has much weight with most people, and often more than reasoning ...'. Yet Boswell's attitude towards Hume was singularly ambivalent; and there were times when he felt that Johnson might have gone a little too far. Provoking Johnson to impressive explosions of wrath was almost as delightful an exercise as securing his approval; and on one occasion, he records in his private papers, he ventured boldly to enquire why his revered friend, whatever he might think of Hume's head, should find it necessary to 'attack his heart'. Johnson's response was splendidly overwhelming: 'Why, Sir, because his head has corrupted it. Or perhaps it has perverted his head. I know not indeed whether he has first been a blockhead and that has made him a rogue, or first been a rogue and that has made him a blockhead.'

Unlike the amiable Dr Adams, Johnson declined to treat his antagonist with conventional civility. They met twice; and, although, when they came face to face, at a dinner-party in St James's Palace, during the summer of 1763, Johnson seems to have controlled his ire*, a year earlier, as the infidel entered a room, he had immediately walked out. For he shared Boswell's belief that Hume was a spiritual brigand who threatened to rob him of the faith he treasured – the faith that, amid the misery of his secret thoughts, provided his only lasting consolation. Nor did his fury subside on Hume's death. It enraged him to learn that the Great Infidel had awaited his end with equanimity.

'I said I had reason to believe [writes Boswell, recording a conversation they had held in September 1777] that the thought of annihilation gave Hume no pain. JOHNSON. "It was not so, Sir. He had a vanity in being thought easy. It is more probable that he should assume an appearance of ease, than that so very improbable a thing should be, as a man not being afraid of going ... into an unknown state, and not being uneasy at leaving all he knew. And you are to consider, that upon his own principle of annihilation he had no motive to speak the truth." The horrour of death which I had always observed in Dr Johnson, appeared strong tonight.'

Upon one subject alone was there an agreement between Hume

*Their host was the Royal Chaplain; which may have accounted for Johnson's good manners. Letter from Thomas Birch, Secretary of the Royal Society, to Lord Royston, quoted by E. C. Mossner: *The Life of David Hume.*

Right David Hume (1711–66); after a difficult youth, he became sturdy and robust 'with a ruddy Complexion & a chearful countenance'. Portrait by Allan Ramsay.

and Johnson – neither would admit that the pretended works of Ossian
were genuine specimens of antique Celtic poetry. Otherwise, an
almost impassable gulf divided the 'easy' philosopher from the
melancholy, self-tormenting sage. Hume accepted the pleasures and
pains of life; such acceptance was entirely alien to Johnson's dark and
anxious spirit. Johnson had achieved virtue by dint of tremendous
effort – he was constantly at war against his own vices; Hume had an
instinctive feeling for goodness and, so far as we can nowadays judge,
much more temperate, or more easily disciplined passions. Johnson
declared that his whole adult existence had been 'radically wretched';
Hume, in early middle age, seemed already to have acquired the art
of living. Though he certainly enjoyed success, reverses left him
unperturbed. A contented man, he chose to share his contentment.
Not without reason did his French admirers entitle Hume '*le bon
David*'.

When Johnson encountered him, and refused to make his acquaintance, the philosopher was fifty-two. Born on 26 April 1711, through
his mother he came of a distinguished legal stock; his father, Joseph
Hume of Ninewells in Berwickshire, who died in 1713, had also
practised as an advocate and belonged to a family of minor Scottish
gentlefolk, said to be relations of the Earl of Home. He had had a happy
childhood; despite the fact that she was still young and handsome,
Mrs Hume, 'a woman of singular Merit', devoted herself to her
children's interests; and David, her younger son, entered Edinburgh
University before he had reached the age of twelve.

He was not a particularly promising boy; his school-fellows are
reputed to have called him 'the Clod', perhaps because he was so
large and heavy; and he grew up into a 'tall, lean, & raw-boned youth',
who suffered frequently from moods of deep depression. But, rather
than give way to hypochondria – a disorder that all his contemporaries
dreaded – once he had recognized the symptoms, he had set about
discovering a cure, and adopted the calming and strengthening regime
recommended by his wise physician, which included regular exercise
on foot or horseback, 'Anti-hysteric Pills' and a daily pint of claret.
The physical results were excellent; as a young man, he became sturdy
and robust, 'with a ruddy Complexion & a chearful Countenance'; and
ruddy and robust he remained at least another forty years.

His moods of depression, however, proved somewhat more difficult
to remedy; he found it hard to concentrate his ideas or follow an
extended train of thought. A cloud enveloped him; until he felt that
he must be suffering from the dread disease that the mystics named
acedia, 'a Coldness & Desertion of the Spirit' which constantly

returns to overcast the mind. But once again he adopted resolute measures, and decided 'that as there are two things very bad for this Distemper, Study & Idleness, so there are two things very good, Business & Diversion. . . .' He then resolved to 'seek out a more active life'; and, since he had already refused his family's suggestion that he should follow the Law like his father and grandfather, in 1734 he moved to Bristol where he entered the office of a merchant, but was soon dismissed because he had made an ill-judged effort to correct his employer's slipshod prose.

Meanwhile, his spirits had shown a great improvement, and he felt capable of resuming his previous studies. Determined to learn French and acquire '*l'Art de Vivre*, the art of society and conversation', he crossed the English Channel in 1735, and took up residence first at Rheims, then at La Flèche, a little Angevin town that housed a celebrated Jesuit college. There he completed the ambitious work that he had 'projected', he said, before he left the University, and had 'planned' before he was yet twenty-one. The first two books of *A Treatise of Human Nature: Being an Attempt to introduce the experimental Method of Reasoning into Moral Subjects* appeared in January 1739, and were succeeded by a third book in November 1740. 'Never', wrote Hume in later years, 'was any literary attempt more unfortunate than my Treatise of human Nature. *It fell deadborn from the Press . . .*'. Hume then quietly retired to his brother's house, where, 'being naturally of a cheerful and sanguine Temper', he remarks, he 'very soon recovered the Blow, and prosecuted with great Ardour my studies in the Country'.

One of the charges brought against Hume's *Treatise* had concerned its alleged 'unintelligibility' and the 'abstruse and perplex'd style' in which he set about his work. This criticism must have been especially wounding; 'the greatest of British philosophers', as he had already shown himself, was a careful literary stylist, and had hoped to deliver his opinions with an 'Elegance & Neatness' that would command 'the Attention of the World'; he 'wou'd rather live & dye in Obscurity', he declared, 'than produce them maim'd & imperfect'. Later, the merits of Hume's style were generally recognized by his admirers – in 1761, Madame de Boufflers, though she admitted that she could not read English, spoke of 'the clearness, the majesty, the touching simplicity' that distinguished his *History of the Stewarts*; and today we can enjoy the famous *Treatise* for the excellencies of the style alone.

Some of Hume's most contentious and destructive passages, such as his attack on the idea of an integrated human personality, are among the most attractive:

204 A GREAT INFIDEL

For my part, when I enter most intimately into what I call *myself*, I always stumble on some particular perception or other, of heat or cold, light or shade, love or hatred, pain or pleasure. I never can catch myself at any time without a perception, and never can observe any thing but the perception. ... If any one .... thinks he has a different notion of *himself*, I must confess I can no longer reason with him. All I can allow him is, that he may be in the right as well as I.... He may perhaps, perceive something simple and continu'd, which he calls *himself*; tho' I am certain there is no such principle in me.

But setting aside some metaphysicians of this kind, I may venture to affirm of the rest of mankind, that they are nothing but a bundle or collection of different perceptions, which succeed each other with an inconceivable rapidity, and are in a perpetual flux and movement. Our eyes cannot turn in our sockets without varying our perceptions. Our thought is still more variable than our sight.... The mind is a kind of theatre, where several perceptions successively make their appearance; pass, re-pass, glide away, and mingle in an infinite variety of postures and situations.... They are the successive perceptions only, that constitute the mind....

Here Hume's style, with its lightness and clarity and occasional touches of pointed irony, is the antithesis of 'Johnsonese'. And then, for a man who shared Johnson's beliefs, Hume's view of the Self was yet more disturbing than his notorious essay upon miracles. If the personality be 'a bundle of perceptions', and the idea of personal identity the merest legend, where do we find room for the human soul? There can be no question of the Soul surviving death; for, once this fortuitous bundle has been broken up, the Ego, of which the Soul is regarded as the spiritual nucleus, must inevitably be annihilated. Johnson not only was a devout Christian, but had a firm conviction of his personal identity. He felt no doubt that he was solid and whole and 'simple'; and, as a determined rationalist for all his religious beliefs, he resented David Hume just as he afterwards resented Bishop Berkeley, whose 'ingenious sophistry' he attempted to put in its place by 'striking his foot with mighty force against a large stone, exclaiming "I refute him *thus* "'.

Both Hume and Johnson had an instinctively sceptical turn; but, whereas Johnson struggled to suppress his doubts, Hume had trained himself to accept them with philosophic fortitude. 'However paradoxical it may sound', writes his biographer and editor[17], 'Hume's scepticism was creative scepticism.' By introducing a strictly empirical method into the study of the moral sciences, he had no desire to diminish the dignity of mankind; and the philosopher, he insisted, amid all his theorizing, should remember to be 'still a man'. Although he had long since abandored Faith, in the conduct of his own life he

had never abandoned Hope and Charity; and these virtues did much
to support him after the apparent failure of his *Treatise*.

First, he became tutor to Lord Annandale, a weak-witted young
peer, then accepted a series of minor secretarial posts, which took him
to Vienna and Turin with various diplomatic missions. Those were
agreeable, if unproductive years; not until 1748 could he resume the
existence of an independent man of letters. His *Enquiry concerning the
Principles of Morals*, which he considered 'of all my writings, historical,
philosophical, or literary, incomparably the best', attracted regrettably
little notice, when it appeared in 1751; but, in 1752, his *Political
Discourses* were a good deal more fortunate. During the following year,
he launched his *Essays and Treatises* – they did not include his *Treatise
on the Human Understanding*, which long remained his most neglected
work. Finally, between 1754 and 1762, having secured a congenial
appointment as Keeper of the Advocates' Library at Edinburgh, he
·produced his enormous *History of England**. By that time, he had
established his reputation as one of the greatest writers of his age.

Meanwhile, his fame had crossed the Channel; and, when in 1763,
at the end of the Seven Years' War, Lord Hertford, the British
Ambassador to the Court of France, chose the famous historian as his
private secretary, he received a wildly enthusiastic welcome. This was
the heyday of Parisian anglomania, when, wrote Gibbon, who also
benefitted from the prevailing craze for all things English, 'our
opinions, our fashions, even our games, were adopted in France; a ray
of national glory illuminated each individual, and every Englishman
was supposed to be born a patriot and philosopher'. Laurence Sterne
had arrived a year earlier; and he, too, had had a cordial reception,
becoming the friend of d'Holbach and Diderot, meeting not only the
Duc d'Orléans but the great financier, La Popelinière, and constantly
arousing 'new emotions in tender hearts by his naïve and touching
sensibility'.

Gibbon and Sterne, however, seem to have been much less fashionable than David Hume, whose triumph lasted over two years, from the
moment he arrived until he finally regained London. The news that
he might soon appear in Paris had given 'a most general & unfeigned
satisfaction' both to the *Philosophes* themselves and to liberal-minded
High Society; and Hume himself, so good-natured, so ready to please,
so learned yet so unpretentious, had surpassed their warmest hopes.
Horace Walpole, another visitor from London, was amazed by Hume's

---

*Voltaire described the *History*, two years after the publication of the closing volume, as
'perhaps the best ever written in any language . . . Mr Hume . . . is neither parliamentarian,
nor royalist . . . he is simply judicial.'

206 A GREAT INFIDEL

success, and evidently somewhat nettled; 'it is incredible', he remarked, 'the homage they pay him'. Hume was treated 'with perfect veneration', whether he attended the drawing-rooms of the famous *salonnières*, or accompanied his ambassador on a ceremonious visit to the Court at Fontainebleau, where the royal children, the duc de Berry, 'a boy of ten Years old', and his brother, the eight-year-old comte de Provence, declared that they were very glad to see him and informed him they had read his books. The King's mistress, too, graciously accepted his homage. 'All the Courtiers, who stood around when I was introduc'd to Mme de Pompadour', he wrote, 'assurd me she was never heard to say so much to any Man.'

In Paris, the 'Place of the world which I have always admired the most', he ate 'nothing but Ambrosia', he said, drank 'nothing but Nectar', breathed 'nothing but Incense', and trod 'on nothing but Flowers'. Among those who scattered flowers were some of the prettiest women in Parisian society; and the fact that he was awkward and stout and plain merely accentuated his native charm. He was also slow-spoken and bad at parlour-games. Madame d'Épinay, for example, writing to M. de Lubière, describes a charade during which the *'grand et gros historiographe d'Angleterre'* had been persuaded to enact the rôle of Sultan, and required to sit on a sofa between two attractive but obdurate slave-girls, – in real life, elegant *femmes du monde* – masterfully overcoming their resistance.*[18] Words failed him; he stared at them fixedly, smote the pit of his stomach and slapped his knee, repeating again and again, *'Eh bien! mesdemoiselles.... Eh bien! vous voilà donc....'* Yet even this ludicrous spectacle, Madame d'Épinay adds, did not diminish Hume's renown; *'toutes les jolies femmes s'en sont emparées; il est de tous les soupers fins, et il n'est point de bonne fête sans lui....,*

One of his most enthusiastic devotees he already knew by correspondence. As early as the spring of 1761, he had received a long letter (including the eulogy that has been quoted above) signed Hyppolyte De Soujon, Comtesse De Boufflers; and he had answered with his customary grace. Two years later, determined to meet him personally, Madame de Boufflers had arrived in London; but, for some reason that remains obscure, Hume, who was in Scotland, had refused to travel south; and she had had to be content with the series of festivities that had been arranged by English friends, visiting Woburn and Lord Shelburne's country house, and touring Horace Walpole's picturesque 'Gothick' castle, at which she breakfasted to the accompaniment of clarinets and French horns.

* *Mémoires et Correspondence de Madame d'Épinay.*

Being a learned woman, she had now seized the opportunity of paying her respects to Hume's arch-opponent, Samuel Johnson. Topham Beauclerk had acted as her escort; and he afterwards described the meeting in his usual 'lively manner'. Johnson had entertained her with his conversation for some time:

When our visit was over, she and I left him, and were got into Temple Lane, when all at once I heard a noise like thunder. This was occasioned by Johnson, who it seems, upon a little recollection, had taken it into his head that he ought to have done the honours of his literary residence to a foreign lady of quality, and eager to show himself a man of gallantry, was hurrying

The comtesse de Boufflers (left) with her friend, the duchesse de Lauzun; a drawing by Carmontelle, 1769.

An English tea-party at the Prince de Conti's apartments in the Temple. A painting by Michel Barthélemy Ollivier, which includes a portrait of the young Mozart.

down the stair-case in violent agitation. He overtook us before we reached the Temple-gate, and brushing in between me and Madame de Boufflers, seized her hand, and conducted her to her coach. His dress was a rusty brown morning suit, a pair of old shoes by way of slippers, a little shrivelled wig sticking on the top of his head and the knees of his breeches hanging loose. A considerable crowd of people gathered round....

Although Madame de Boufflers' elegance attracted the London crowd, who hailed her affectionately as 'Madame Blewflower', and no one could have been better received by her fellow grandees, she was at last obliged to leave London without meeting her philosophic idol. They did not finally come face to face until November or December 1763; for, on Hume's first appearance in Paris, she was suffering an attack of measles. But, once they had met, they felt an immediate affinity. Neither was young; Hume had passed his fiftieth birthday; Madame de Boufflers was now thirty-eight. Moreover, she was the mistress of another man – the prince de Conti, a Prince of the Blood, in the hereditary position he occupied only two degrees lower than the King himself; and with Conti she had been living, as his *maîtresse-en-titre*, since the year 1752.

This was the period of French history when, as Talleyrand recorded, social barriers had begun to crumble. One of Conti's chaplains was the Abbé Prévost, author of that demoralizing story, *Manon Lescaut*; and he had extended his generous patronage to Jean-Jacques Rousseau, the bold exponent of the egalitarian theories that were already hastening his order's downfall. At his splendid modern apartments behind the walls of the medieval Temple – afterwards the prison of Louis XVI and Marie Antoinette – he and Madame de Boufflers held a weekly court. There they observed the English custom of offering their guests tea, exchanged gossip and subversive small talk, and sometimes listened to a concert. In Ollivier's picture of a typical gathering at the Prince de Conti's, the musician who amuses the party is the ten-year-old Wolfgang Amadeus Mozart.

Madame de Boufflers, as her portrait by Carmontelle shows, was unusually graceful and attractive; and Hume, like Johnson, had always loved women. From time to time, he experienced a grand passion; and, during his stay at Turin, he had become violently enamoured of a twenty-four-year-old Italian countess, 'a Lady of Great Beauty', unhappily married to 'an old decrepid Man, whom Family Convenience had compelled her to espouse'. An English acquaintance, James Caulfield, the future Lord Charlemont, claimed that he had watched Hume's courtship from a hiding-place where the treacherous Countess had installed him, seen him collapse heavily on his middle-aged knees, and heard him gasping out, '*Ah, Madame, j'étouffe avec l'amour. Chère, chère dame, je suis désolé – abimé – anéanti!*' The spectacle, Caulfield afterwards wrote, suggested Silenus 'on his knees to one of the Graces', or a bear doing its best to make love to an Italian greyhound. When the Countess finally dismissed him, tears could be seen coursing down his florid cheeks.

Madame de Boufflers was a great deal less evasive. Not only was she prepared to overlook his stoutness and his ugliness – 'his Face', said Caulfield, 'was broad and fat, his Mouth wide, and without any other expression than that of Imbecility'; and, whether he spoke English or French, he had a 'vulgar Scottish accent' – but, thanks to the deep respect she had already conceived for his mind, she met his passion half way. There followed one of those love-affairs that seem so characteristic of eighteenth-century Europe, an *amitié amoureuse**, in which physical passion, sentimental affection and intellectual admiration were each allowed to take a share, and both friends, as their relationship changed and developed, would frequently analyze their own feelings – a pursuit they found even more agreeable than the enjoyment they derived from love itself.

The relationship between Hume and Madame de Boufflers was further complicated by her *amour propre*. Though she worshipped her adoring philosopher, she was still determined to marry the prince de Conti; and the Prince hesitated to wed an old friend of comparatively undistinguished birth, who, despite her position at the Temple, was his mistress nowadays in name alone. Nothing that Hume said could persuade the Countess that she should release her hold upon her one-time lover. Why, he protested, should she think with reluctance of a private life in Paris? 'It is the situation for which I thought you best fitted, ever since I had the happiness of your acquaintance. The inexpressible and delicate graces of your character and conversation, like the soft notes of a lute, are lost amid the tumult of company, in which I commonly saw you engaged. A more select society would know how to set a juster value upon your merit.'

At an earlier stage of their relationship, when briefly perhaps she may have been his mistress, he had declared that he would never leave her side; 'you may cut me to pieces, limb by limb; but like those pertinacious animals of my country, I shall expire still attached to you, and you will in vain attempt to get free'. Alas, Madame de Boufflers' neurotic tergiversations, displayed at formidable length in her letters, gradually wore down his patience. Not that she lost his love; he remained a faithful admirer; but he ceased to expect that he could ever join their lives. They parted for the last time in January 1766, when his duty called him back to England.

He was accompanied thither by the prince de Conti's protégé; Hume's association with Jean-Jacques Rousseau was the only unfortunate result of the happy years he spent in Paris. After their original meeting, Rousseau's patrons reported that the good-natured English philosopher 'dotes on his nice little man'; but Rousseau's air of 'niceness', of modesty and persecuted simplicity, very soon evaporated, and he reappeared in the lurid colouring of an aggressive paranoiac. The fierce quarrel that presently exploded need not be discussed here. But it shook Hume's philosophic calm; and he went

---

* In *Tristram Shandy*, Sterne writes of 'that tender and delicious sentiment which ever mixes in friendship, where there is a difference of sex'.

so far as to compose a justificatory pamphlet, published both in English and in French, under the title of *A Concise and Genuine Account of the dispute between Mr Hume and Mr Rousseau*.

Once he was rid of the 'nice little man', and of Rousseau's detestable concubine, or *gouvernante*, Mademoiselle Thérèse Le Vasseur (whom Boswell, while he escorted her across the Channel, had thought that it would be an interesting experience to seduce *en route*), Hume had quietly settled down. From 1769, he played the part of 'petty Statesman' as Under-Secretary of State in the Northern Department; but, once the opportunity occurred, he was glad to leave London and regain Edinburgh, the city that, after Paris, he had always most liked. There, against the dignified classical background of the New Town, in the house that he had built himself, he lived out his remaining years, held elegant supper-parties, conversed with learned men and 'modest women', and entertained the celebrated Dr Benjamin Franklin, who discoursed to him at length about 'the natural advantages of America'; at which Hume gently but firmly reminded his guest that, besides manufacturing commodities, it was also necessary to manufacture men – a detail he had quite omitted.

Then, in 1772, he began to show signs of weakness, which gradually grew more and more apparent, until, early in 1776, he recognized that he was facing death, the disorder of the bowels from which he suffered being 'mortal and incurable'. James Boswell visited him on

Jean-Jacques Rousseau (1712–88); the 'nice little man', whose association with David Hume resulted in a bitter quarrel. Portrait by Allan Ramsay.

7 July, as soon as he heard that the 'great infidel' had not very long to live. Hume's biographer suggests that Boswell 'came to visit the dying man more out of morbid curiosity than out of sympathy';[19] but this seems a little unfair. Notwithstanding Johnson's grave objections, he was genuinely devoted to his fellow Scot; and one of Boswell's least discreditable traits was his passionate determination to enlarge his knowledge, and to prosecute his researches, which were already extensive, into the mysteries of the human mind and soul.

Like Johnson, Boswell dreaded death; and he confronted the spectacle of a hardened unbeliever, who knew that he was about to die, in a speculative and philosophic, rather than in an inquisitive and morbid spirit. He found the great historian propped up on a drawing-room sofa, and at once noted his sadly changed appearance. Though at an earlier period he had been so plump and large and rosy that he was said to have resembled 'a turtle-eating alderman', Hume's aspect was now lean and ghastly, and his skin of quite an 'earthy' hue. 'Drest in a suit of grey cloth with white metal buttons, and a kind of scratch wig', he was reading a new book, the Reverend George Campbell's Philosophy of Rhetorick. 'He seemed to be placid and even cheerful. He said he was just approaching his end. I think', Boswell adds, 'these were his words.'

They inspired Boswell to talk of the immortality of the soul – a subject that had long obsessed him; but the change that had occurred in Hume's appearance was not reflected in his conversation, which remained as gay and free as ever. He had accepted no religious system, he said, since he had begun to read the works of Locke and Clarke*. 'He then said flatly that the Morality of every Religion was bad', remarking that 'when he heard a man was religious, he concluded he was a rascal ...'.** Was it not possible there might be a future state, the anxious Boswell now demanded; but Hume immediately brushed his hopes aside, announcing that he considered it 'a most unreasonable fancy'. Nothing that Boswell said could shake his disbelief; 'for he was indecently and impolitely positive in incredulity', and argued and joked with all his old ebullience.

'The truth is', Boswell was obliged to admit, 'that Mr Hume's

---

*The Reverend Samuel Clarke, a renowned Rationalist, author of a treatise On the Being and Attributes of God.

**In his agnosticism, as in other aspects of his character, Hume was, for the most part, surprisingly liberal; and we are told that, when he took a friend's young sons to visit St Paul's Cathedral and, wishing to ingratiate themselves, they remarked 'how foolish it was to lay out a million on a thing so useless', Hume sharply reproved them, adding 'St Paul's, as a monument to the religious feeling and sentiment of the country, does it honour and will endure'.

pleasantry was such that there was no solemnity in the scene; and Death for the time did not seem dreadful. It surprised me to find him talking of different matters with a tranquillity of mind and clearness of head, which few possess at any time.' Boswell momentarily forgot his own fears; but he was dismayed to find that he could not answer Hume as he felt that an agnostic should be answered. 'A sort of wild, strange, hurrying recollection' of the early lessons he had learned from his mother, and of Johnson's admirable advice, rushed confusedly across his mind; he groped around him, 'like a man in sudden danger', for the spiritual weapons that he needed, and left Hume's presence bearing a burden of doubts that long continued to disturb him. The philosopher died on 25 August. 'True to the End' had been his motto; and he had a dignified and easy passing.

The English writer who had preceded Hume to Paris, though less dangerous as a spiritual opponent, was almost equally exasperating in Johnson's eyes. He had detested Hume; he despised and ridiculed Sterne. The former was a redoubtable adversary; the latter, merely a

David Hume in later life; 'so plump and large and rosy that he was said to have resembled "a turtle-eating alderman"'. Portrait by Allan Ramsay.

profligate parson, who sometimes allowed himself to gibe at a faith
he ought to hold sacred. In *Tristram Shandy*, he condemned not only
the fantastic tale but its general air of oddity. 'Nothing odd will do
long. *Tristram Shandy* did not last', he observed in 1776; and, when
'the lively Miss Monckton', afterwards the famous hostess Lady Corke,
'insisted that some of Sterne's writings were very pathetick', and that
she, personally, had found them so, 'Why, (said Johnson, smiling,
and rolling himself about,) that is because, dearest, you're a dunce.'

There was an additional link between Sterne and Hume that may
have, now and then, troubled Johnson; for both of them treated the

Laurence Sterne (1713–68); from a drawing by Carmontelle in 1762.

human character, not as a separate, well-established whole, but as a
fortuitous 'bundle of perceptions'. Hume had announced that, if he
looked into himself, he could discover nothing that implied the
existence of a separate, simple and continuous identity; and Sterne
wrote that 'there is not a more perplexing affair in life to me than to set
about telling any one who I am, – for there is scarce any body I cannot
give a better account of than myself...'. Body and soul are so closely

interconnected – 'exactly like a jerkin and jerkin's lining; – rumple the one, – you rumple the other' – that, although this is an inference Sterne does not pursue, the soul is bound to perish with the body.

Nor would Johnson have much appreciated Sterne's minute analyses of character, or his descriptions – almost Proustian in their complexity – of his personages' varying moods and passions. Here, for example, is his picture of Mr and Mrs Shandy at a somewhat awkward moment:

> ... As he turned his head, he met her eye: – Confusion again! he saw a thousand reasons to wipe out the reproach, and as many to reproach himself: – a thin, blue, chill, pellucid crystal, with all its humours so at rest, the least mote or speck of desire might have been seen at the bottom of it, had it existed; – it did not. ...

Both Sterne's vision of human conduct, and the method he employs to depict it, is a perpetual 'zig-zaggery', which he emphasizes by means of the strange typographical devices that often interrupt his text. Only Mr Shandy's obstinate conservatism – 'he pick'd up an opinion, sir, as a man in a state of nature picks up an apple', and thereafter will not let it go – enables him to see life steadily and see it whole: 'What a shuttlecock of a fellow would the greatest philosopher that ever existed be wisk'd into at once, did he read such books, and observe such facts, and think such thoughts, as would eternally be making him change sides!' For Sterne, every element of human life was elusive and deceptive; and, although its author said that his *Treatise of Human Nature* had fallen still-born from the press and never reached a large public, Sterne must surely have read the passage in which the mind is compared to a 'theatre, where several perceptions successively make their appearance; pass, re-pass, glide away...'. Heracleitus' doctrine that all things are in a state of flux, and that 'nothing stands still', may also have inspired the novelist, who devoted one of his most eloquent passages to the idea of mortal transience:

> I will not argue the matter: Time wastes too fast: every letter I trace tells me with what rapidity Life follows my pen; the days and hours of it more precious, – my dear Jenny, – than the rubies about thy neck, are flying over our heads like light clouds of a windy day, never to return more; every thing presses on, – whilst thou art twisting that lock! – see! it grows grey; and every time I kiss thy hand to bid adieu, and every absence which follows it, are preludes to that eternal separation which we are shortly to make. –
> Heaven have mercy upon us both!

The first volume of *The Life and Opinions of Tristram Shandy, gentleman* had appeared in 1760, when Sterne was forty-six years old; and, that year, the adventurous parish priest, hitherto almost unknown outside the confines of a remote cathedral city, had become the pampered favourite of the London world, kindly received by Lord Chesterfield; praised by the aged Lord Bathurst, once the friend of Pope and Swift; complimented by David Garrick; painted by Sir Joshua Reynolds at the request of Lord Ossory; and so beset with callers and invitations that, he told Catharine Fourmantelle, the beautiful songstress who had followed him from York, 'I am as much a prisoner as if I was in Jail...'.

Johnson he encountered on only one occasion – exactly when we do not know; and Sterne had produced a very bad effect; for his sole 'attempt at merriment', Johnson recalled, 'was the display of a drawing too grossly indecent to have delighted even in a brothel'. But, several years after Sterne's death, when Goldsmith, hearing Johnson speak of the novelist's popularity, remarked that he had been 'a very dull fellow', he received a rapid snub; which suggests that, had it not been for the unlucky incident of the erotic drawing, Johnson might have found him tolerable company. In *Thraliana* Sterne is rarely mentioned; though the authoress records that he had disappointed Murphy, and repeats a joke, which would certainly have shocked Johnson, on the Christian sacrament of marriage:

'Says a Gentleman who listen'd while Sterne was abusing Matrimony – Come, Come, Jesus Christ once honoured a Wedding with his presence – but between you & I replies Sterne, that was not the *best* thing he ever did.'

Sterne's triumphant visit to Paris began in January 1762. A year later, the youthful Edward Gibbon, having just escaped from a 'wandering life of military servitude' with the militiamen of South Hampshire, first made his way into Madame Geoffrin's salon. There, and afterwards at the houses of Helvétius and the Baron d'Holbach, he listened to 'more conversation worth remembering', and observed 'more men of letters among the people of fashion', than 'in two or three winters in London'. But Gibbon was still an obscure young pilgrim; he had not yet visited Rome, or experienced the tremendous revelation from which his life-work was to take its source. He arrived modestly and departed unobtrusively; not until February 1776, would the opening volume of *The History of the Decline and Fall of the Roman Empire* suddenly raise him to the heights of fame.

Meanwhile, in 1774, as a literary man-about-London, and a member both of Parliament and of White's, Brooks's and Boodle's clubs, he had been elected to The Club itself. Boswell, who had joined in 1773,

Laurence Sterne, painted by Reynolds when, as the author of *Tristram Shandy*, he first appeared in London.

immediately detested him; Gibbon, he exclaimed, was an 'ugly, affected, disgusting fellow'; and his attendance poisoned every meeting. Johnson, the tutelary genius of The Club, proved a formidable antagonist; and, when Johnson spoke, Gibbon held his peace or delivered acid comments *sotto voce*. Their differing styles of talk and contrasted physical appearance have been described by the younger George Colman. Whereas Gibbon affected a flowered velvet coat and a fashionable wig and sword, Johnson wore his old brown suit and customary black worsted stockings. 'Johnson's style was grand, and Gibbon's elegant.... Johnson marched to kettle-drums and trumpets, Gibbon moved to flutes and hautboys.' Johnson had brutally put down Colman, then a shy and nervous youth; Gibbon condescended, 'once or twice, in the course of the evening to talk with me'. But 'still his mannerism prevail'd; still he tapp'd his snuff-box ... and rounded his periods with an air of good breeding.... His mouth, mellifluous as Plato's, was a round hole, nearly in the centre of his visage.'

Though Johnson had tolerated Gibbon at The Club, he did not spare him in his conversation. On 20 March 1776, soon after the appearance of the *Decline and Fall*, he and Boswell:

... talked of a work much in vogue at that time, written in a very mellifluous style, but which, under pretext of another subject, contained much artful infidelity.... The authour had been an Oxonian, and was remembered there for having 'turned Papist'.* I observed, that as he had changed several times ... I did not despair yet of seeing him a methodist preacher. JOHNSON (laughing) 'It is said, that his range has been more extensive, and that he has once been Mahometan. However, now that he has published his infidelity, he will probably persist in it.'

Thus did Johnson casually dismiss the book that had delighted and astonished Hume, who, about the same time, hastened to inform Gibbon that, 'whether I consider the Dignity of your Style, the Depth

Edward Gibbon (1737–94); portrait by H. Walton. The historian as a young man. In conversation at The Club, 'Johnson marched to kettle-drums and trumpets; Gibbon moved to flutes and hautboys.'

of your Matter, or the Extensiveness of your Learning, I must regard the Work as equally the Object of Esteem....' He added jokingly that, if he had not already had the happiness 'of your personal Acquaintance, such a Performance, from an Englishman in our Age, would have

* During the spring of 1760, Boswell had himself been briefly converted to the Catholic faith.

given me some Surprise. . . . It seems to me that your Countrymen, for almost a whole Generation, have given themselves up to barbarous and absurd Faction, and have totally neglected all polite Letters. . . .'

Just as Voltaire had praised the impartial – the 'simply judicial' – tone that Hume adopted in his *History*, so Hume applauded the cool deliberation with which he felt that Gibbon viewed his subject. Here, perhaps, he was somewhat over-partial. Though Gibbon's style is cool and calm and measured, strong emotions, even violent prejudices, frequently boil beneath the surface. As an agnostic, he could not recognize the sincerity, or appreciate the beauty, of a strongly-held religious faith; and, while he applauded the Empire of Antonine Rome,

Edward Gibbon; a caricature by Lady Diana Beauclerk.

which had once comprehended the fairest regions of the earth 'and the most civilized portion of mankind', protected by 'ancient renown and disciplined valour', and unified by the 'gentle but powerful influence of law and manners', he had nothing but contempt and disgust for the Holy City of Byzantium, which, he would have us believe, 'subsisted one thousand and fifty-eight years, in a state of premature and perpetual decay'.

The civilization of the Byzantine Empire offended Gibbon because, despite its many moral defects, it had remained profoundly Christian; and Gibbon, observes a modern critic,[20] was an eighteenth-century Humanist, determined to show 'that the dignity and nobility of the human spirit are possible only under conditions of political and spiritual freedom'. By temperament, Gibbon was no democrat; and the outbreak of the Revolution in France – an explosion of 'popular madness', he called it – would one day astonish and alarm him. But, like many contemporaries, he worshipped the idea of freedom, if not on the political, at least on the intellectual and the moral plane; and such a cult was deeply abhorrent to Johnson, who, having seen more of his fellow men, could not believe that they deserved their liberty, and had always supported the aristocratic principle and 'the grand scheme of subordination'.

Thus, Gibbon, from the moment his book appeared, was yet another noxious infidel, whom he was ready to demolish by any means he could. Boswell dreaded the historian's literary artifice: 'I said … he should have warned us of our danger, before we entered his garden of flowery eloquence, by advertising, "spring guns and man-traps set here"', and asserted that an infidel should 'not be treated handsomely by a Christian, merely because he endeavours to rob us with ingenuity. … I think ridicule may be fairly used against an infidel; for instance, if he be an ugly fellow, and yet absurdly vain of his person, we may contrast his appearance with Cicero's beautiful image of Virtue….' Johnson assented. Both were thinking of Gibbon, the stout, affectedly ceremonious little man, in his fashionable velvet coat.

Yet Johnson, as Mrs Thrale had observed, could, at times, be oddly 'ductile'; and Boswell had even persuaded him to dine at the same table as the notorious demagogue, John Wilkes. Their meeting took place at the Dillys' house on 15 May 1776; and Wilkes, having won his greatest battle, been elected Lord Mayor in 1774, and in 1775 returned to Parliament, which had once expelled him from its midst, was no longer a fire-breathing patriot. Yet the violent campaign he had launched in 1763, with a fierce criticism of the King's Speech, was still a fairly recent memory; nor had his opponents forgotten the 'Wilkite' riots of the Spring of 1768, when London streets had rung to the cry of 'Wilkes and Liberty', bonfires had blazed, windows were broken, and the mob had dragged an ambassador from his carriage and severely manhandled a passing duke.

The main issue involved was the freedom of the British press, which, Wilkes proclaimed, was 'the birthright of a Briton' and 'the firmest bulwark' of our national liberties. On this subject, Johnson, the inveterate Tory, had already discoursed at length to Boswell:

He talked in his usual style with a rough contempt of popular liberty. 'They make a rout about *universal* liberty without considering that all that is to be valued, or indeed can be enjoyed by individuals, is *private* liberty. Political liberty is good only as far as it produces private liberty. Now, Sir, there is the liberty of the press…. Suppose you and I and two hundred more were restrained from printing our thoughts: what then? What proportion would that restraint upon us bear to the private happiness of the nation?'

Later, in 1770, when Wilkes, after going into voluntary exile and suffering a period of not uncomfortable imprisonment, had been thrice re-elected to the House of Commons but refused admission by his fellow Members, who illegally seated the unsuccessful candidate, Johnson had published a pamphlet entitled *The False Alarm*, defending the government's outrageous attitude towards a major constitutional issue. All this he must have vividly remembered on 15 May 1776; and Boswell could persuade him to accept Edward Dilly's invitation only by employing an ingenious strategem:

JOHNSON. 'Sir, I am obliged to Mr Dilly. I will wait upon him – '
BOSWELL. 'Provided, Sir, I suppose, that the company which he is to have, is agreeable to you.' JOHNSON. 'What do you mean, Sir? What do you take me for? Do you think I am so ignorant of the world, as to imagine that I am to prescribe to a gentleman what company he is to have at his table?'

From that moment, it would have been hard to withdraw; and, once Boswell had managed to overcome the objections petulantly raised by Miss Williams, heard Johnson bellow, 'Frank, a clean shirt', and 'had him fairly seated in a hackney-coach', he 'exulted as much as a fortune-hunter who has got an heiress into a post-chaise ... to set out for Gretna Green.' The sight of Mr Arthur Lee, who 'was not only a *patriot* but an *American*', seated in Dilly's parlour, considerably disconcerted Johnson, and produced uneasy mutterings. 'And who', he next enquired, 'is the gentleman in lace?' 'Mr Wilkes, Sir', Boswell bravely replied – information that 'confounded him still more; he had some difficulty to restrain himself, and taking up a book, sat down in a window-seat and read, or at least kept his eye upon it intently for some time', until he had regained composure.

To have arranged this confrontation was one of Boswell's most brilliant and successful *coups*; and his account of the meeting, when he came to write the *Life*, exhibits all his talents as a literary chronicler. No abbreviated version can do the story justice. It must be enough to say that the rakish 'gentleman in lace', who was sitting beside Johnson, 'gained upon him insensibly', not only by his charm and good humour, but by the diplomatic attention that he paid to Johnson's appetite, carving for him succulent slices of veal, and offering him stuffing, gravy and a squeeze of orange – 'or the lemon, perhaps, have more zest'; at which Johnson bowed 'with a look for some time of "surly virtue", but, in a short while, of complacency'.

Nor did the conversation flag; they talked of Garrick and the comedian, Samuel Foote, of Colley Cibber and the art of biography; of Shakespeare and the present Duke of Argyle; of Horace and

Homer, Scots and Americans and Wilkes' old enemy, the Attorney General. It was an harmonious evening; and Johnson took no offence when Wilkes, an experienced *homme à femmes*, 'held a candle to shew a fine print of a beautiful female figure ... and pointed out the elegant contour of the bosom with the finger of an arch connoisseur'. All their differences were forgotten and forgiven. 'Jack', said Johnson a year later, 'has great variety of talk, Jack is a scholar, and Jack has the manners of a gentleman. . . . I could do Jack a kindness, rather than not. The contest is now over.'

With another adversary Johnson was less fortunate. From Boswell's biography we often gain the impression that his ascendancy was undisputed; but there were some who continued to deny his genius, and to question the critical authority that Johnson exercised in the world of modern letters. He did not please an aristocratic taste; and none of the *beau monde* found him more displeasing than the patrician dilettante Horace Walpole, a man who had arranged his own life to resemble an harmonious work of art, from which he had always done his best to banish every hint of discord.

For Walpole, we are assured by Boswell, his hero felt a mild regard, allowing 'that he got together a great many curious little things, and told them in an elegant manner'. But Walpole shared the views of Chesterfield, who, when he wrote of 'respectable Hottentots', was generally assumed to have had in mind the author of the *Dictionary*; and, unlike Chesterfield, he would never concede that Johnson possessed some intellectual merit, but wrote him off as merely a 'saucy Caliban', a typical representative of contemporary literature at its dullest and its least distinguished. 'Indolent Smollett! trifling Johnson! piddling Goldsmith!' he cried in February 1781, 'how little have they contributed to a period in which all arts, all sciences are encouraged and rewarded'.

Year after year, Walpole's complaints persist. Johnson is a 'sycophant old nurse' and 'a babbling old woman', whose life of Pope is a 'most trumpery performance ... stuffed with all his crabbed phrases and vulgarisms.... He seems to have read the ancients with no view but of pilfering polysyllables...'. The Dean of Derry appeared to have published a poetic retort to 'a gross brutality of Dr Johnson.... A properer answer', Walpole exclaimed, 'would have been to fling a

Right John Wilkes (1727–97), drawn from the life, and 'Etch'd in Aquafortis', by one of his bitterest opponents, William Hogarth, May 1763. 'Jack', decided his old adversary, Johnson, a year after their first meeting, 'is a scholar, and Jack has the manners of a gentleman ...'

glass of wine in his face. I have no patience with an unfortunate monster trusting to his helpless deformity for indemnity for any impertinence that his arrogance suggests, and who thinks that what he has read is an excuse for everything he says.'

Walpole had had many middle-class friends, notably his schoolfriend Thomas Gray. But he was sufficiently conscious of his own birth to resent this rough intruder, wearing rusty brown and black, who settled down with such ponderous self-assurance in Mrs Montagu's accomplished circle. Walpole had never visited Streatham; nor had he the smallest wish to do so. It was not the kind of milieu he usually cared to frequent; the rich brewer's huge and splendid meals, though they might be served on 'massy plate', were no substitute for elegant little breakfasts, accompanied by clarinets and French horns. Of Johnson's beloved hostess, after her second marriage, Walpole heard some vague reports. 'That ridiculous woman', he told a correspondent, to crown her foolish existence had now married 'an Italian fiddler'.

There were also deeper reasons for Walpole's dislike of Johnson; they belonged to different literary periods – Johnson to the neo-classic age, where Pope and Dryden still presided; while Walpole, however remotely and vaguely, had already been privileged to catch a glimpse of the Romantic Revolution, which, before the century had ended, would reveal a new heaven and a new earth. Johnson feared his dreams – 'the first corruption that entered into my heart was communicated in a dream', he had once told Mrs Thrale*; and it was from the world of sleep that the Romantics would draw some of their most moving visions.

Both Walpole's *Castle of Otranto* and William Beckford's *Vathek*, as the novelists themselves declared, were projections of their own dreams; and each is an attempt to overleap the barriers that surround our ordinary waking lives. Johnson, on the other hand, detested mystery, abhorred any kind of extravagance, whether emotional or intellectual, and believed that 'nothing odd will do long'. Because he dreaded death, and often looked forward with horror to the prospect of eternal punishment, he revolted angrily against any suggestion that the world he now inhabited was not supremely solid.

* '"What was it, Sir?" said I. "*Do* not ask me", replied he with much violence, and walked away in apparent agitation.' Piozzi: *Anecdotes*.

Right Horace Walpole (1717–97); engraving after Reynolds' portrait of 1757. Walpole dismissed Johnson as a 'sycophant old nurse' and a 'saucy Caliban'.

7 'The Horrour of the Last'

Mrs Thrale, as she frequently proclaimed, had never been a jealous wife; and Mr Thrale had made no attempt to appear a faithful husband. Then, towards the end of 1778, Thrale began to fall in love – this time not with an expensive kept woman, whom he would carry off to some 'Paphian bower' and there enjoy in peace and quietude, but with one of his wife's friends, an attractive, decorous, highly-accomplished girl, only twenty-four years old. Her name was Sophia Streatfield. Although her widowed mother had both a London house and a country house near Tonbridge, she spent a good deal of her life travelling; and the Thrales were friends she often visited. Every member of Hester Thrale's entourage admired 'the charming S.S.'; her beauty, her gentleness and her knowledge of Greek and Latin appeared equally remarkable. Moreover, despite her erudition, she was extraordinarily good-natured.

Mrs Thrale had first encountered the Streatfields at Brightelmstone in the autumn of 1777, having previously heard that she and Sophia Streatfield had been educated by the same tutor – the eccentric Dr Arthur Collier, a learned and kindly man, but so perverse and odd that, if he were pressed to talk 'on some Critical or Metaphysical Subject', he would immediately proceed to expatiate 'on the skill of curing Hams, or making Minced Pyes, or say what pains he had taken to invent an universal Pickle'. As Sophia Streatfield's guide to the classics, he had unquestionably done his work well; and not only had he taught her the dead languages, but he had also reared her 'in the strictest Principles of Piety & Virtue'.

Such was Sophy's charm and the 'attractive Sweetness' of her manner, 'which claims and promises to repay one's confidence', that she had soon elicited from Mrs Thrale 'the secret of my keeping a Thraliana to deposit all kinds of Nonsense in'. Before long she had been allowed to see the book; and, when its authoress opened a new volume, Sophy displayed her penmanship and her command of the gothic script by adding an exquisitely lettered title. Thenceforward Mrs Thrale's pages are thickly scattered with affectionate references to her new friend. The Streatham circle was fond of parlour-games; and in December 1778, we read, they amused themselves 'with Goldsmith's Idea of everybody's being like some Dish of Meat...'. Johnson, they then agreed, was a solid haunch of venison; William Seward, a ham; Sir Philip Jennings, a roasted sweetbread; and Miss Streatfield, a white fricassee.

Later, in February 1779, they decided that all their closest friends could be likened to a silk and colour. Fanny Burney resembled 'a lilac Tabby'; Mrs Thrale, 'a gold-Colour'd Watered Tabby'; the delicate Miss Streatfield, 'a pea Green Satten'; while Johnson, 'who helped this folly foward', recalled a sober chestnut-brown fabric. 'The next Nonsense was Flowers'; and here Fanny Burney was a modest buttercup, and Sophy figured as a jasmine. In Mrs Thrale's careful evaluation of her friend's qualities, Sophy received twenty marks for 'Worth of Heart'; ten for 'Conversation Powers'; sixteen for 'Person, Mien & Manner'; twenty for 'Good Humour'; and twelve for 'Ornamental Knowledge'. Though for 'Useful Knowledge' she was awarded none at all, she achieved a particularly high score, being outdistanced only by Lady Frances Bourgoyne and a certain Fanny Brown, of whom we know comparatively little, except that, in 1779, she 'scampered off with a Cornet of Horse', and that Johnson once complained that her treatment of him had been 'very cruel'.

At Streatham, both Dr Burney and his daughter found 'the S.S.' strangely captivating; and to the Doctor was attributed a copy of verses, published in a daily paper, which sang the praise of well-bred English beauties, as opposed to the disreputable heroines whom the *Morning Herald* often celebrated, and, besides eulogizing Mrs Thrale herself –

> Thrale, in whose expressive eyes
> Sits a soul above disguise

referred appreciatively to Miss Streatfield –

> Smiling Streatfield's iv'ry neck,
> Nose, and notions – *à la Grecque*!

Fanny's earliest meeting with this female paragon occurred on 13 June, while she was paying a visit to the Thrales:

After church, we all strolled round the grounds, and the topic of our discourse was Miss Streatfield. Mrs Thrale asserted that she had a power of captivation that was irresistible; that her beauty, joined to her softness, her caressing manners, her tearful eyes and alluring looks, would insinuate her into the heart of any man she thought worth attacking.

Sir Philip [Jennings Clerke] declared himself of a totally different opinion, and quoted Dr Johnson against her, who had told him that, taking away her Greek, she was ignorant as a butterfly.

Next morning, at the breakfast table, Fanny witnessed a scene, 'of its sort, the most curious I ever saw'. Among Miss Streatfield's well-advertised accomplishments was the art of weeping beautifully; and Mrs Thrale, not perhaps without a shade of malice, had urged her to display her gift. 'Yes, do cry a little, Sophy', she begged her in a 'wheedling' tone, 'pray do! Consider now, you are going today, and it's very hard if you won't cry a little; indeed, S.S., you ought to cry.' The S.S. was far too good-mannered a young woman not to fall in with her hostess' wishes:

When Mrs Thrale, in a coaxing voice, suited to a nurse soothing a baby, had run on for some time ... two crystal tears came into the soft eyes of the S.S., and rolled gently down her cheeks! ... She offered not to conceal or dissipate them: on the contrary, she really contrived to have them seen by everybody. She looked indeed uncommonly handsome; for her pretty face was not ... blubbered; it was smooth and elegant, and neither her features nor her complexion were at all ruffled; nay, indeed, she was smiling all the time....

Loud and rude bursts of laughter broke from us.... Yet we all stared, and looked and re-looked again, twenty times, ere we could believe our eyes. Sir Philip, I thought, would have died in convulsions; for his laughter and his politeness, struggling furiously with one another, made him almost black in the face.

Later that year, Fanny was privileged to meet the S.S. at her country home. Travelling with the Thrales on an expedition to Bath, she was taken to visit Mrs Streatfield, a very small woman, 'but perfectly well made, thin, genteel and delicate ... very lively, and an excellent mimic'. Mrs Streatfield was clearly a born actress; 'she has a kind of whimsical conceit, and odd affectation, that, joined to a very singular sort of humour, makes her always seem to be rehearsing some scene in a comedy. She takes off ... all her own children, and, though she quite adores them, renders them ridiculous. . . .' Thanks to this treatment, the sensitive S.S., at least in Mrs Thrale's opinion, did not really love her mother; though she was 'Dutyful & attentive ... 'tis done to please God & not herself'. But then, Mrs Thrale, whose feelings for the daughter were becoming somewhat mixed, had no great liking for her parent: 'How should she love a silly, drunken, old painted Puss Cat? ... To confer Benefits will seldom procure Affection; one must either give Pleasure, or enforce Esteem.'

Meanwhile, Mrs Thrale was gradually becoming aware of her husband's significant sighs and glances. It was during the summer of 1778 that Mrs Thrale drew up her list of qualities; in December, recollecting how she and her friends had once compared the S.S. to a white fricassee, she added: 'Sophy Streatfield will make a *Brown Fricassee* of me soon – I see, I see, my Husband is in Love with her!' A more detailed note was committed to *Thraliana* on 10 January 1779. Mr Thrale, she wrote, had 'fallen in love *really and seriously* ...'. This was scarcely surprising. The S.S. was 'very pretty, very gentle, soft & insinuating'. She hung about him, cried when they parted, slyly squeezed his hand and gazed 'so fondly in his Face – & all for *Love of me* as she pretends; that I can hardly sometimes help laughing ...'.

When, after an enjoyable Christmas party, the S.S. was obliged to quit Streatham, her new admirer, as he bade her goodbye, appeared pitiably disconsolate. 'My poor Master', Mrs Thrale observed, 'is left to pine for his fair Sophia', whom he would have no opportunity of seeing again until the next session of Parliament allowed him to return to London, and he could spend every evening at the Streatfields' house in Clifford Street, while his carriage awaited him opposite his sister's door – 'that no enquirer', his wife remarked acidly, 'might hurt his favourite's reputation ...'.

Mrs Thrale herself had now begun to fret; but neither Johnson nor Murphy, she noted, gave the slightest sign of disapproving. Johnson, who invariably hesitated to criticize Mr Thrale, and who believed that a virtuous wife should always countenance her husband's whims, made a little joke upon the subject – he had heard, he said, that Mr Thrale lived in Clifford Street throughout the winter; and Murphy, Mrs Thrale supposed, "approves my silent and patient endurance of what I could not prevent by more rough & sincere Behaviour'; for men invariably 'admire a Woman who tho' jealous does not rave about it ...'.

Hitherto, she had managed to keep her jealousy – her first experience of that horrid disease – under fairly strict control. But, on rare occasions, she was apt to drop the mask – for example, at a large dinner-party where, as hostess, she was sitting between Burke and Johnson; and Mr Thrale, 'very unceremoniously', suggested that she should give up her place to Sophy, 'who was threatened with a sore throat', and whose health might perhaps be imperilled by sitting uncomfortably near the door. At the time, Mrs Thrale was once again *enceinte*, 'and dismally low-spirited'. Hearing her husband's thoughtless request, she burst into tears, 'said something petulant', and rose and hastened to the drawing-room.

There Burke and Johnson eventually joined her; and she resolved to give them 'a *jobation*'. Of Johnson she demanded whether he had noted the incident and, given the present state of her nerves, if he considered she was much to blame? Johnson temporized. 'Why, possibly not', he replied; 'your feelings were outraged.' Mrs Thrale, however, declined to be put off: 'I said, "Yes, greatly so"', and added, moreover, that she could not help observing 'with what blandness and composure you *witnessed* the outrage'. Had this story been told of someone else, his anger surely would have known no bounds; 'but, towards a man who gives good dinners &c, you were meekness itself'. Her indignant outburst produced the effect she desired; 'Johnson coloured, and Burke, I thought, looked foolish. . . .' It was an occasion that she often remembered, particularly after Thrale's death, when her attitude towards her old friend had become a great deal less indulgent. Johnson, she wrote, 'was, on the whole, a rigid moralist; but, at times, he could be ductile' – she might even say, 'servile'.

Both in Thrale's autumnal passion for the S.S. and in Miss Streatfield's juvenile affection for her host, as Mrs Thrale no doubt perceived, there was an element of tragedy. An aura of doom, of hopes frustrated and promises unfulfilled, seems to hover around every beauty's head. Though well aware of the precious gift she owned, the S.S. was perpetually uncertain how she should dispose of it; and after a long series of fruitless conquests, which included 'Bishops, & Brewers, & Directors of the East India Company' – even 'poor dear Dr Burney', whose infatuation sadly vexed his children – she was destined to die, still irreproachable and still unmarried, at the age of eighty-one. No less pathetic was Henry Thrale's plight. Since Harry's death only two years earlier, he had lived a life of gluttonous indifference, which may have helped him to forget his loss. Now, suddenly smitten by romantic love, he had begun yet again to feel and suffer.

As for Mrs Thrale, her emotions varied daily; and she alternated between moods of good-humoured cynicism and moments of the deepest gloom. The situation had certainly a comic side. It was ludicrous enough to see the S.S. seated modestly beside her host, recommending that he should read Spenser's poems, not a single word of which she could repeat; horribly painful, however, from an older woman's point of view, to reflect that, were she herself to die during her next unwanted pregnancy, the S.S., young and fresh and beautiful, would probably succeed her in her husband's bed.

Meanwhile, there was evidently no question of the young woman becoming Thrale's mistress. She had not observed 'with any *Pleasure*', wrote Mrs Thrale in January 1780, that her husband now preferred 'Miss Streatfield to *me*, tho' I must acknowledge her both Younger, handsomer, & a better Scholar'; but of her chastity she had 'never had a doubt.... She not only knows She *will* always be Chaste, but she knows *why* She will be so....'

Thus, the S.S. continued to guard her virtue – faced with a strictly modest girl, Thrale may have been an ineffective lover; and, eventually, it was the breakdown of his own health, rather than Miss Streatfield's virtuous resistance, that brought his courtship to an end. The doctors, who had warned Thrale against immoderate eating, proved to have diagnosed his case correctly. On 8 June 1779, he experienced his first stroke as he sat at dinner with his sister, and was carried home 'apparently Paralytick'. The seizure passed; and, by 22 June, Dr Heberden thought him 'wholly out of Danger'. But, privately, Mrs Thrale suspected that he would have 'another of these strokes *some-time*'. Nor were her suspicions unfounded. That autumn, having caught a severe chill, he temporarily lost the power of speech; and in February 1780, he was once more struck down, 'with another Stroke of the Apoplexy or Palsy or some dreadful Thing!'

Even now, although his family often despaired, the sufferer himself did not entirely lose hope. He had 'such a Desire of Life', Mrs Thrale reported; his romantic passion burned as bright as ever; and, just two days before he was taken ill, he had sat next to his beloved amid a crowded evening party, and, pressing her hand to his heart – it was Miss Streatfield who afterwards told the tale – exclaimed, 'Sophy, we shall not enjoy this long, and tonight I will not be cheated of my *only comfort*.' Listening to Sophy's ingenuous account of the episode, Mrs Thrale was genuinely moved; 'Poor Soul!' she commented, 'how shockingly tender!'

He showed the same tenderness while he was recovering from his stroke, and saw the faithful S.S. near his bed. 'Oh says he "who would not suffer even all that I have endured, to be pitied by *you*!".' Other members of his family who were attending him, and 'had never been treated with a kind Word', felt naturally a little put out; but his wife, since she had ceased to expect gratitude and knew his cool, phlegmatic ways, 'thought it rather good', she assures us, 'that he had *some* Sensibility for *some* human Being'.

Thrale passed his convalescence at Bath, attended by Mrs Thrale and Fanny Burney. There they remained until the early days of June, and thus escaped the terrifying explosion of the bloody Gordon Riots, which paralysed London for a whole week, between 2 June and 9 June 1780*. On 6 June, the anti-Papist mob, which had already broken into Newgate Gaol, released the prisoners and fired the prison, appeared at Thrale's brewery, dragging the chains that they had captured. 'Nothing but the astonishing Presence of Mind shewed by Perkins', Thrale's invaluable chief clerk, 'in amusing the Mob with Meat & Drink & Huzzaes', and offering them the service of a dray-horse to help them carry off their booty, saved the fabric from complete destruction**. Langdales' distillery near Holborn was a great deal less fortunate. Vats were broached; the warehouse went up in flames; many of the rioters were shot or bayoneted, or drank themselves to death on the cobblestones as they lapped up the escaping flood of spirits.

It was news of the dissolution of Parliament that, at length, recalled the Thrales to Streatham. Early in September, during the General Election that followed, Thrale courageously began his canvass; but, after a few days, the effort exhausted him; and, on Sunday morning, at a service in the parish church, his wife was dismayed to behold him 'seized with such Illness as made him look a perfect Corpse in full View of an immense Congregation assembled to see the Gentlemen who wished to represent them'. Although he soon rallied, and re-appeared at the hustings 'amidst the deafening Acclammations of his Friends', Thrale knew that he had lost the day; and, reluctantly, he was obliged to concede the election before the final votes were counted. Nevertheless, he soon regained his calm; his 'Desire of Life' had not yet weakened; and, for the winter season of 1781, he engaged a splendid furnished house in Grosvenor Square.

Mrs Thrale had done her best to dissuade him – she dreaded the unnecessary expense; but he, 'Dear Creature',.she lamented, was 'as absolute' as he had always been, 'ay and ten Times more so ... since he suspects his Head to be suspected...'. Nor would he pay the slight-est attention to his doctors' joint advice. He still ate and drank with his usual frantic greed; and, at the end of September 1780, when the defeated candidate had temporarily retired to Streatham, Samuel Crisp describes a mangificent dinner-party in the Thrales' palatial 'Eating

* The Thrales left Bath for Brighthelmstone on 10 June, when a report appeared in a local newspaper, asserting that Henry Thrale was a secret Papist.

** Mrs Thrale estimated the value of the property they might then have lost as £150,000. The Gordon Riots had been provoked by a bill, passed two years earlier, that allowed some small relief to Catholics in matters of education and the right to hold property. As President of the Protestant Association, Lord George Gordon, a religious enthusiast, afterwards converted to the Jewish faith, had helped to whip up public feeling.

Parlour', which included 'two courses of 21 Dishes each, besides Removes'*, succeeded by 'a dessert of a piece with the Dinner – Pines and Fruits of all Sorts, Ices, Creams, &c., &c., &c.', every dish being served on massy plate.

Thrale's unbridled appetite continued to alarm his friends throughout the spring of 1781; and on 2 April, at the house in Grosvenor Square, when the guests were Johnson, Baretti and Sir Philip Jennings Clerke, 'Mr Thrale eat voraciously – *so* voraciously' that his wife felt that she must try to check him; and Johnson added, 'Sir, after the denunciation of your physicians this morning, such eating is little better than suicide!' Yet Thrale refused to lay down his knife and fork; even Johnson's 'remarkable words' had no effect upon the stubborn gourmand. Next day, Thrale was in excellent spirits. 'He eat however more than enormously', washing down a long succession of dishes with heavy draughts of strong beer, until 'the very Servants were frighted'; and the Thrales' favourite medical adviser, Sir Lucas Pepys, having arrived at Grosvenor Square to pay his customary visit, announced firmly that 'this could not last'. Thrale would succumb, unless he were committed to a private mad-house; 'either there must be *legal* Restraint or certain Death'.

The moment of retribution descended even sooner than Sir Lucas feared. The same evening, Queeney visited her father in his room, and found him lying on the floor. 'What's the meaning of this?' she cried 'in an Agony'; but Mr Thrale was unaccustomed to being questioned by his children; and he gave a short, dismissive answer. 'I choose it', he replied sternly, 'I lie so o'purpose'; and, when Queeney hastened to fetch a servant, he no less sternly sent the man away. Sir Lucas was followed and recalled; but, before he reappeared, Thrale was already in the throes of 'a most violent fit of the Apoplexy from which he only recovered to relapse into another...'.

Meanwhile, Johnson, who had hurried to Grosvenor Square, was sitting beside Thrale's bed, and watching his 'strong convulsions' gradually grow weaker as his strength began to ebb away. About five o'clock on the morning of Wednesday, he afterwards wrote among his *Prayers and Meditations*, 'I felt almost the last flutter of his pulse, and looked for the last time upon the face that for fifteen years had never been turned upon me but with respect or benignity....'

It was a double blow; in Henry Thrale, Johnson had lost not only a beloved friend – a man whose solid merits, he felt, far outnumbered

*'The act of taking away a dish or dishes. ... Hence a dish thus removed, or brought on in place of one removed': *Oxford English Dictionary*. 'A dish to be changed while the rest of the course remains': *Johnson's Dictionary*. During the eighteenth century, the number of 'removes' indicated the splendour of the meal.

a few venial errors – but the dignified pivot of a household that had become the mainstay of his own life. Changes were bound to follow; and Boswell suggests that, although Johnson 'did not foresee all that afterwards happened', he may have experienced some dark misgivings– he was 'sufficiently convinced that the comforts which Mr Thrale's family afforded him, would now in a great measure cease'. But he 'continued', Boswell adds, 'to shew a kind attention to his widow'; and Mrs Thrale gave not the slightest sign that his attentions were no longer welcome. During the previous year, she had mentioned him with peculiar tenderness in the pages of her commonplace book. Recently, she wrote, they happened to have been much apart; yet 'our mutual Regard does not decay ... how should it?' founded as it was on 'Religion, Virtue, & Community of Ideas'. Once 'my master' had finally removed his support, she more than ever needed Johnson.

Among the other qualities she had always admired was his un-expected grasp of business. Thrale had left behind him a carefully-drawn-up will, in which, apart from a series of small bequests (including a legacy of £200 to Johnson) he divided his substantial fortune between his widow and his daughters. Mrs Thrale would receive a yearly income of £2,000 if she elected to retain the brewery; should the brewery be sold, the lump sum of £30,000. She decided to sell; and, as one of the executors of Thrale's estate, Johnson proved a shrewd assistant. He immensely enjoyed performing the role of energetic modern businessman; and on the day of the sale (Lord Lucan informed Boswell) he 'appeared bustling about, with an ink-horn and pen in his button-hole ...'. Asked what he considered the real value of the property to be disposed of, he gave a characteristically sententious answer: 'We are not here to sell a parcel of boilers and vats, but the potentiality of growing rich, beyond the dreams of avarice.'

The purchasers were John Perkins, the Thrales' resourceful head-clerk, and a London banker, David Barclay, who agreed to pay £135,000, over a period of four years. Mrs Thrale was relieved to throw off her 'Golden Millstone' – and, being a direct descendant of the noble Adam of Salzburg, equally relieved to sever her connection with the odious world of commerce. 'I long to salute You', she wrote a friend, 'in my restored Character of a Gentlewoman' – a gentle-woman, too, both adequately rich and still relatively young and handsome. Her friends imagined that she was certain to marry again; there were those who boldly conjectured that she might now proceed to marry Johnson; and, the day after her husband's burial at Streatham, Boswell produced a collection of singularly unattractive stanzas, *Ode by Samuel Johnson to Mrs Thrale upon their supposed approaching nuptials*, which he handed round among their intimates.

Johnson, however, did not disclose his feelings; he merely wished 'my mistress' to be happy; and whatever seemed likely to promote her happiness he accepted with complete approval. Throughout the summer months, her spirits had remained low; and early that autumn she was temporarily afflicted with an irritating nervous rash. Thus, when Johnson heard that a gifted Italian acquaintance, Signor Gabriel Piozzi, Queeney's one-time music-master, whom he knew that Mrs Thrale liked, was due shortly to return to London, he expressed the warmest satisfaction. He himself was then away in Staffordshire; but, as soon as '*he* comes and *I* come', Johnson wrote, 'you will have two

Vauxhall gardens, 1784; a drawing by Thomas Rowlandson. The singer is Madame Weischel; Johnson, Boswell and Mrs Thrale, all grossly caricatured, are seated in a supper-box. To their left stands Wilkes quizzing the assembly.

about you that love you'; though no one could love her better, he said, or honour her more than her devoted old friend. Content in his own love, absorbed in his own emotions which brimmed and overflowed his heart, Johnson appears never to have suspected that he might one day have a rival.

Yet a rival was already materializing, even before the death of Henry Thrale; and, like most rivals, he came under a harmless guise, from an entirely unexpected quarter. The attachment that now preoccupied Mrs Thrale had originally sprung up at Brighthelmstone, whither the Thrales had gone in July 1780, to enjoy the benefits of sea-air, and Piozzi, the well-known musician, to stage a series of impromptu concerts. But their first friendly encounter, on the threshold of a local bookshop, had been preceded, in 1777 or 1778, by a very different introduction – at Dr Burney's London house, where Mrs Thrale, far from admiring Piozzi, had positively held him up to ridicule, until the good Doctor, always a considerate host, had found it necessary to intervene.

Dr Burney's disastrous musical evening was long remembered by his children; and, in the *Memoirs of Dr Burney* that Fanny subsequently put together, this remarkable soirée would provide the material for a particularly felicitous piece of comic narrative*. Dr Burney had undertaken to arrange the party at the request of his early patron, Fulke Greville, who, elsewhere, on a different social plane, had often heard his friend, Topham Beauclerk, applauding Samuel Johnson's virtues, and had lately signified a polite desire to make the acquaintance of the Streatham circle. So, that evening, Johnson arrived with the Thrales; Greville, with his wife, authoress of a well-known *Ode to Indifference*, and his fashionable daughter, Mrs Crewe.

He himself was eminently a man of fashion; but, owing to unlucky gambling 'at the clubs and on the turf', his pristine splendour was growing somewhat tarnished; while Mrs Greville, once a distinguished *élégante*, had lost a good deal of her former beauty, 'from the excessive thinness that had given to her erst fine and most delicate small features, a cast of sharpness so keen and meagre, that, joined to the shrewdly intellectual expression of her countenance, made her seem fitted to sit for a portrait... of a penetrating, puisant, and sarcastic fairy queen'. Only Mrs Crewe looked fresh and sleek and young, with her clear roseate complexion and 'her happy and justly poised *embonpoint*...'.

Both the Grevilles and the blooming Mrs Crewe evidently expected homage; but none was much inclined to talk. The ladies sat back, surveying the middle-class company; and Mr Greville, superb and stately as ever, planted himself upon the hearth, coolly examining the 'leviathan of literature', who, since he seldom troubled to open a dialogue, but preferred to seize upon a line of talk once it was already

---

* See Virginia Woolf's essay, 'Dr Burney's Musical Party' in *The Common Reader. Second Series*, a delightful adaptation of Fanny Burney's narrative, with some picturesque details added.

under way, confronted him in philosophic silence. Mrs Thrale, however, observing Mr Greville's patrician stares, soon became extremely restive. He might trace his descent from a line of Brookes and Grevilles; 'but she had a glowing consciousness that her own blood, rapid and fluent, flowed in her veins from Adam of Salzburg'; and her rebellious spirits 'rose ... above her control'.

Meanwhile, Dr Burney, embarrassed by his taciturn guests, had decided that the time had come for music. Piozzi had been engaged to harmonize the gathering; but, soon after he had made his bow and taken his place at the keyboard, she rose and softly stole behind him, just as he was in the midst of 'an animated *arria parlante*', and 'ludicrously began imitating him by squaring her elbows, elevating them with ecstatic shrugs of the shoulders', and wildly casting up her eyes. 'This grotesque ebullition of ungovernable gaiety', we are told, 'was not perceived by Dr Johnson.' But Dr Burney was profoundly shocked; and, gliding around to Mrs Thrale, 'with something between pleasantry and severity', begged she would at once desist.

It was now [writes Fanny Burney] that shone the brightest attribute of Mrs Thrale, sweetness of temper. She took this rebuke with a candour, and a sense of its justice the most amiable: she nodded her approbation ... and, returning to her chair, quietly sat down, as she afterwards said, like a pretty little miss, for the remainder of one of the most humdrum evenings that she had ever passed.

This was an encounter that she had certainly not forgotten when she and Piozzi next came face to face. Nor had Piozzi forgotten that terrible soirée. On hearing her claim acquaintance at the Brighthelmstone bookshop, he had been distinctly cold and unresponsive; but Mrs Thrale had refused to accept the snub, and had soon persuaded him, not only to sing at her house, but to undertake the musical training of her cultivated eldest daughter. She herself had never been versed in music; but she found his talents strangely inspiring, even curiously disquieting; 'his Hand on the Forte Piano' was 'so soft, so sweet, so delicate', that 'every Tone goes to one's heart ... and fills the Mind with Emotions one would not be without, though inconvenient enough sometimes'.

Thereafter, she renewed her friendly attentions; and, in December, 'that delightful Mortal Piozzi' had joined a house-party at Streatham Place, where, as the house was full of young people, he condescended, 'for the 1st Time of his Life', to amuse them by playing country dances. Later, he appeared at Grosvenor Square; and a woman friend, who heard him sing and play, sharply exclaimed, 'You know, I suppose, that that Man is in Love with you'; to which Mrs Thrale, having more immediate problems – this was on 2 April, the day before her husband's final stroke – merely answered, 'I am too irritated to care who is in Love with me'; and there the matter was allowed to rest.

Piozzi, however, had constantly haunted her mind during the weary and gloomy weeks that followed. Though Johnson might comfort and reassure, he alone could touch her heart, and bring back thoughts of youth and happiness. In April 1781, Gabriel Mario Piozzi was a man of nearly forty-one, a robust, dignified, good-looking person with a high intelligent forehead, a large well-shaped, slightly aquiline nose, and a neatly modelled mouth and chin. It was a sensitive rather than a sensuous face; Piozzi was no crafty Italian adventurer, of the kind then often to be found wandering round Northern Europe. Born in the Veneto, the son of a large middle-class family who had expected he would become a priest, he had left them to study music at Milan; but, discovering that his voice lacked sufficient strength for success upon the operatic stage, he had eventually made his way to England, where, despite the insolence of some of his noble patrons – at a famous country-house he visited he was so teased by hostile guests and servants that he was obliged to barricade his bedroom door – he had quickly made his mark among the *cognoscenti*. Though Piozzi's voice might be small, it is described as sweet and nicely trained; and Dr Burney, a keen supporter of his gifts, would declare, in his usual generous way, that listening to Piozzi had first taught him 'what good singing was'.

He had not been spoiled by success. There seems no doubt that Gabriel Piozzi had a sensitive, warm-hearted nature. Clearly, he responded to Mrs Thrale's attachment, which she was soon displaying with all her customary brio; but it is no less clear that he was also a little alarmed; and, after Thrale's death, he rapidly decided that his safest plan would be to leave England, until Mrs Thrale's emotions, and the excitement they aroused in her inquisitive friends, had had time to settle down. Thus, he announced that he must visit his aged parents and, having paid his admirer a ceremonious Italian farewell, quietly took his departure in the early days of July.

The move was ill-judged; Piozzi's absence served merely to accentuate Mrs Thrale's disturbing passion. Her health suffered. At the beginning of September, she records that she is now 'erisypelatous, & scorbutic, & I know not what'; in October, that she had become 'excessively anxious'. Then, before the close of November, 'I have got my Piozzi home at last', she writes. Alas, the poor man looked 'thin & battered, but always kindly upon me I think'. That winter, he was again a housemate, with her eldest daughter as his pupil. Johnson, too, had safely returned to Streatham, and was once more tutoring Queeney in the classics.

It was a moment of general relief; and Mrs Thrale's resolutions for the New Year were appropriately wise and firm. She regretted to hear that 'poor dear Doctor Burney' had become Miss Streatfield's latest victim. But 'let me not', she added, while censuring the Behaviour of others ... give Cause of Censure by my own...'. She was starting the year in a new character, which she trusted she could support with dignity. She must be careful not to alienate her daughters

Gabriel Maro Piozzi (1740–1809); drawing by George Dance, 1793. He united, said his wife, 'the Spirit of a Gentleman with the talents of a Professor'.

by seeming too severe and 'rigid', and herself must not appear 'wild, & give them Reason to lament the Levity of my Life'. Resolutions, however, were vain – we could only pray, she wrote, for God's grace; and none of the good intentions she announced on New Year's Day was destined to outlast the summer. Piozzi's gentle presence proved even more unnerving than his previous six-months' absence. She could not escape from her growing infatuation, which soon possessed her heart and soul. It was no pleasing romantic whim she felt, but a ravening appetite that had both engaged her emotions and painfully involved her senses.

Hitherto she had affected to despise love. 'My Peace has never been disturbed by the *soft Passion*', she had claimed in 1777; and it seems improbable that Henry Thrale's embraces had satisfied her very deeply. If Piozzi was the lover she had long been denied, or had prudently denied herself, she also cast him for the fatherly rôle that had hitherto been played by Johnson. But, whereas Johnson, at their earliest encounter, was already fifty-five, she and Gabriel Piozzi had entered the world within the same twelve months; and Piozzi, at the age of forty-one, was still comparatively young and vigorous. On meeting him again, she had made a significant note: 'he is amazingly like my Father'. And this chance resemblance – no doubt it was largely physical; in character, no two men could have been less alike than the mild Piozzi and the rough, ill-tempered Salusbury – may have provided the secret point of attraction around which her feelings slowly crystallized.

Meanwhile, she did not forget Johnson. He remained her 'Friend, Guardian, Confident'; and, were she to lose him, she declared in February 1782, her condition would indeed be desperate. In April, Robert Levett had died, greatly lamented by his old protector; and, in May, Johnson himself was 'so very ill' that she bore him off to Streatham Place. That autumn, having decided that, for reasons of economy, it was advisable to let her country house*, she moved her family to Brighthelmstone. Johnson accompanied them; and, early in October, he dined at Streatham for the last time. He bade the beloved house and the neighbouring church, where he had so often worshipped, a pathetic farewell. It affected him strongly – as he had once written in *The Rambler*, he had a 'secret horrour of the last'; and, when he arrived at Brighthelmstone, he was gloomy and dispirited. Fanny Burney, a fellow guest, observed that he was sadly out of temper – so irascible that his sudden explosions of wrath were apt to drive away their friends. Dr Delap was actually afraid to visit them; 'poor Mr Pepys' had been treated with such severity that he had seized his hat and 'walked out of the room in the middle of the discourse . . .'.

Mrs Thrale, too, had become increasingly irritable; under the strain of a passion she could not disguise, all the patience she had shown in

* It was let for three years to the famous politician, Lord Shelburne, who needed a *pied-à-terre* near London.

her married life was gradually deserting her. Johnson continued to love and trust 'my mistress'; but, exasperated by the old man's quirks and oddities, his rudeness and greed and the offensive table-manners that had evidently grown worse with age, Mrs Thrale was beginning to regard him from a far less sympathetic point of view.

Soon the unworthiest suspicions crossed her mind. Had not his professed attachment been 'merely an interested one'? True, she believed that Johnson had really loved her husband; in her, she felt, all he had ever needed was 'a careful Nurse & humble Friend for his sick and his lounging hours'. She had formerly imagined that he enjoyed her conversation. Today she suspected that 'he cares more for my roast Beef & plumb Pudden which he now devours too dirtily for endurance...'. When she talked of 'going abroad – her latest plan was to 'shew Italy to my Girls, and be shewed it by Piozzi' – Johnson seemed surprisingly reluctant to join them on a foreign tour. Although she had not yet issued a definite invitation, he had told Queeney that, were she to ask him, he would undoubtedly refuse to go.

Piozzi, however, had behaved 'like an Angel, he will go with us, or follow after us, or any thing...'. To treat such a man unkindly, she must be a monster of ingratitude; but the danger, she added, was surely 'on the *other* Side' – that she might allow her affection for Piozzi to exceed all proper limits. Until now, except for an occasional pleasantry, even her closest friends had remained discreetly silent; though 'that little discerning Creature Fanny says I'm in love with Piozzi', she recorded at the end of August. Fanny's remark had provoked a lengthy interior debate as to why she should, or should not marry. Piozzi, she argued, was both amiable and honourable, above her in understanding, despite their inequality in birth.

In that respect, he was certainly below her; but then, 'so is almost every man I know...'. At the same time, he 'united warm notions of Honour, with cool attention to Oeconomy; the Spirit of a Gentleman with the talents of a Professor'. Had her first husband come of a more distinguished family? Yet it was Mrs Salusbury who had made the match. Having married for the first time to please her mother, should she marry now to please her daughters? Since, in the past, she had 'always sacrificed my own Choice', was it reasonable to expect that she should sacrifice it yet again? As to her five daughters, how would such a marriage injure either their morals or their financial prospects? Piozzi was a virtuous and upright man; and each now possessed an independent fortune.

In the meantime, she determined to 'resolve on nothing ... take a Voyage to the Continent; enlarge my Knowledge, & repose my Purse'.

But once more her resolutions failed. When November came, and she was still at Brighthelmstone, Queeney, noticing that her mother looked ill, chose to 'force me to an explanation'. She could have avoided it; but 'my heart was bursting', she writes; and, partly from an instinctive desire to unload her feelings, but also partly from a sense of duty, 'I called her into my Room & fairly told her the Truth', describing 'the strength of my Passion for Piozzi', the impossibility of living without him, 'the opinion I had of his Merit, & the Resolution I had taken to marry him'. Queeney, who, her mother thought, 'could not have been ignorant before', seemed as usual calm and clear-headed. Piozzi himself was called in, quickly followed by 'my own Bosom Friend, my beloved Fanny Burney', who happened to be visiting them, and whose 'Skill in Life and Manners is superior to that of any Man or Woman in this Age or Nation . . .' . From Fanny Burney, however, Mrs Thrale expected little help. She knew that Fanny was already deeply prejudiced against her friend's outrageous plan.

Once Mrs Thrale had fairly told the truth, and even her disapproving daughter had been admitted to her confidence, she could no longer hope for mercy. None of her circle approved; and particularly stern in her attitude was the eldest Miss Thrale. Even as a child, this formidable young woman had been strangely unaffectionate; and, during adolescence, she had managed to acquire an almost alarming degree of self-possession. When Reynolds painted her, sitting at her mother's knee, she was only fifteen; but it is Queeney, with her reddish short-cut hair, her small pursed mouth and her coolly determined eyes, who somehow dominates the portrait. By comparison, Mrs Thrale herself looks surprisingly remote and pensive. Though Queeney is gazing up at her mother, whose hand rests lightly on her arm, their relationship seems oddly formal. Queeney is deep in her own thoughts; and she has her own opinion – not necessarily a very high opinion – of the parent she is studying.

At nineteen, she was fully prepared for life, and had developed both a keen sense of her personal importance and an iron-clad sense of right and wrong. She had never liked her mother – such affection as she possessed had, no doubt, been spent upon her father; and, though Mrs Thrale admired and respected Queeney, she had always found her difficult to love. If Queeney had but 'made herself more amiable to me', and had taken 'the proper Methods', she wrote in the autumn of 1783, she might well have given up her dear Italian. Queeny, however, despite her determination to do her best, was plainly the reverse of amiable and, by refusing the sympathy that her love-stricken mother demanded, drove her back towards Piozzi. He,

Mrs Thrale (1741–1821) and her eldest daughter, 'Queeney', by Sir Joshua
Reynolds. 'It is Queeney . . . who somehow dominates the portrait. By comparison,
Mrs Thrale herself looks surprisingly remote and pensive.'

at least, was unfailingly kind and tender. His 'angelic' disposition
seemed to grow more apparent as the internal crisis worsened.

Yet, for all his deep devotion, Gabriel Piozzi was not courageous,
and, in January 1783, after a long impassioned scene, he suddenly
abandoned hope. Mrs Thrale had left him alone with Queeney, who,
as she subsequently learned, had 'touch'd on the Magic String, by
telling him *My Honour* was concerned in our immediate Separation...'.
Piozzi then hastened home to the London rooms he occupied, and,

returning with Mrs Thrale's letters and her 'Promises of Marriage', thrust them dramatically into Queeney's hands. Let Queeney take her Mother, he cried; and marry her off, if she thought good, to some important English nobleman. 'It shall kill *me* never mind – but it shall *kill her too!*' Once again, he announced that he would leave England; Mrs Thrale was obliged to acquiesce; and, on 6 April, the unhappy lovers said goodbye. They parted 'courageously'; for, at his beloved's suggestion, Piozzi had brought along an old friend, 'to keep the Meeting from being too tender, the Separation too poignant'; and in the presence of this same friend, Francisco Mecci, who was accompanying Piozzi across the Channel, they plighted their troth and registered solemn vows, which, notwithstanding 'Absence, Adversity, and Age', they resolved to hold sacred.

April was a disastrous month. While Mrs Thrale miserably retired to Bath, her youngest children, Caecilia and Henrietta, had been left behind at Streatham. Soon afterwards, she learned that both were ill; and, on the 18th, Henrietta died. None of her surviving daughters made any effort to console their mother. They went quietly about their own affairs; now that Henrietta's death had increased their fortunes, their insolence was 'extream, and their hardness of Heart astonishing'. Nor could she count on Piozzi's support. Although he had not yet left for Italy, she felt that she could not risk a further interview; and early in May, when a 'dreadful Wind' had arisen – 'God protect my best beloved, my Piozzi!' she exclaimed – she learned that he was due to set sail. 'Shall I never see him more? Never hear him more?' Were she allowed herself to be possessed by such thoughts, they would 'cost me my Reason or my Life'.

Piozzi was to remain in Italy until the summer of 1784; once he had reached his home and rejoined his humdrum family, he showed an understandable reluctance to venture back into the terrifying English world, with its savage newspapers, its censorious moralists and its horde of rabid social gossips. Meanwhile, his beloved's lamentations assumed an increasingly operatic tone. A modern Dido, she yearned for her absent Aeneas, '*Sposo promesso! Amante adorato! Amico senza equale.*' Now and then, grief discovered in her nature an unexpected vein of poetry, as when she observed that breaking her heart would serve very little useful purpose. It was if one broke a looking-glass; 'the Figure still lives in every broken Piece...'.

The day before she parted from Piozzi, she had already bidden Johnson farewell, presumably expecting to see him as soon as she returned to London; but there is no reference in the pages of *Thraliana* that would suggest they ever met again. They continued, however, to correspond. At Bath, she heard that, on 17 July, he had experienced a minor stroke; and, when he had partly recovered, he sent her a touching message, in which he summed up their relationship and pleaded for a renewal of their understanding:

I have loved you with virtuous affection; I have honoured you with sincere esteem. Let not all our endearments be forgotten.... You see I yet turn to you as a settled and unalienable friend; do not, do not drive me from you, for I have not deserved either neglect or hatred.

'My mistress', however, was no longer in a state of mind that permitted her to feel for others; she was too wretched, as she afterwards confessed, to look beyond her own miseries. The woman whom Johnson had once loved – brisk, sharp-tongued, full of 'ebullitions of ungovernable gaiety' – had become a very different creature. 'Dear, lost, infatuated Soul' – Fanny's description to Queeney of her mother's tragic plight – she was now stumbling on the verge of breakdown. Gone were her courage and her common sense. Noble-minded as she was, Fanny demanded, 'how *can* she suffer herself ... to be thus duped by ungovernable Passion?' It was the fact that Mrs Thrale's feeling for Piozzi was not only emotional, but strongly, undisguisedly physical, that caused her friends the deepest horror. And, while Miss Burney deplored her abject condition, and her daughters coldly disapproved, the whole formidable phalanx of Bluestockings voted her an odious renegade. '... There must be', declared Mrs Chapone, 'really some degree of *Insanity* in that case.... It has given great occasion to the Enemy to blaspheme and to triumph over the Bas Bleu Ladies.'

Such strictures, though she keenly resented them, had ceased to have any effect upon her conduct. At Bath, despite some occasional gaieties, she had lapsed into a mood of neurasthenic desperation; and, when November came and Sophia fell ill – with a series of 'Fits, sudden, unaccountable, unprovoked' – once she had nursed her daughter back to health, she reached the limit of endurance. Even Queeney, who had behaved 'inimitably' during Sophia's illness, now showed signs of giving way, and agreed that, since her mother's passion defied cure, their best plan was to accept the doctors' advice and call Piozzi back to England. But would be return? Summoned by Mrs Thrale towards the end of December, he displayed a strange unwillingness to set forth; and, early in January, Queeney herself despatched an invitation, to which Piozzi replied by pleading the state of the roads and the horrid dangers of the wintry Alps.

Not until June, after seven months' excruciating anxiety, could Mrs Thrale at last confide to her journal that 'he is set out sure enough'; and by that time Queeney and her sisters had adapted themselves to the situation with sufficient good grace. When their mother remarried, they had decided that, naturally under proper chaperonage, they would form a separate household. There must be no public breach, they determined; no scandal to attract the journalists; and, late in June, at the end of a sight-seeing tour which had taken the family to Stonehenge, Fonthill and Wilton House, they quietly parted from her on the road. Alone, she travelled back to Bath, where, at the beginning of July, dawned 'the happiest Day of my whole Life I think'. Yes, indeed, it was '*quite* the happiest, my Piozzi came home Yesterday...'. When he reappeared, she had been 'too painfully happy'. To-day, her sensations were 'more quiet ... & my Felicity less tumultuous'.

On 30 June, she had already informed her children's guardians that she meant to re-marry. Among them was Samuel Johnson; and to her formal letter she added, for Johnson's benefit, a brief reminder of their old affection; she would feel, she said, that she was 'acting without a parent's Consent' until she had received a kind reply. But Johnson's reply proved to be as unkind as pride and injured love could make it. Hitherto, he had stoically held his peace. Now his pent-up fury and misery were permitted full expression:

Madam, [he wrote on 2 July] if I interpret your letter right, you are ignominiously married: if it is yet undone, let us once [more] talk together. If you have abandoned your children and your religion, God forgive your wickedness; if you have forfeited your fame and your country, may your folly do no further mischief. If the last act is yet to do, I who have loved you, esteemed you, reverenced you, and served you, I who long thought you the first of Human kind entreat that, before your fate is irrevocable, I may once more see you. I was, I once was,

Madam, most truly yours,
Sam. Johnson

Mrs Thrale responded with a spirited defence of the man she loved

Mrs Piozzi in 1810, a year after her second husband's death.

and honoured, whose birth, sentiments and profession, she observed, were 'not meaner' than those of the man whom she had first married. 'It is the want of fortune then that is ignominious; the character of the man I have chosen has no other claim to such an epithet.' Thereupon Johnson's rage subsided as quickly as it had arisen:

Dear Madam, [he wrote on 8 July] What you have done, however I may lament it, I have no pretence to resent, as it has not been injurious to me; I therefore breathe out one sigh more of tenderness, perhaps useless, but at least sincere.

I wish that God may grant you every blessing, that you may be happy in this world for its short continuance, and eternally happy in a better state; and whatever I can contribute to your happiness I am very ready to repay, for that kindness which soothed twenty years of a life radically wretched....

I will come down, if you will permit it.

This letter he signed 'with great affection', and concluded with a note that he was 'going into Derbyshire', whither he hoped 'to be followed by your good wishes'. But they could not be reconciled; he had finally broken the tie; and when, in November, Fanny Burney visited him at Bolt Court, she heard him, for the last time, speak of his beloved *Thralia dulcis*. Both of them had lately seen Miss Thrale. Did he, the novelist innocently asked, ever hear from Queeney's mother?

'No', cried he, 'nor write to her. I drive her quite from my mind. If I meet with one of her letters, I burn it instantly. I have burnt all I can find. I never speak of her, and I desire never to hear of her more. I drive her, as I said, wholly from my mind.'

By now, Mrs Piozzi was travelling abroad, and, at the moment, comfortably established in a sumptuous Milanese palazzo. She had married Piozzi, according to the rites of the Roman Catholic Church, in London on 23 July; and, despite the grave objections that her friends had often advanced – his foreign descent, his Catholicism and his lack of any proper fortune – he became a faithfully devoted spouse. Having secured him, she soon recovered her spirits, her gaiety, her animation, her endless flow of sense and nonsense. She was once more the vivid, impulsive character who, during the heyday of their friendship at Streatham, had captured Samuel Johnson's heart. She was a happy woman; and happy she remained so long as her second husband lived. Piozzi, always the less robust of the two, died, after nearly twenty-five years of marriage, on 30 March 1809; and Mrs Thrale recorded his death in the closing passage of her *Thraliana*. She herself survived, gay, lively and irreverent to the end, until 2 May 1821.

8 Epilogue

For James Boswell, an inveterate man of moods, 1784 had begun dully and continued rather gloomily. A few years earlier, he had had sanguine hopes. Although, in 1781, Johnson had thought it his duty to comment on his old friend's selfish gloom, had warned him against the 'hypocrisy of misery' and had declared, 'I love everything about you but your affectation of distress', in 1782 Boswell had enjoyed such good spirits that he believed his customary attacks of depression had at last been put behind him, and, indeed, had almost forgotten he had once been afflicted with this 'direful malady'. He was now a free man and, into the bargain, comparatively prosperous. During August, his father had died – a loss, Johnson pointed out, accompanied by 'every circumstance that could enable you to bear it'; and, as the new laird of Auchinleck, he could look forward to a comfortable middle age. He also imagined that he had finally overcome the habit of excessive drinking.

Then, somehow, his hopes had dwindled and faded. He discovered that, despite all his bouts of passionate remorse, all his subsequent resolutions, he was still a chronic toper. 'I drank very liberally', he wrote on 5 August 1783, 'just to dissipate dreary dullness. I came home somewhat intoxicated....' And, on the 6th: 'I was in such miserable spirits that I resolved to drink a great deal of wine. I did so. ... It was a day not to be remembered with satisfaction.' Should he refrain from drinking, 'my mind was affected with a kind of dull indifference, a sort of callous stupor'. True, he presently rallied, and felt so well, as he sat at his ease among his Scottish neighbours, 'that, while I kept up the highest pitch of jollity, I at the same time maintained the peculiar decorum of the Family of Auchinleck'. Yet, before long, he had another serious relapse, was 'irritable in a sad degree; and upon some careless expression of my dear Wife's which hurt my pride, I burst into a paroxysm of horrible passion...'. Earlier, the memories of his carefree romantic youth had often comforted him and cheered his heart. Yet, in October 1783, when he was travelling with his wife across the Lowlands, 'I did not have at Hamilton the fine sensations I once had at that place. I *must* submit', he noted pathetically, 'to life losing its vividness.'

Nor did Christmas Day pass very cheerfully; 'the rigour of the season chilled my good feelings, and the consciousness of disease vexed me ...'. Between 26 November and 12 December, some pages have been cut out of Boswell's manuscript; but the disease that helped to spoil his Christmas had probably a venereal origin, and been contracted during one of his frequent expeditions into the

Left 'OLD WISDOM. Blinking at the Stars'; Johnson caricatured by Gillray, after the publication of *Lives of the Poets*.
Right Caricature by Sir Thomas Lawrence of Boswell at the end of his career.

dangerous back-streets of the Old Town. Meanwhile, his sleep was apt to be troubled by nightmares; and, at the beginning of January, he records that he had 'awaked in horror, having dreamt that I saw a poor wretch lying naked on a dunghill in London, and a blackguard ruffian taking his skin off with a knife ... and that the poor wretch was alive and complained woefully. How so shocking a vision was produced I cannot imagine'; but, as a result, he had been 'dismal the whole day'.

Soon afterwards, another dream, though it reveals an equally neurotic frame of mind, had proved considerably more consoling. He could never forget the 'indecent' and 'impolite' manner in which he had seen David Hume confronting death; and now he dreamt that he had been reading the philosopher's unpublished diary, 'from which it appeared that though his vanity had made him publish treatises of scepticism and infidelity, he was in reality a Christian and a very pious man'. During the same month, and the months that followed, he often quarrelled with his patient wife, who, to increase her own uneasiness – she was already tubercular, and spat blood – frequently delved into his secret journals. 'There was an unhappy renewal of domestick disturbance', he wrote on 12 March, 'which vexed me exceedingly.'[21]

All this time, Boswell was living in Scotland, either in Edinburgh or at Auchinleck; and, although he longed to regain London, he was obliged to postpone his departure until May, 1784. Johnson, he knew, had been in bad health, suffering, he heard, from dropsy; but Boswell was delighted to find him 'greatly recovered', having felt, he said, 'extraordinary relief' after a day 'employed in particular exercises of religion' – a fact that he imparted to his disciple with a 'solemn earnestness'.

Yet it was clear that he constantly thought of death and, although the idea seemed as terrible as ever, was gradually preparing for it. Robert Levett's death in January 1782, had been succeeded by that of his cross, devoted housemate, Anna Williams, in September 1783. Life at Bolt Court was now especially desolate; but Johnson was still well enough to dine out; and Boswell was able to collect some memorable conversations. Nor did he omit the characteristic snub, with which the old man, arguing *ad hominem* and using the butt-end of his pistol,* had temporarily left him speechless:

One of the company [Boswell himself] had provoked him ... by doing what he could least of all bear, which was quoting something of his own writing, against what he then maintained.... His anger burst out in an un-justifiable retort, insinuating that the gentleman's remark was a sally of ebriety; 'Sir, there is one passion I would advise you to command: when you have drunk out that glass, don't drink another.'

That same evening, however, at the Essex Head Club, Boswell managed to forget the insult; and Johnson was 'in fine spirits', talking of the Bluestockings and Edmund Burke, and calling out 'with a sudden air of exultation, as the thought started into his mind, "O!

---

* 'There is no arguing with Johnson,' Goldsmith had said; 'for if his pistol misses fire, he knocks you down with the butt end of it.'

Gentlemen, I must tell you a very great thing. The Empress of Russia has ordered the Rambler to be translated into the Russian language, so I shall be read on the banks of the Wolga. Horace boasts that his fame would extend as far as the banks of the Rhone; now the Wolga is further from me than the Rhone was from Horace".' The information, he admitted, had pleased him much. But, a little later, when one of the guests 'mentioned his having seen a noble personage driving in his carriage', and looking remarkably well, although he was a very old man, 'Ah, Sir,' Johnson remarked, 'that is nothing. Bacon observes, that a stout healthy old man is like a tower undermined.'

Once, when they were alone together, he spoke to Boswell of his feelings for Mrs Thrale, declaring 'with much concern', that she 'done everything wrong, since Thrale's bridle was off her neck'. But 'elegant and accomplished' young ladies were still capable of interesting him. He paid a 'most delicate and pleasing compliment' to a Miss Helen Maria Williams, author of a 'beautiful *Ode on the Peace*'*; and, during the journey that, early in June, he and Boswell made to Oxford, where Dr Adams was expecting them, he 'talked a great deal' to a pair of American visitors, named Beresford, who travelled in the same coach – the wife and daughter, though luckily he did not suspect it, of an American Congressman – teasing Mrs Beresford about the 'knotting'** with which she whiled away the time. 'Next to mere idleness (said he) I thinking Knotting is to be reckoned in the scale of insignificance.' He admitted, however, that he himself had once attempted to learn it, but had shown very little aptitude.

Johnson had borne the journey well, and 'seemed to feel himself elevated as he approached Oxford, that magnificent and venerable seat of Learning, Orthodoxy, and Toryism'; and, at Pembroke, they were received by Dr Adams 'with the most polite hospitality'. Both Boswell and Johnson seem to have enjoyed their stay. But it was on this occasion that Johnson spoke with such passionate vehemence about his prospects in the next world, and his fears that he might be one of those who were destined to eternal punishment; from which 'we passed to discourse of life, whether it was upon the whole more happy or miserable. Johnson was decidedly for the balance of misery'; while Boswell maintained that 'no man would choose to lead over again the life he had experienced. Johnson acceded to that opinion in the strongest terms.'

* She afterwards shocked Boswell by defending the French Revolution and, on a visit to Paris, walking, 'without horror', among the corpses of the massacred Swiss Guard.

** 'Knotting' is defined by the *Oxford English Dictionary* as 'the knitting of knots for fancy-work, similar to Tatting; and 'Tatting', as a kind of knotted lace . . . netted from stout sewing-thread; used for edging or trimming . . .'

Of the fortnight he spent with the amiable Master, Johnson after-wards remarked that Dr Adams had treated him with all the kindness he could 'expect or wish; and he that contents a sick man, a man whom it is impossible to please, has surely done his work well'. About 19 June, the travellers returned to London; and, although Boswell's hero, General Paoli, with whom they dined on 25 June, observed that the Doctor was looking 'very ill', he ate so greedily of a number of his favourite dishes that Boswell 'was afraid he might be hurt by it...'. On 30 June, a 'friendly and confidential dinner with Sir Joshua Reynolds took place, no other company being present'; and they dis-cussed a visit to Italy, which Johnson thought might possibly restore his health. His well-wishers hoped that the government, either by increasing his pension or making 'one large donation', would help him defray the cost of the long, expensive journey; and Johnson informed them that he would prefer to have his pension doubled rather than accept a grant of a thousand pounds*; 'for, (said he,) though probably I may not live to receive a thousand pounds, a man would have the consciousness that he should pass the remainder of his life in splendour...'.

More general conversation followed. They talked over the benefits and drawbacks of embarking on a country life, 'which Johnson, whose melancholy mind required the dissipation of quick successive variety, had habituated himself to consider a kind of mental imprisonment'. Boswell objected that many country people seemed content enough. 'Sir', replied Johnson, 'it is in the intellectual world as in the physical world; we are told by natural philosophers that a body is at rest in the place that is fit for it; they who are content to live in the country, are *fit* for the country.' Boswell quickly introduced another subject, bound to put the sage upon his mettle. 'Talking of various enjoyments, I said that a refinement of taste was a disadvantage, as they who have attained to it must be seldomer pleased than those who have no nice discrimination.... JOHNSON. "Nay, Sir; that is a paltry notion. Endeavour to be as perfect as you can in every respect."'

Boswell's account of how they parted for the last time is one of his greatest biographical feats; not a single word is wasted, and every phrase he employs makes the cumulative effect more deeply moving:

I accompanied him in Sir Joshua Reynolds' coach, to the entry of Bolt-court. He asked me whether I would not go to his house; I declined it from an apprehension that my spirits would sink. We bade adieu to each other affectionately in the carriage. When he had got down upon the foot-pave-

* The plan miscarried; and when Thurlow, then Lord Chancellor, offered him a personal loan of £500, Johnson courteously refused it.

ment, he called out, 'Fare you well'; and without looking back, sprung away with a kind of pathetick briskness ... which seemed to indicate a struggle to conceal uneasiness, and impressed me with a foreboding of our long, long separation.

Boswell remained another day in London, then dejectedly returned to Edinburgh. 'Soon after this time', he adds, 'Dr Johnson had the mortification of being informed by Mrs Thrale, that ... she was actually going to marry Signor Piozzi, an Italian musick master.'* This he learned from a letter written on 30 June, the day he said goodbye to Boswell; and, as we know, he replied in two letters, the first savagely ungenerous, though he concluded with the pleading postscript, 'I will come down, if you will permit it'; the second, tenderly affectionate. Mrs Thrale replied, on 15 July, that his last letter had been 'sweetly kind', and that not only her 'good wishes but my most fervent Prayers for your Health and Consolation' would accompany 'my dear Mr Johnson'. But evidently she did desire a meeting; and he left London, to revisit Lichfield and his old school-fellow, Dr Taylor, at Asbourne, about the middle of the month.

Neither of these journeys afforded him much relief; for Taylor, an affluent country clergyman, less interested in the affairs of the Church than in the successful management of his own estates – 'his talk is of bullocks', Johnson observed gloomily – proved a good-humoured but rather dull companion; while his middle-aged step-daughter, Lucy Porter, was neither intelligent nor entertaining. By way of diversion, however, he paid a visit to Chatsworth, where, for the first and last time, he set eyes on the beautiful Duchess of Devonshire and the stout, lethargic Duke, and 'was very kindly received, and honestly pressed to stay: but I told them that a sick man is not a fit inmate of a great house'.

Sickness had made him increasingly self-centred. 'What can a sick man say, but that he is sick?' he wrote in August to the well-known politician William Windham, who had despatched a sympathetic message. 'His thoughts are necessarily concentrated in himself; he neither receives nor can give delight; his inquiries are after alleviations of pain, and his efforts are to catch some momentary comfort.' To the symptoms of dropsy were added attacks of asthma, which, alas, showed 'no abatement'. But he noted, as an encouraging sign, that his appetite was 'keen enough; and ... I have a voracious delight in

*'Poor Thrale!' Johnson wrote to Hawkins during his subsequent holiday at Asbourne, 'I thought that either her virtue or her vice would have restrained her from such a marriage. She is now become a subject for her enemies to exult over, and for her friends, if she has any left, to forget or pity'.

raw summer fruit . . .' . Nor had he completely abandoned literature; but, on sleepless nights, he would translate into Latin verse epigrams he had selected from the *Greek Anthology*.

At last, during mid-November, after a brief visit to an old friend at Birmingham and yet another glimpse of Oxford, he wandered back again to Bolt Court. 'I have', he had already told Boswell, 'this summer sometimes amended, and sometimes relapsed, but, upon the whole, have lost ground very much.' His legs were weak; his breathing was difficult; and his dropsical condition was becoming more and more apparent. He no longer expected to live; yet only after much persuasion could Sir John Hawkins, a lawyer with a strong sense of legal decorum, persuade him, on 27 November, to sign a properly executed will. On the 30th, he had a sudden resurgence of energy; and Hawkins 'was informed, that he had, for his dinner, eaten heartily of a duck pie and a pheasant'. Then, on 1 December, he began to burn the papers that he had heaped up in his archives, among them, presumably, being the 'two quarto volumes, containing a full, fair, and most particular account of his own life, from his earliest recollection', that Boswell had once 'accidentally seen' when Johnson was his guest at Edinburgh.

Now there was little more to do. 'The prospect of his dissolution was very terrible to him', he had already told his friends; and to Dr Robert Warren, who ventured to hope he was better, he replied briefly, 'No, Sir; you cannot conceive with what acceleration I advance towards death.' Yet, even on his death-bed, he remained a master of language; and, a man having been hired to sit up with him, he remarked next morning, in his most incisive style, that the fellow was an idiot, 'as awkward as a turn-spit when first put into the wheel, and as sleepy as a dormouse'. Similarly, on William Windham offering him a new pillow, 'That will do, – all that a pillow can do'; and, as his servant brought him a note, 'An odd thought strikes me: we shall receive no letters in the grave.'

Meanwhile, he continued to pray fervently and, it seemed, to hope against hope. Though he was in pain, he refused all opiates – he was anxious to confront his Maker with a perfectly unclouded vision; but, during the temporary absence of the four doctors and the surgeon who attended him, according to Hawkins, whose informant was Johnson's devoted negro servant, Frank, 'he got at a pair of scissors that lay in a drawer, and plunged them deep in the calf of each leg . . .'. Though some biographers have suggested that Johnson may perhaps have contemplated suicide, it seems far more probable that, impetuous and courageous as ever, despairing of the doctors' skill, he had decided himself to perform a rough-and-ready operation. He died at a quarter past seven, on 13 December 1784, 'without a groan, or the least sign of pain or uneasiness ...'. *'Jam moriturus'* are said by Hawkins to have been the last intelligible words he uttered.*

During the next six years, three of his old friends drew the great man's literary portrait. Mrs Piozzi's *Anecdotes of the late Samuel Johnson LL.D* appeared in March 1786; Hawkins' biography, *The Life of Samuel Johnson, LL.D*, in March 1787; and Boswell's, after agonizing delays, on 16 May 1791. Boswell, of course, resented both his

Left Sir John Hawkins by James Roberts; an 'unclub-able' man, Johnson once complained. *Right* Mrs Piozzi in 1793; drawing by George Dance. Her *Anecdotes of the late Samuel Johnson* had appeared in 1786.

rivals – not only because their books had preceded his own**, but because each could very well claim to have had a deeper knowledge of

*Boswell, however, anxious so far as possible to avoid resembling Hawkins, asserts that they were 'God bless you, my dear!' addressed to 'a Miss Morris, daughter to a particular friend of his', who visited his sick-room some time on the 13th.

**They had themselves been preceded by William Cooke and William Shaw, whose less important studies of Johnson's life and work both appeared in 1785.

their hero. Mrs Piozzi had observed Johnson, day after day and month after month, while Boswell was detained at home; Hawkins, the crusty retired magistrate, who had been first associated with Johnson as early as 1749, though they had never been dear friends – he was an 'unclub-able' man, Johnson once complained, unlike the eminently 'club-able' Boswell – had know him very much longer.

Of the three, it was undoubtedly James Boswell who had toiled and suffered most; for him, Johnson's death was a personal bereavement that left him bewildered, lost and wretched. Mrs Piozzi, when she published her recollections, had already shaken off the great man's

A war of words between biographers; Mrs Piozzi upbraids a figure who seems intended to represent Sir John Hawkins; while her husband, on the right, tries in vain to keep the peace.

influence; though Hawkins had long admired Johnson, he had never been his pupil. But, in Boswell's life since 1763, Johnson had continued to play a variety of major rôles – not only as a chosen friend and guide, but also as a second father, who gave the spiritual support that his

Johnson and Boswell in Edinburgh, 1773; caricature by Thomas Rowlandson, published after the appearance of Boswell's *Journal of a Tour to the Hebrides* in 1791.

real father, the hard-headed Scottish law-lord, had persistently refused him.

Boswell had needed a father. 'Was really in a comfortable frame', he had noted at the age of thirty-six, after he and his 'honoured parent' had passed a busy day gardening, 'and felt more agreeably under parental awe than when unrestrained. It put a lid on my mind and kept it from boiling vehemently. Being thus kept quiet, I was happier than when agitated, with ebullitions.' Johnson, too, had often clamped down the lid – and then not always very gently; but, whereas Lord Auchinleck had declined to love his heir, whom he considered absurdly weak and foolish, the sternness that Johnson sometimes showed had been the by-product of real affection.

Without a fatherly director to keep his mind from boiling, Boswell's ebullitions soon defied control and, during the six years it took him to finish his masterpiece, he was seldom calm or happy. His *Journal of a Tour to the Hebrides*, the lively record of one of his most successful Johnsonian adventures, appeared in 1785; but, in the same year, he abandoned his Scottish law-practice and decided he would move to London – a disastrous mis-step; he failed at the English bar, just as he failed to secure a Parliamentary seat; while the temptations of London life proved particularly demoralizing.

In 1789, Margaret Boswell died; and he was overwhelmed with a poignant sense of guilt. 'How often and often', he wrote, 'when she was very ill ... have I been indulging in festivity ... and have come home late and troubled her repose.' Before very long, it is true, he had begun to plan a second marriage, and greatly enjoyed making his bow at Court, 'in a suit of imperial blue lined with rose-coloured silk, and ornamented with rich gold-wrought buttons'. But such consolations were slight and transitory; he was once again a prey to fits of 'hypochondriack' gloom. 'I get bad rest at night', he informed a favourite correspondent, William Temple; 'and then I brood over all my complaints – the *sickly mind* which I have had from my early years ... the irrevocable separation between me and that excellent woman who was my cousin, my friend, and my wife ... nay, the want of *absolute certainty* of being happy after death, the *sure prospect* of which is *frightful*.'

Meanwhile, he had completed a preliminary draft of his book; and, although the 'labour', 'perplexity' and 'vexation' of 'arranging a prodigious multiplying of materials' and 'searching for papers, buried in different masses', were sometimes almost more than he could bear – and, after a night's drinking, his hand was often so unsteady that he found it difficult to correct the proofs – he slowly struggled on towards the last page. But, once he had sighted the end, his depression lifted, and he uttered a momentous prophesy. He was sure, he announced, that 'my mode of biography, which gives not only a *history* of Johnson's *visible* progress through the world ... but a *view* of his mind ... is the most perfect that can be conceived, and will be *more* of a *Life* than any book that ever yet appeared'.

His claims were justified; when his book finally emerged in the early summer of 1791, he would revolutionize the whole technique of modern biographical writing; and, compared with Boswell, neither Hawkins nor Mrs Piozzi was an imaginative literary artist. Yet, considering how much the rival biographers vary, both in method and in outlook, it is remarkable how closely the portraits they draw blend into the same majestic figure. At times, they provide opposing versions of a single incident or scrap of dialogue; but nothing they may choose to add or subtract can change the figure's general outline. From beyond the tomb, Johnson controls the narrative, and projects his tremendous shape on our imagination.

This he does through the native strength of his genius, his overwhelming force of character. Yet his character, if we examine it detail by detail, appears to abound in inconsistent traits; and, although he regarded himself as a supremely reasonable man, his passions and prejudices, rather than the faculty of reasoning, seem to have deter-

Johnson in the travelling-dress he wore on his journey to the Hebrides with
Boswell; 'drawn from life'. A print of 1786.

mined many of his views. Numerous lists have been made of Johnson's apothegms; and together they form a very strange assembly; at some point, every reader of his sayings must inevitably take offence. During an age of liberal thought, he might well have declared, like Ruskin, that he remained a firm 'illiberal'. Under any guise, the idea of human freedom excited his contempt or hatred; for civilized society, he believed, must always be based on 'the grand principle of subordination', and man ineluctably subjected to man, as in the sixteenth-century 'Chain of Being'.

Towards his fellow human creatures, Johnson's attitude was sometimes harsh and often cynical. He sympathized with, and yet despised the poor; 'a poor man', he said, 'has no honour' – presumably because it was beyond his means; and we are all of us moulded and limited, he thought, not by our inward needs but by our mundane circumstances. Man was invariably the prisoner of circumstance, and, having been cast into a grim, unfriendly world, provided that he did not offend against Christian ethics, must relieve the tedium of life as best he could. Life, he asserted, was a bitter pill, 'which none of us can bear to swallow without gilding'; and, while the poor deserved their rations of gin and tobacco, the rich might excusably fall back on wine, food and conversation. There was nothing discreditable about seeking pleasure; to have achieved some degree of innocent enjoyment, however slight and frivolous the form it took, was unquestionably a lasting gain.

'The business of the wise man was to be happy', he instructed the often unhappy Boswell; and much of the pleasure that he himself had enjoyed had been derived from the company of 'modest women'. Yet he had always refused to exaggerate their mental gifts, and continued to judge the sexes by different moral standards. Weaknesses excusable in a man – just as 'you don't call a man an ironmonger', he remarked, 'for buying and selling a pen-knife ... you don't call a man a whoremonger for getting one wench with child' – were utterly inexcusable in a woman; and, although a woman's adultery could never be forgotten or condoned, if a man (he assured Boswell, who eagerly snapped up the good news) 'from mere wantonness of appetite' should steal into her maid's bed, 'a wife ought not greatly to resent this'. A wife owed her husband implicit obedience. 'The grand principle of subordination' he applied, no less vigorously and indiscriminately, to the relationship of man and woman.

His political views are well-known. Johnson was a High Tory; and, again, the opinions he held had a deeply pessimistic colouring. The human lot might be irksome and wretched; but, given the characteristics of human nature, it was almost impossible to ameliorate. 'So, Sir, you laugh at schemes of political improvement', protested Boswell in 1769, after a discussion about oppressive landlords; to which Johnson had merely replied: 'Why, Sir, most schemes of political improvement are very laughable things.' Yet the State, he felt, must protect its poorer citizens; 'a decent provision for the poor is the true test of civilization'; and 'the poor in England were better provided for, than in any other country of the same extent'.

Otherwise, human society, as it was now organized, should be allowed to continue on its present course. He strongly supported the doctrine of *laissez-faire*; and, as a keen royalist, he refused to agree with Boswell, that the growing authority of the Crown might eventually curtail the people's liberties. But he added a typical Johnsonian proviso: 'And then, Sir, there is this consideration, that *if the abuse be enormous, Nature will rise up, and claiming her original rights, over-turn a corrupt political system.*' Until then, presumably, it was wiser and easier to accept the system that we had inherited.

There was an element of perversity in Johnson's character. 'When I was a boy', he had confessed to Boswell, 'I used always to choose the wrong side of a debate, because most ingenious things, that is to say, most new things, could be said upon it'; and, since he had long had the habit of 'talking for victory', not every opinion that Johnson advertised did full justice either to the acuteness of his intelligence or to the natural goodness of his heart. Hence the chaotic impression we often receive as we scan his published dicta. No great man has ever been less consistent, or displayed in his private life so many contra-dictory attributes. Yet the cumulative effect his portrait produces is one of solid human strength.

Perhaps the quality that unified Johnson's character was more spiritual than intellectual. Oscar Wilde is said by André Gide to have claimed that he had put his genius into his life, and that for his work he had reserved his talents. The same remark might surely be applied to Johnson, who, on a far nobler scale, expended his genius in living*, and employed his subsidiary gifts in writing. His books reflect his genius, yet seldom so richly and accurately as his reported conversa-tion. 'There is in this world', he believed, 'no real delight (excepting those of sensuality), but the exchange of ideas in conversation; and whoever has once experienced the full flow of London talk, when he retires to country friendships and rural sports, must either be con-tented to turn baby again ... or he will pine away like a great fish in a little pond....'

*In his *Dictionary*, Johnson defines 'genius' as, among other things, a 'Disposition of nature by which any one is qualified for some peculiar employment.'

Although his range was, of course, remarkably wide, and – except for history, which he regarded as an arrant waste of time; 'sooner than hear of the Punic War', Arthur Murphy remembered, 'he would be rude to the person that introduced the subject.' – covered the whole

James Boswell two years before his death; drawing by George Dance, 1793. Of Boswell in later life, once he had published his biography of Johnson, we are told that 'his joke, his song, his sprightly effusion . . . did not appear to possess upon all occasions their wonted power of enlivening social joy'.

extent of literature and scholarship, the conversationalist was perpetually reverting to some familiar human problem. No question was too large or too small for him; and he refused always to draw a pendantic distinction between the important and the unimportant. The least important fact might increase his knowledge of life, and was consequently worth discussion; and upon any theme that Johnson happened to discuss he brought to bear all the resources of his intellect and all his powers of human sympathy.

'Men and women are my subjects of enquiry', he had once told Henry Thrale; and the Roman dramatist's phrase, 'I am a man, and nothing human do I consider alien to myself', might well have been pronounced by Johnson. The extensive landscape of his mind enclosed no desert-regions of indifference; everything concerned, agitated, amused him, aroused either his furious scorn or his equally energetic approbation. His idea of misery was to be obliged to sit alone; his greatest happiness, to join his friends; and when, as he often did, he declared that he 'loved' a friend, he used the word in its most valuable meaning. Through his friends he exercised his native genius; and some, like Boswell (who succeeded triumphantly upon one plane, though he failed miserably upon another) he had taught to live and work and think. Johnson's affections were never merely static; whether their object was Boswell or Bet Flint, they arose from his imaginative appreciation of a fellow human being. Because he loved, he understood; and, because he understood, his friendship grew. Johnson's large heart and his noble head formed a peculiarly close alliance.

Johnson as a septuagenarian;
bust by E. H. Bailey after Joseph
Nollekens. At the age of sixty-
nine, he remarked that, since his
first nervous breakdown fifty
years earlier, 'my health has been . .
such as has seldom afforded me
a single day of ease'.

Notes

1 Joseph Wood Krutch, *Samuel Johnson*, 1945
2 Charles Vereker, *Eighteenth-Century Optimism*, 1967
3 James L. Clifford, *Hester Lynch Piozzi*, 1952
4 James Baretti, quoted by James L. Clifford, *Op. Cit.*
5 Rylands English manuscript 543/1, quoted by Katherine C. Balderston in her notes to *Thraliana*. Mrs Thrale's reply, also quoted by Dr Balderston, is catalogued as 539/30
6 Ellis Waterhouse, *Sir Joshua Reynolds*, 1941
7 See 'Reynolds on Johnson': *Portraits* by Sir Joshua Reynolds, in the Yale Edition of the Private Papers of James Boswell
8 Recollections of Garrick by G. C. Lichtenberg, translated by John Newell, *History Today*, March 1972
9 *Portraits* by Sir Joshua Reynolds, *Op. Cit.*
10 See *The Letters of Sir William Jones*, edited by Garland Cannon, 1970
11 Diary of a Visit to England in 1775 by an Irish man. First published in Sydney, 1854
12 See Joyce Hemlow, *The History of Fanny Burney*, 1958
13 Joyce Hemlow, *Op. Cit.*
14 Joseph Wood Krutch, *Op. Cit.*
15 See E. L. MacAdam Jr & George Milne: *Johnson's Dictionary: A Modern Selection*
16 See G. M. Young's note on the poem, in *Johnson: Prose and Poetry*, selected by Mona Wilson, 1950
17 See Ernest C. Mossner, *Introduction to a Treatise of Human Nature*, 1969
18 *Mémoires et Correspondence de Madame d'Épinay*, 1818
19 See Ernest C. Mossner, *Op. Cit.*
20 See Harold E. Bond, *The Literary Art of Edward Gibbon*, 1960
21 Quotations all derived from *The Journal of James Boswell, 1783–1786*; in *The Private Papers of James Boswell*, edited by James Scott and Frederick A. Pottle, 1932

Bibliography

BAILEY, JOHN. *Dr Johnson and his Circle*, 1944

BOND, HAROLD E. *The Literary Art of Edward Gibbon*, 1960

BOSWELL, JAMES. *Life of Johnson*, edited by R. W. Chapman; a new edition corrected by J. D. Fleeman, 1970

BOSWELL, JAMES. *The Private Papers of James Boswell, from Malahide Castle*, edited by Frederick A. Pottle and Geoffrey Scott, 1938

BOSWELL, JAMES. *Yale Edition of the Private Papers of James Boswell*, edited by Frederick A. Pottle and others. 10 vols, 1950–71

BOSWELL, JAMES. *Letters of James Boswell*, edited by C. B. Tinker, 1924

BURNEY, CHARLES. *Memoirs*, arranged from his own manuscripts by Madame d'Arblay, 1832

BURNEY, CHARLES. *Music, Men, and Manners in France and Italy, 1770.* edited by H. Edmund Poole, 1969

BURNEY, FANNY (Mdme d'Arblay). *Diary and Letters*, 1778–1840, edited by Charlotte Barrett, 1904

CECIL, LORD DAVID. *Poets and Storytellers*, 1960

CLIFFORD, JAMES L. *Hester Lynch Piozzi (Mrs Thrale)* 1952

CLIFFORD, JAMES L. *Young Samuel Johnson*, 1955

CLIFFORD, JAMES L. *From Puzzles to Portraits*, 1970

DELANY, MRS (Mary Granville). *Mrs Delany's Autobiography and Correspondence*, 1861–62; compiled and edited by George Paston, 1900

ELIOT, T. S. *On Poetry and Poets*, 1957

d'ÉPINAY, LOUISE-FLORENCE. *Mémoires et Correspondence*, 1818

GEORGE, MARY DOROTHY. *England in Johnson's Day*, 1928

HALLIDAY, F. E. *Dr Johnson and his World*, 1968

HARRIS, R. W. *Reason and Nature in Eighteenth-Century Thought*, 1968

HAWKINS, SIR JOHN. *The Life of Samuel Johnson, LL.D.*, edited by Bertram H. Davis, 1961

HAWKINS, LAETITIA MATILDA. *Memoirs*, 1824

HEMLOW, JOYCE. *The History of Fanny Burney*, 1958

HIBBERT, CHRISTOPHER. *The Personal History of Samuel Johnson*, 1971

HILLES, F. W. *The Literary Career of Joshua Reynolds*, 1936

HUDSON, DEREK. *Sir Joshua Reynolds: A Personal Study*, 1958

HUME, DAVID. *A Treatise of Human Nature*, edited by E. Campbell, 1969

JOHNSON, SAMUEL. *Johnson's Dictionary*, A Modern Selection by McAdam and George Milne, 1963

JONES, SIR WILLIAM. *Letters*, edited by Garland Cannon, 1970

KETTON-GREMER, R. W. *Horace Walpole*, 1940

KINGSMILL, HUGH. *Samuel Johnson*, 1933

KRUTCH, JOSEPH WOOD. *Samuel Johnson*, 1945

KINGSMILL, HUGH. *Samuel Johnson*, 1935

KINGSMILL, HUGH. *Johnson without Boswell*, 1940

LANSDOWNE, MARQUIS OF. *Johnson and Queeney. Letters from Dr Johnson to Queeney Thrale*, edited, 1932

LONSDALE, ROGER. *Dr Charles Burney*, 1965

MORE, HANNAH. *Works*, 1830

MOSSNER, ERNEST CAMPBELL. *The Life of David Hume*, 1954

NICHOLS, JOHN. *Literary Anecdotes of the Eighteenth Century*, edited by Colin Clair, 1967

NORTHCOTE, JAMES. *The Life of Sir Joshua Reynolds*, 1819

OMAN, CAROLA. *David Garrick*, 1958

PIOZZI, HESTER LYNCH (see also Mrs Thrale). *Anecdotes of the late Samuel Johnson, LL.D.*, 1786

PIOZZI, HESTER LYNCH (see also Mrs Thrale). *Autobiography, Letters and Literary Remains*, edited by A. Hayward, 1861

PIOZZI, HESTER LYNCH (see also Mrs Thrale). *Observations and Reflections, Made in the Course of a Journey through France, Italy, and Germany*, edited by Herbert Barrows, 1967

QUENNELL, PETER. *The Singular Preference*, 1952

QUENNELL, PETER. *Four Portraits*, 1965

REYNOLDS, SIR JOSHUA. *Portraits* (Yale Edition of the Private Papers of James Boswell), edited by Frederick W. Hilles, 1952

RUDÉ, GEORGE. *Hanoverian London*, 1971

ROGERS, SAMUEL. *Table-Talk*, edited by Marchard Bishop, 1952

SCOTT, WALTER S. *The Bluestocking Ladies*, 1947

STEEGMAN, JOHN. *The Rule of Taste*, 1968

SWAIN, JOSEPH WARD. *Edward Gibbon the Historian*, 1966

TINKER, CHAUNCEY B. *Dr Johnson and Fanny Burney*, 1912

TOMPKINS, J. M. S. *The Popular Novel in England, 1770–1800*, 1932

THRALE, HESTER LYNCH (see also Mrs Piozzi). *Thraliana: The Diary of Mrs Hester Lynch Thrale, 1776–1809*, edited by K. C. Balderston, 1951

VEREKER, CHARLES. *Eighteenth-Century Optimism*, 1967

VULLIAMY, C. E. *James Boswell*, 1932

WALPOLE, HORACE. *Letters*, edited by Mrs Paget Toynbee, 1903–5

WATERHOUSE, ELLIS. *Sir Joshua Reynolds*, 1941

WATERHOUSE, ELLIS. *Painting in Britain, 1730 to 1790*, 1954

WILLES, FREDERICK W. *The Literary Career of Sir Joshua Reynolds*, 1936

WOOLF, VIRGINIA. *The Common Reader: Second Series*, 1933

Index